DISCOVERING PROPHECY AND WISDOM

Discovering the Living Word

These four volumes provide an excellent beginner's introduction to understanding the Bible. Keyed to the questions that uninformed adults ask about biblical stories and claims for belief, this series brings the scriptures alive in very concrete and practical ways for today's world. The volumes are designed to encourage maximum participation by the entire group, and each lesson both explains an aspect of biblical interpretation and invites further discussion on its relevance and spiritual value for contemporary society. With two volumes on the Old Testament and two on the New Testament, the series is flexibly designed to be used in classes over a one or two year period as the teacher decides, or in discussion groups without the feel and limits of a textbook. The series is appropriate for Juniors in high school, or anyone older. **Discovering the Living Word** is simply one of the finest introductory tools available today to engage people's interest in the Bible.

DISCOVERING THE GOSPELS: Four Accounts of the Good News

DISCOVERING THE FIRST CENTURY CHURCH: The Acts of the Apostles, Letters of Paul and the Book of Revelation

DISCOVERING OLD TESTAMENT ORIGINS: The Books of Genesis, Exodus and Samuel

DISCOVERING PROPHECY AND WISDOM: Isaiah, Job, Proverbs, Psalms

(all volumes by Margaret Nutting Ralph)

DISCOVERING PROPHECY AND WISDOM

The Books of Isaiah, Job, Proverbs, Psalms

MARGARET NUTTING RALPH

PAULIST PRESS
New York/Mahwah

Library of Congress Cataloging-in-Publication Data

Ralph, Margaret Nutting.
    Discovering prophecy and wisdom : Isaiah, Job, Proverbs, Psalms / Margaret Nutting Ralph.
        p.   cm. — (Discovering the Living Word ; v. 4)
    Includes index.
    ISBN 0-8091-3402-0 (pbk.)
    1. Bible. O.T. Isaiah—Textbooks.   2. Bible. O.T. Job—Textbooks.   3. Bible. O.T. Proverbs—Textbooks.   4. Bible. O.T. Psalms—Textbooks.   I. Title.   II. Series: Ralph, Margaret Nutting. Discovering the Living Word : v. 4.
    BS1515.5.R36 1993
    223'.061—dc20   93-10245
                                                                CIP

Published by Paulist Press
997 Macarthur Boulevard
Mahwah, New Jersey 07430

Printed and bound in the
United States of America

Contents

Job

Proverbs

In gratitude:

"Let the words of my mouth and
the meditation of my heart
be acceptable to you,
O Lord, my rock and my redeemer."
Psalm 19:14

Preface

Are you one of those people who reads the last chapter of a mystery book first? Do you want to know "the rest of the story" before you know the beginning of the story? Do you wish God had given God's people the ability to see into the future and to comprehend all mystery?

No matter what your answers to these questions, the fact is that human beings, through the centuries, have had to struggle to comprehend the truth. In real life no one can read the last chapter first. God did not give God's people the ability to see into the future or the ability to comprehend all mystery.

However, many Christians somehow have the impression that God did just that. Aren't the prophets those whom God let see into the future? Don't the inspired authors of wisdom literature reveal those mysteries which were hidden from others who lacked inspiration? People who hold such opinions have not read the prophets or wisdom literature.

The book which you now hold in your hand, *Discovering Prophecy and Wisdom,* is based on the premise that the first thing you should do to discover "prophecy" or "wisdom" is to actually read a prophet, such as Isaiah, or a wisdom book, such as Job or Proverbs. Read the biblical text before you read the book you now hold. Let the prophet or the wisdom author speak to you first before anyone else tries to tell you what the biblical author had to say.

True, there is much that you will read that you will not understand, particularly if you come to this first reading with many misperceptions, false ideas or expectations which you impose on the text without any conscious knowledge that this is what you are doing.

As you read, jot down every question which comes to mind. Don't try to find answers to the questions as they arise. Just jot down the questions and read on. Let yourself get an impression of a whole book, with each verse in the context in which it appears in the Bible.

Over the years I have collected the questions which students ask when reading Isaiah, Job, Proverbs and the first book of Psalms for the first time. This book is a collection of short articles written in response to those questions.

It is my experience that the content of these articles is appropriate and useful for juniors in high school and anyone older. I do not recommend this book for most younger students. I have found that one must have developed beyond the very "literal" way of thinking which is normal in the early teen years before one is able to understand the points made in these articles.

The quantity of material is appropriate for a variety of religious education settings. If two articles were discussed every class meeting, this book would be a one-quarter course for an in-school class that meets every day, a semester course for an in-school class that meets two to three times a week, and a year-long course for an out-of-school class that meets once a week. One may, of course, go faster or slower, depending on how much time is spent on the review and discussion questions. The material is also appropriate for adult education groups.

The format of question and response may tempt the students to skip responses to questions which have not occurred to them. This would be a mistake. One question often leads to related questions which do not appear in the heading but which are addressed in the articles.

Despite the question and answer format the short articles written in response to specific questions are not pat answers. I have tried to respond to the questions in such a way as to teach a methodology, so as to enable students to think. The goal is to equip students with the tools they will need to search out answers to questions which do not appear in these articles.

The fact that the responses deal with methodology is an additional reason to read the articles in order. Methodological points made in early articles are usually not repeated in subsequent articles.

It may be that a student will be unfamiliar with a word or concept in a given article which has been presumed to be known and so is not explained. The glossary in the back of the book has been designed to help the student in such a situation. Students should remember to use the glossary if unfamiliar words appear or to review concepts which were explained in earlier articles.

In addition to a glossary, the book contains an index of biblical passages. This will help both teacher and student locate comments on given passages.

Both teacher and student may expect, and even want, to read more introductory material before reading the specific Old Testament text. This desire is purposely thwarted in this book in an attempt to let the texts themselves have the first word. Some background information is provided in various articles as the need arises. However, the student is urged to read the biblical text first so that questions are not explained away before the student has had an opportunity to ask them. All commentary is secondary to actually reading the biblical text.

Of course not all questions which students raise will be addressed in this book. This is all to the good. To grow in one's ability to raise the questions, to explore answers and to live with mystery are goals in themselves. While it is wonderful to reach a degree of understanding as we read the prophets and wisdom literature, no one of us will ever succeed in completely understanding the mysteries which these books probe.

THE BOOK OF ISAIAH

ARTICLE 1

The Book of Isaiah: An Edited Anthology

Question: "When did Isaiah's vision occur? Four kings are mentioned." (Is 1:1)

When the book of Isaiah begins with the words, "The vision of Isaiah son of Amoz, which he saw concerning Judah and Jerusalem in the days of Uzziah, Jotham, Ahaz, and Hezekiah" (Is 1:1), the setting named is the second half of the eighth century B.C.

Isaiah, son of Amoz, was a prophet who lived and worked in Jerusalem, the capital of what was at that time the southern kingdom, Judah. As you may know, the nation Israel had been a united nation when David was its king (ca. 1000 B.C.). However, the kingdom later divided (922 B.C.) into the northern kingdom, Israel, and the southern kingdom, Judah. All the kings mentioned are kings of Judah.

In chapter 6 you will read that the prophet Isaiah received his call "in the year that King Uzziah died" (Is 6:1) or in 742 B.C. Jotham was king of Judah from 742 to 732 B.C., Ahaz from 732 to 715 B.C., and Hezekiah from 715 to 686 B.C.

Since the book of Isaiah begins by placing the prophet Isaiah so clearly in his political context, you might assume that you are reading a collection of prophecies which are arranged chronologically through the reign of these four kings. In fact you will not find such a chronological order, nor will you find that the book contains only the words of the prophet Isaiah.

The book of Isaiah might more accurately be called an edited anthology than a book. While the setting for the first chapters is the second half of the eighth century B.C., the setting for later chapters is some two hundred years after the time of Isaiah of Jerusalem,

7

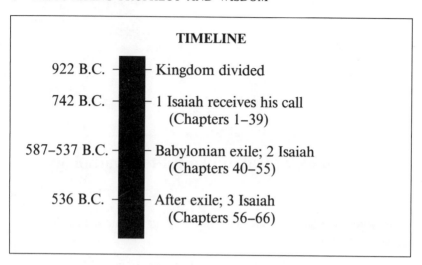

during the time when the Israelites were exiles in Babylon (587–537 B.C.). Still later chapters are set in the time after the Babylonian exile when the Israelites returned to the holy land and faced the momentous task of resettling and rebuilding. Because the setting of the book changes, scholars refer to chapters 1–39 as First Isaiah, chapters 40–55 as Second Isaiah, and chapters 56–66 as Third Isaiah.

However, if we acknowledge that the book of Isaiah is an anthology and that only chapters 1–39 involve the setting of Isaiah of Jerusalem, we still should not read these chapters as though we are reading a chronological arrangement of the words of this one historical person. Remember, prophets spoke rather than wrote. So a prophet's words were heard, remembered, treasured, written down, discussed, elaborated upon, applied to recent events, seen in the light of hindsight, handed on, edited and preserved. When we read the first chapters of the book of Isaiah we are reading such an edited arrangement.

For instance, the first chapter of Isaiah is not simply one prophecy from Isaiah's earliest ministry. Rather it is a collection of prophecies from various times in Isaiah's ministry. The prophecies have been selected and arranged to introduce the reader to Isaiah's core teaching.

So as we read the "vision" of Isaiah of Jerusalem we will have to

---

CONTEXTS TO CONSIDER

- Historical prophet

- Hindsight view of prophet's disciples

- Editor of book of Isaiah

- Readers of Isaiah who live after Jesus' resurrection

---

keep several things in mind. First we will remember the time of the historical prophet and will try to put his words in the political context in which they were spoken. Only then will we begin to understand what Isaiah was saying to his contemporaries. We will also remember that the editor of the book of Isaiah had access not only to Isaiah's words but to what those words had come to mean to Isaiah's disciples in the light of events. In passing on the prophecies of Isaiah the editor would naturally include the insights and elaborations of his disciples.

In addition to these contexts we will take into consideration the context which a Christian brings to a reading of the book of Isaiah, a context formed by events which were unknown to Isaiah of Jerusalem, Isaiah's disciples, or to the person who selected and arranged the contents of the book of Isaiah. These events, which we read about in the New Testament, add an additional layer of meaning to the prophetic words in the mind of Christian readers.

Because of the added significance which we Christians have attributed to the prophet's words, we read the book of Isaiah in the context of our own lives, also a context completely unknown to the original prophet or the original editor.

When did Isaiah's "vision" occur? It occurred in the second half of the eighth century B.C. However, the significance of Isaiah's vision relates not only to the eighth century but to every century. Isaiah's words have meaning not only for their historical time but for all time.

Review Questions

1. When did Isaiah of Jerusalem live?
2. What was the name of the northern kingdom? The southern kingdom? When did the two kingdoms split?
3. When was the Babylonian exile?
4. How do scholars divide the book of Isaiah? Why do they divide it this way?
5. Are the words in chapters 1–39 the exact words of Isaiah of Jerusalem? Explain.
6. Name four distinct contexts in which we can look at the words of a prophet.

Discussion Questions

1. Did anything you read in this essay surprise you? If so, what?
2. Have you ever thought of putting a prophet's words in the context in which they were said? Why or why not?
3. Are you familiar with any anthologies? Explain. What are characteristics of an anthology?
4. How does material that has been edited with hindsight insight differ from a daily diary? What does this have to do with the book of Isaiah?

ARTICLE 2

The Role of a Prophet

Question: "I don't understand why you conclude that the book of Isaiah contains the work of three prophets of three different historical times just because the book pictures three different historical settings. Since a prophet can see into the future, couldn't one prophet have foreseen all three settings?" (Is 2:6; Gen 12:1–2; 2 Sam 7:16)

Behind this question is a misunderstanding of the role of a prophet. We will try to define clearly the role of a prophet because, if one brings a false presumption of prophecy to a reading of the book of Isaiah, one will misunderstand the book. One will conclude that Isaiah, or the editor of Isaiah's work, is saying things which, in fact, never entered either of their minds.

A prophet is not a fortune teller, a person who can see into the future and accurately predict historical settings two hundred years in the prophet's future. In fact, to involve oneself with "fortune tellers," "diviners" or "soothsayers" was considered a sin by the Israelites (see Is 2:6). Such people were considered to be part of the occult, and to confer with them was to turn away from Yahweh, the true God.

Rather, a prophet's spiritual gift is the ability to understand the ramifications of being in a permanent loving relationship with God.

By the time of Isaiah of Jerusalem the Israelites had come to understand themselves to be in a "covenant" relationship with God for one thousand years, ever since 1850 B.C. when God first called Abraham, the Israelites' father in faith. A "covenant" relationship is a permanent relationship of love which can never be dissolved and in which both parties have mutual obligations.

11

In the book of Genesis we read that when God called Abraham and established a covenant with him, God said, "Go from your country and your kindred and your father's house to the land that I will show you. I will make of you a great nation, and I will bless you, and make your name great, so that you will be a blessing" (Gen 12:1–2). So God is pictured, as part of God's covenant love, as having promised the people a nation.

When the great King David united the twelve tribes of Israel into a single nation and defeated their enemy, the Philistines, the people understood these events to be the fulfillment of God's promise to Abraham. God had made them a great kingdom as God had said God would.

Not only did the Israelites believe that the kingdom established under David was the fulfillment of God's promise, they believed that God had promised to secure the future of that kingdom forever. We read of this hope and expectation in 2 Samuel when God is pictured as saying to David, "Your house and your kingdom shall be made sure forever before me; your throne shall be established forever" (2 Sam 7:16).

However, a "covenant" is a loving relationship with mutual obligations. Just as God promised to love the Israelites and give them a nation, so the Israelites promised to love God and obey God.

A prophet is one who has a deep understanding of the mutual obligations of covenant love and who views current events in the light of that understanding.

Current events at the time of the call of Isaiah of Jerusalem revolved around the fact that Assyria was becoming a mighty nation and was a threat to the very existence of both the northern and the southern kingdoms. How was one to understand this threat? Because Isaiah was a great prophet he understood events in the context of covenant love.

So, while Isaiah was not a fortune teller who predicted historical events two hundred years in his future, he was a person who saw the ramifications of covenant love. If people were sinning, thus being unfaithful in covenant love, Isaiah warned of the ramifications of such behavior. However, his point was not to predict inevitable future events. Rather, his point was to call people to repentance. If people had responded to a prophet's warning and had returned to

Yahweh, the events of which he had warned would not have occurred. The events were not inevitable but avoidable, if only people would live in faithful covenant love.

So, if the setting for a prophetic book is the eighth century B.C. or the sixth century B.C., we know that the setting informs us of the historical context of the prophet. It tells us when that prophet lived.

The prophet's role was to speak to the nation about the ramifications of covenant love in the light of those current events. The prophet understood that God was a loving, powerful presence in the lives of God's people, and so the prophet tried to pass on that understanding by helping others to see the meaning of current events in the light of covenant love.

Review Questions

1. Were fortune tellers held in high regard by the Israelites? Explain.
2. What is a prophet's spiritual gift?
3. What is a covenant relationship?
4. What did God promise Abraham?
5. What did God promise David?
6. What is the people's responsibility in a covenant relationship with God?
7. What were "current events" at the time of the call of Isaiah of Jerusalem?
8. Are the events of which a prophet warns inevitable? Explain.
9. What is the prophet's role?

Discussion Questions

1. Do you know of any relationships between people which are relationships of covenant love? Explain.
2. Do you believe that God's power and presence are felt in current events? Explain.
3. Do you believe that events are inevitable or rather that human beings' choices determine events? Explain.

ARTICLE 3

A Sinful People

Question: "What did the people do to make God so angry?" (Is 1:1–17; Is 1:19–20; 1:27 also discussed)

Remember that in this first chapter of Isaiah we are not reading a single prophecy from a single occasion. Rather we are reading an arrangement of prophecies which introduce us to Isaiah's major themes.

We get an idea of the kind of event which precipitated Isaiah's prophetic ministry in Isaiah 1:7–9 when we read:

> Your country lies desolate,
>   your cities are burned with fire;
> in your very presence aliens devour your land;
>   it is desolate, as overthrown by foreigners (Is 1:7).

Scripture scholars believe that this is a description of Judah at the time that the Assyrian king, Sennacherib, devastated the country, crushing a revolt by Judah's king, Hezekiah, in 701 B.C. As we will see when we read the other prophecies which come from this later period of Isaiah's ministry, Hezekiah had ignored Isaiah's advice to trust Yahweh, and catastrophe had followed. The editor of Isaiah is looking at Isaiah's prophetic words in hindsight. He knows not only what Isaiah prophesied but the disaster that followed when Isaiah was ignored. In the first chapter the editor, with his hindsight point of view, gives us a good idea of what the people had done to bring disaster upon themselves.

The first charge against the people is that they have failed in their covenant relationship with God. God has loved Judah and has

14

treated Judah as a beloved child, but the people have revolted against God. God claims that the people do not even know the God who created them and who loves them.

> The ox knows its owner,
>> and the donkey its master's crib;
> but Israel does not know,
>> my people do not understand (Is 1:3).

Israel has become so sinful that she despises "the Holy One of Israel" (Is 1:4). As we will see, Isaiah often refers to God as "the Holy One of Israel." In fact, Isaiah's keen perception of God's holiness is one of his most striking characteristics.

God is too holy to allow sin to continue uncorrected. It is God's desire to correct God's people that motivates God's actions, not anger. Isaiah understands tragic events such as the devastation wrought by the Assyrians as the way God chooses to correct the people. These events are evidence that the people have broken their covenant with Yahweh.

The first specific charge which is made is that the people's worship has become empty ritual because the ritual is not accompanied by love of God and neighbor. God rejects religious observances such as burnt offerings, the observation of festivals and of the sabbath, and even prayer because the people's hands are full of blood.

> Wash yourselves; make yourselves clean;
>> remove the evil of your doings from before my eyes;
> Cease to do evil,
>> learn to do good;
> Seek justice,
>> rescue the oppressed,
> Defend the orphan,
>> plead for the widow (Is 1:16–17).

Isaiah makes it clear that he warns the people of disaster not in order to foretell inevitable events but to call them to repentance.

> If you are willing and obedient,
>> you shall eat the good of the land;
> but if you refuse and rebel,

APPROXIMATE TIMELINE FOR 1 ISAIAH

* 742 B.C. — Isaiah receives his call

733 B.C. — Northern kingdom suffers first defeat at the hands of the Assyrians

732 B.C. — Syro-Ephramite War at height; King Ahaz and Immanuel prophecy

722–721 B.C. — Samaria, capital of northern kingdom, conquered

715 B.C. — Hezekiah, Ahaz's son, comes to throne (Judah a vassal of Assyria)

714 B.C. — Philistines revolt against Assyria (Egyptians try to get Hezekiah to join but he doesn't)

705 B.C. — Babylonians revolt against Assyria (Egyptians try to get Hezekiah to join; he finally does)

* 701 B.C. — Sennecherib crushes Hezekiah's revolt; Jerusalem is spared

---

you shall be devoured by the sword;
for the mouth of the Lord has spoken (Is 1:19–20)

If the people do not repent they will face terrible suffering, not because God is angry and wishes to destroy them, but because God wishes to purify them.

Zion will be redeemed by justice,
and those in her who repent, by righteousness (Is 1:27).

So while the prophet warns of terrible destruction if sin prevails, he also holds out great hope for those who repent. Hope is always realistic in a covenant relationship because God is too holy to withdraw God's love. God is always calling the people back to covenant love through the events in their lives.

"What did the people do to make God so angry?" The people failed to love God and their neighbor. Instead they sought political solutions which showed that they did not trust Yahweh. Instead of love and trust they offered Yahweh empty ritual, unaccompanied by love of God and neighbor. However, God does not act through events merely to punish. Rather God is calling God's people back to covenant love. For Isaiah, God is motivated not by anger but by love.

Review Questions

1. What event, late in Isaiah of Jerusalem's ministry, resulted in devastation for the people of Judah?
2. What is the first charge against the people?
3. How does Isaiah often refer to God?
4. What does Isaiah suggest is God's motive in letting a devastating event occur?
5. Why does God reject the people's religious observances?
6. What is Isaiah's motive in warning of disaster?
7. Why is hope always realistic in the context of covenant love?

Discussion Questions

1. How do you refer to God? Do you name a particular characteristic of God's? Do you like the way Isaiah refers to God? Why or why not?
2. Do religious observances sometimes appear to you to be empty ritual rather than real worship? Explain.
3. What does the phrase "seek justice" mean to you? Do you think it is possible to pray well and to fail to seek justice? Explain.

Oracle: A Literary Form

Question: "How do you know that the first chapter of Isaiah is a collection of prophecies from different periods in Isaiah's career? It seems all of a piece to me." (Is 1)

One way we can tell that the first chapter of Isaiah is a collection of prophecies rather than a single prophecy is by looking at the form in which the prophet's words appear. This form is called an "oracle."

An oracle is a highly stylized literary unit which can be clearly defined and identified in terms of both its form and its function. The oracle's form grows out of its function.

As we have already said, a prophet is a person whose spiritual gift is the ability to see the meaning of events within the context of covenant love. A prophet not only understands the ramifications of covenant love but passes on this understanding to others. Since the prophet's insights are a spiritual gift which enables the prophet to make God's will known to God's people, the prophet is understood to be God's messenger, to speak for God.

The form which the prophet uses in speaking for God grows out of this sense which the prophet has that he is merely a messenger passing on God's message. The oracle begins, "Yahweh says this," or with a similar formula which attributes the prophet's words to God. Isaiah 1:2 says, "The Lord speaks." Any messenger naturally attributes the message to its source. The source of the prophet's message is God.

The oracles which the prophets deliver in the Old Testament traditionally have four functions, all of which we have seen in the first chapter of Isaiah. Oracles denounce empty religious practices

---

ORACLE

Form: "Yahweh says this . . ."
   (A prophet is one who speaks for God)

Function: • Denounces empty religious practices and social
            injustices
          • Calls people to repentance
          • Warns of destruction
          • Promises restoration

Characteristics: • Uses poetic line: parallelism
                 • Uses traditional images

---

or social injustices, they call the people to repentance, they warn of destruction, or they promise restoration.

In addition to employing a standard linguistic formula and having standard functions, oracles use common images. We will have ample opportunity to discuss these images as we read Isaiah. An example which we have already encountered is the image of God as a parent and Israel as a child who has failed to respond with love and obedience.

Prophetic oracles as they appear in the Old Testament take the form of poetry. Hebrew poetry has unique characteristics which, if defined, will help us understand prophetic oracles.

Poetry in English is usually distinguished from prose by its internal form. A poetic line usually contains a regular number of syllables with a regularly recurring accent. The ends of poetic lines might rhyme. Hebrew poetry is distinguished from prose not by internal form but by logical relationships. The structure comes from the balance of units of thought rather than from the number of syllables or the arrangement of accents.

The word used to describe this characteristic of Hebrew poetry is "parallelism." There are many kinds of parallelism. For purposes of illustration, though, we will name the most simple: synonymous parallelism. Synonymous parallelism is present when two adjacent lines contain the same thought but in different words. This first chapter of Isaiah is full of synonymous parallelism.

> The ox knows its owner,
>> and the donkey its master's crib (Is 1:3a).

> Offspring who do evil,
>> children who deal corruptly (Is 1:4a).

Since an oracle is a linguistic unit with a definable form and function and with identifiable poetic characteristics, it is usually possible to distinguish where one oracle stops and another starts. In Isaiah 1:2–3 the function of the oracle is to denounce Israel for her lack of loving response. In Isaiah 1:4–9 the function of the oracle is to describe or warn of destruction. In Isaiah 1:10–17 the function of the oracle is to blame Israel both for empty religious practices and for social injustices. Each change in function represents a probable moving on to another oracle.

For a modern reader the more pressing question is usually not how one can distinguish one oracle from another. This becomes obvious since the change in function is often abrupt and seems illogical to us. Our question is often: "Why did the editor arrange the oracles in this particular order?" We will not always be able to come up with a satisfactory answer to this question.

As we continue to read Isaiah, then, we must remember that we are reading an edited arrangement of oracles which are in poetic form. In order to understand their meaning we must put them in their appropriate historical context. But since their source is God, we may find, in hindsight, that the words take on a meaning in the light of subsequent events which transcends their original meaning, the meaning intended by the prophet. Events "fulfill" or "give fuller meaning" to the words of the prophet.

Review Questions

1. What is the name of the form in which the prophetic words appear?

2. What does it mean to say that a prophet "speaks for God"?
3. How is this function of a prophet apparent in the form of an oracle?
4. What four functions do prophetic oracles traditionally have?
5. What is a traditional prophetic image which we have already read in Isaiah?
6. How is Hebrew poetry distinguished from prose?
7. What is synonymous parallelism?
8. What is one obvious way of distinguishing one oracle from another?
9. In what way might events "fulfill" the words of a prophet?

Discussion Questions

1. When you read "Yahweh says this . . ." are the words that follow a direct quotation from God? Explain.
2. Do you like the image of God as a parent and we as God's children? Why or why not? What other images might describe the relationship between God and God's people?
3. Why is each of the four functions of prophetic oracles pertinent to covenant love? Can you think of a modern setting in which each of these kinds of oracles would be appropriate? Name some.

ARTICLE 5

The Mountain of the Lord: God's Dwelling Place

**Question: "Is 'the mountain of the Lord' in Zion or in Jerusalem?"
(Is 2:1–2; Ex 15:17)**

Two of the facts which we learned in our previous article on
"oracles" will help us respond to this question.

Notice that the questioner has presumed that Zion and Jerusalem are two different places, probably because in Isaiah 2:3b we
read:

> For out of Zion will go forth instruction,
>   and the word of the Lord from Jerusalem" (Is 2:3b).

These lines are an example of synonymous parallelism. The
same thought is expressed in each line, using different words but in
reverse order. Once we recognize the synonymous parallelism, we
realize that the prophet is using Zion and Jerusalem as synonyms.
Zion is another way of referring to Jerusalem. So, in answer to the
question, we can say that "the mountain of the Lord" is in
Jerusalem.

But what is "the mountain of the Lord"? Again, our knowledge
of synonymous parallelism will help us, for the prophet says:

> Come, let us go up to the mountain of the Lord,
>   to the house of the God of Jacob" (Is 2:3a).

"The mountain of the Lord" is a poetic image used to refer to "the
house of God," or to "God's dwelling place." This image pre-dated
Isaiah of Jerusalem. In fact, we find the same image in the book of

Exodus in a song which Moses and the Israelites are pictured as singing after their escape from Egypt at the time of the exodus.

> You brought them [the Israelites] in and planted them on the
>   mountain of your own possession;
> the place, O Lord, that you made your abode,
> the sanctuary, O Lord, that your hands have established (Ex
>   15:17).

Perhaps the image of God's dwelling as "the mountain" was originally influenced by the Canaanite culture in which the gods were thought to assemble on the mountain top. However, God's "dwelling," God's "mountain," eventually came to refer to Jerusalem, and specifically to the hill on which the temple was built and to which the ark of the covenant was brought. God was understood to have chosen Jerusalem, Zion, as God's dwelling place, God's holy mountain.

So, "the mountain of the Lord" is in Jerusalem, not because there is actually a very high mountain there but because Jerusalem is the city in which God chooses to dwell.

When Isaiah says that there will come a day when

> The mountain of the Lord's house
>   shall be established as the highest of the mountains,
>   and shall be raised above the hills.
> All the nations shall stream to it (Is 2:2),

Isaiah is reminding the people that God has chosen them to be witnesses to the truth which God has revealed to them. When the people are faithful witnesses, all nations will come to Jerusalem because it is from Jerusalem that nations will be taught God's ways.

In what context did Isaiah proclaim this oracle? There are several possibilities. One is that Isaiah is saying that those in the northern kingdom, who suffered their first defeat at the hands of the Assyrians in 733 B.C., should come to Jerusalem and be faithful to Yahweh. Isaiah would have seen the defeat of the northern kingdom as evidence that those in the north had failed to live up to their responsibilities as people in a covenant relationship with Yahweh.

The defeat of the northern kingdom should serve as a sobering example for the southern kingdom who might suffer the same fate.

Once this passage became part of the prophetic tradition (evidence of this is that the passage also appears in Micah 4:1–3), it would have also had pertinent meaning after the Babylonian exile (587–537 B.C.). In that context it would have been urging people to return from foreign nations and come back to Jerusalem, the center of worship for the Jews, the chosen dwelling place of Yahweh.

After Jesus rose from the dead, the idea that Jerusalem would be the source of knowledge about God for all nations was understood in the context of Jesus' ministry. That Jesus is the revelation of God's truth to all nations is the idea behind Matthew's beautiful gospel image of three wise men (i.e. all nations) following a star to find the infant Jesus. Jesus as the revelation of the Father is finally recognized as the source of truth for all nations.

Even in our day this imagery from Isaiah is held up to teach the idea that God would have all nations be at peace with each other.

> They shall bear their swords into plowshares,
>   and their spears into pruning hooks;
> Nation shall not lift up sword against nation,
>   neither shall they learn war any more (Is 2:4b).

The mountain of God, God's dwelling place, is the source of truth. Whether we understand this truth in the context of eighth century B.C. Jerusalem, in the context of sixth century B.C. Jerusalem, in the context of the first century A.D., or in the context of the twentieth century, Isaiah's spiritual insight remains true. The hope of nations rests in understanding and obeying God's will. Peace will come when all nations approach "the mountain of the Lord."

Review Questions

1. What does "Zion" mean?
2. What traditional image is used to refer to the place where God dwells?
3. Why is Jerusalem referred to as "God's holy mountain"?

4. What does it mean to say that the Lord's house will be established as the highest mountain so nations will stream to it?
5. What would Isaiah's words have meant to his contemporaries shortly after 733 B.C.? Why?
6. What would Isaiah's words have meant when heard shortly after 537 B.C.? Why?
7. To whom does Matthew apply the image of the truth to which nations stream? How?
8. How have modern writers used Isaiah's images?

Discussion Questions

1. Have you ever been on top of a mountain? Why do you think people imagine a mountain as a place where God dwells?
2. Do you think nations stream to God's holy mountain? Why or why not? Does our nation? Explain.
3. Do you agree that if all nations truly listened to God, nations would be at peace? Why or why not?

ARTICLE 6

The Day of the Lord

Question: "Is the day of the Lord" which Isaiah predicts in Isaiah 2:11–12, 17 the second coming of Christ?" (Is 2:6–22)

This questioner has made two mistakes which are very hard to avoid if one has been raised Christian and has heard Old Testament prophetic passages only in the context of a Christian liturgy.

The first mistake is one which we have already tried to correct, and that is the presumption that a prophet is predicting far-off future events rather than warning of imminent contemporary events. Isaiah is speaking to his contemporaries about their lives. We must first look for his message in that social context.

The second mistake is to take an idea that developed after the prophet and to impose it on the prophetic words as though that were the prophet's intent. The idea that Christ will come again is a New Testament concept and not one with which Isaiah would have been dealing. To equate Isaiah's "day of the Lord" with our idea of Christ's second coming would be to lose what Isaiah was teaching his contemporaries.

What would "the day of the Lord" have meant to Isaiah's contemporaries? Scripture scholars believe that the Israelites had a popular belief in a "day of the Lord," a day on which Yahweh would make them supreme and victorious since they are God's chosen people. The prophet Amos, a contemporary of Isaiah's of Jerusalem who prophesied in the northern kingdom, warned that "the day of the Lord" would not be a day of victory for the Israelites because they would be held accountable for their actions. Amos says:

26

> Alas for you who desire the day of the Lord!
>   Why do you want the day of the Lord?
> It is darkness, not light (Am 5:18).

Isaiah, like Amos, teaches his people that the day of the Lord will be a day on which God's people are found wanting. Why? Isaiah uses the northern kingdom as his example. He claims that the reason God had forsaken the northern kingdom, the "house of Jacob," was that the northern kingdom had sinned. They had turned to diviners and soothsayers (see Is 2:6). They had accumulated wealth (Is 2:7). They had placed their trust in horses and chariots rather than in Yahweh (Is 2:7b). They had committed idolatry by making and worshiping idols (Is 2:8). In other words, people had trusted to their own devices rather than to God. They had become proud.

Isaiah pictures the day of the Lord as the day on which this pride will be made manifest and will be destroyed.

> For the Lord of hosts has a day
>   against all that is proud and lofty,
>   against all that is lifted up and high (Is 2:12).

As Isaiah describes the day he universalizes it, giving it cosmic significance. Even the pride of nature will be brought low (see Is 2:13–14), and also the pride of other nations (Is 2:16):

> The haughtiness of people shall be humbled,
>   and the pride of everyone shall be brought low;
>   and the Lord alone will be exalted on that day (Is 2:17).

While Isaiah universalizes his message, his specific warning to his contemporaries is that they, like the northern kingdom, are held accountable for their actions. Disaster will come to the south as it did to the north unless the people live in right relationship with God and each other.

The warning which Isaiah gives his people is, of course, very similar to the warning which we read in the gospels concerning "the day of the Son of Man" (see Lk 17:22–37). And, since the imagery of "the day of the Lord," along with its cosmic upheavals, is part of the inherited tradition of the gospel editors, Old Testament imagery is used in describing this "day of the Son of Man."

Nevertheless, we should not simply equate Isaiah's "day of the Lord" with Luke's "day of the Son of Man." To do so is to misunderstand the role of a prophet as well as to ignore the message which Isaiah is giving to his contemporaries in Jerusalem.

Review Questions

1. In popular tradition what did the Israelites expect to be accomplished on "the day of the Lord"?
2. What did "the day of the Lord" mean to the prophet Amos?
3. What does Isaiah expect to happen on "the day of the Lord"?
4. What imagery does Isaiah use to universalize his message?
5. Why is the description of "the day of the Lord" similar to the description of "the day of the Son of Man"?
6. What is lost if we simply equate the two "days"?

Discussion Questions

1. What do you imagine God thinks of the American culture? In what ways would God praise us? In what ways would God correct us?
2. Isaiah wanted the southern kingdom to learn something from the fall of the northern kingdom. What do you think a modern day prophet might want the United States to learn from events in Russia?
3. Are you expecting a "day of the Lord"? Explain. If so, what will it be like? What images can you think of to describe it?

ARTICLE 7

The Daughters of Zion

Question: "Why is Isaiah so hard on women? (Is 3:16–27) Why does he say that the Lord will wash away 'the filth of the daughters of Zion'?" (Is 4:4; Is 3–4 also discussed)

Isaiah 3–4, as the oracles are now arranged, do seem to come down hard on women. However, once we take into account what we know about synonymous parallelism, about poetic images, and about an edited text, we will see that this first impression may be exaggerated.

For instance, in the particular passage to which our questioner refers, the prophet speaks of God washing away "the filth of the daughters of Zion." When we read this phrase in context, we read: "Whoever is left in Zion and remains in Jerusalem will be called holy, everyone who has been recorded for life in Jerusalem . . . once the Lord has washed away the filth of the daughters of Zion and cleansed the bloodstains of Jerusalem from its midst by a spirit of judgment and a spirit of burning" (Is 4:3–4).

Notice that the phrase, "washed away the filth of the daughters of Zion," is in synonymous parallelism to the phrase, "cleansed the bloodstains of Jerusalem." In other words, in this passage the phrase "daughters of Zion" refers to the inhabitants of Jerusalem, not just to the female inhabitants.

Note too that the prophet personifies the city of Jerusalem as a female when he says:

> And her gates shall lament and mourn;
> ravaged, she shall sit upon the ground" (Is 3:26).

This passage is not saying that the women will be ravaged, but that the whole city will be ravaged.

29

The devastated city has previously been personified as female in the introductory chapter to Isaiah:

> And daughter Zion is left like a booth in a vineyard,
>   like a shelter in a cucumber field, like a besieged city (Is 1:8).

Here, "daughter Zion" refers to the whole city of Jerusalem and its inhabitants, not just to the women.

Nevertheless, the women of Jerusalem, as distinct from the men, do come in for special criticism, for the women as well as the men who are in politically powerful positions (i.e. "elders" and "princes"—see Is 3:14a) contribute to the abuse of the poor by their rich lifestyles. Isaiah is criticizing the wealth of the women in Jerusalem when he describes them as

> haughty . . . glancing wantonly with their eyes,
> Mincing along as they go,
>   tinkling with their feet (Is 3:16).

Scripture scholars believe that Isaiah 3:18–23, verses which elaborate on the kinds of rich adornments which the women wore, were inserted by the editor because of their logical connection to the "mincing" and "tinkling" daughters of Zion.

The chapter ends with the rich women, "the daughters of Zion" (Is 3:16a), being absorbed into the inhabitants of Jerusalem. For it is not just the women but all the inhabitants of the city who are in danger of being politically defeated, clothed in sackcloth, tied in ropes, and led through the city in shame. This is the kind of treatment one might expect from a conquering army.

Although the rich women, as well as the ruling men, are warned that disaster lies ahead for them, the washing away of the filth from the inhabitants of Jerusalem will not end in total destruction. God will cleanse rather than destroy Jerusalem because Jerusalem is God's chosen dwelling place. The images used to describe God's presence dwelling in the city are the same images used to describe God's presence with the Israelites during the exodus, a cloud by day and fire by night. "Then the Lord will create over the whole site of

Mount Zion, and over its place of assembly, a cloud by day and smoke and the shining of a flaming fire by night" (Ex 4:5).

Jerusalem will be ravaged but not abandoned, cleansed but still loved. Jerusalem and her "daughters," her inhabitants, will one day be purified, and the remnant left in Jerusalem will be called "holy" (see Is 4:3). It is in order to save Jerusalem, not destroy her, that God must wash away "the filth of the daughters of Zion."

Review Questions

1. To whom does the phrase "the daughters of Zion" sometimes refer?
2. What is "daughter Zion"?
3. Why does Isaiah criticize both the men and the women in Jerusalem?
4. What are the women doing to contribute to the problem?
5. To what will this kind of behavior lead?
6. Does Isaiah believe that God will completely destroy Jerusalem? Why or why not?
7. What images does Isaiah use to describe God's presence with the Israelites?
8. To what does the word "remnant" refer?

Discussion Questions

1. What do we mean by "Lady Liberty"? By "mother earth"? Can you think of other ways in which we personify ideas or things as female? Why do we do this?
2. Do you think a rich lifestyle contributes to the injustices done to the poor? Why or why not?
3. If you wanted to describe God's presence, what image would you use? Why?
4. How do you imagine God "feeling" when we sin? Angry? Sad? Unloved? Give reasons for your answers.

ARTICLE 8

The Song of the Vineyard

Question: "Why is a song about a vineyard called a 'love song'?" (Is 5:1–7)

The "love song" about the vineyard is not really about a vineyard. Rather, the love song is about the relationship between God and God's people. We know this because at the end of the song we hear:

> For the vineyard of the Lord of hosts is the house of Israel,
> and the people of Judah are his pleasant planting (Is 5:7).

The way in which this song is constructed, with the intent of the speaker understandable only at the end, is characteristic of a literary form found in both the Old and the New Testaments. This literary form is called a "parable."

When telling a parable the speaker keeps his real intent hidden until the end of the story for a reason. The speaker is actually telling a story which will correct the audience. However, he tells the story in such a way that the people in the audience do not realize that the story is about them. The audience passes judgment on the characters in the story. Only in hindsight do they realize that the judgment they have passed is a judgment on themselves.

When Isaiah begins the parable:

> Let me sing for my beloved my love-song concerning his vineyard:
> My beloved had a vineyard in a very fertile hill (Is 5:1),

he immediately captures the interest of his listeners. There is something mysterious about this beginning, a hint that the story ends

> **PARABLE**
>
> **(A story told to an audience which is actually about the audience)**
>
> *Function:* To challenge the audience and call the people to conversion

unhappily. The prophet is singing for the beloved about a vineyard which the beloved *had.* Who is this beloved and what has happened?

The foreboding that this is a sad love song, perhaps about unrequited love, persists in verse 2 as we read of the care which the beloved lavished on his vineyard, and the disappointment he experienced in the results.

> He expected it to yield grapes,
>   but it yielded wild grapes (Is 5:2b).

Next the narrative voice changes and the owner of the vineyard invites the audience, "the inhabitants of Jerusalem and people of Judah," to judge between him and his vineyard. The vineyard owner, through his questions, makes it clear that he has done all he could possibly have done for his vineyard. The blame for the fact that the vineyard yielded only "wild grapes" cannot be laid at the feet of the vineyard owner.

Now that the audience can only have judged in favor of the owner, the angry owner tells his audience exactly what he will do to that vineyard.

> I will make it a waste;
>   it shall not be pruned or hoed,
>   and it shall be overgrown with briers and thorns (Is 5:6).

The next voice we hear is not the voice of the vineyard owner but the voice of the prophet who is singing the song of his beloved, God. The prophet tells those in the audience that this song is about them:

> For the vineyard of the Lord of hosts is the house of Israel,
>   and the people of Judah are his pleasant planting;
> He expected justice but saw bloodshed;
>   righteousness, but heard a cry (Is 5:7).

In these lines the prophet is telling his audience not only that they will be destroyed but why. Because God had so loved God's people, God had expected the people to act lovingly toward each other. God had expected "justice," a society in which the rich would not exploit the poor. Instead he has found violence. God had expected "righteousness," "right relationships," but instead God has heard the cry of those who are being mistreated.

Both the form of this song, "parable," and its central image, "the vineyard of the Lord" as God's people, are traditional and are found with regularity in both the Old and the New Testaments. In fact Jesus is pictured as telling a very similar story with a similar purpose in the gospels of Matthew, Mark and Luke (see Mt 21:33–42; Mk 12:1–10; Lk 20:9–18).

So, in this instance, a song about a vineyard is a love song. It is a love song sung by God through the voice of the prophet in which God, whose love has been unrequited, warns God's people that the ramifications of life lived outside of covenant love can only be suffering.

Review Questions

1. What is the song of the vineyard about?
2. Why, in a parable, does the author keep the real intent behind the story hidden?
3. What about the beginning of the parable of the vineyard catches the listener's interest?
4. How does the narrative voice, the voice telling the story, change?
5. How is the audience invited to pass judgment?
6. Who does the "beloved" turn out to be?
7. Why is the song about the vineyard a love song?
8. What does the song teach?

Discussion Questions

1. Do you like the image of a vineyard owner and a vineyard as an image of God's relationship with God's people? Why or why not? What can this image teach that the image of a parent and child cannot teach?
2. What do you think God should do about the fact that people sin? Explain.
3. Do you ever think of God as an unrequited lover? Do you like this image? Why or why not?
4. Do you know of any parable that you experience as correcting you? Explain.

ARTICLE 9

The Call of Isaiah

Question: "Why did the Lord tell Isaiah (Is 6:10) to make the mind of the people dull and to stop their ears?" (Is 6:1–13)

The prophet Isaiah, as is nearly always true with prophets, spoke to a people who were so resistant to his message that they refused to listen to him. Despite the fact that the people were not going to listen, Isaiah was sent to preach. Why would God send Isaiah to do something that would end in failure? Did people perhaps ignore Isaiah because he was not a true prophet? Or was Isaiah a true prophet who, even though he was ignored, faithfully carried out and accomplished God's will? Was Isaiah's prophetic ministry a total waste or would good finally result? The story of Isaiah's call (Is 6:1–13), including the difficult passage, "Make the mind of this people dull," is designed to respond to these questions.

First, was Isaiah a true prophet even though people didn't listen to him? The call story of Isaiah confirms the fact that Isaiah was not self-appointed but was called by God and sent by God as a messenger.

In describing his call Isaiah centers in on an insight which is core to all that Isaiah has to say. For Isaiah, God is the holy one of Israel. This insight is revealed to him as he sees the seraphs in God's heavenly throne room, and hears them say:

> Holy, holy, holy is the Lord of hosts;
> the whole earth is full of his glory (Is 6:3)

Because Isaiah understood God's holiness, he also understood the difference in holiness between God and God's people, including himself. The sinfulness of people was crystal-clear to Isaiah

36

when seen in contrast to God's holiness. "Woe is me! I am lost, for I am a man of unclean lips, and I live among a people of unclean lips; yet my eyes have seen the King, the Lord of hosts" (Is 6:5).

However, in addition to experiencing God's holiness and humankind's sinfulness, Isaiah experienced God's desire and power to save, for instead of rejecting Isaiah, God cleansed him by having the seraph touch Isaiah's lips with a live coal.

After being cleansed, Isaiah hears the Lord ask, "Whom shall I send?" (Is 6:8a). Isaiah is immediately responsive to God's query and so is commissioned by God to be God's messenger.

But why does God tell Isaiah to "dull the mind, stop the ears, and shut the eyes"? This wording is the narrator's way of attributing to God, who is the ultimate cause of all, the behavior of those who would ignore Isaiah's preaching. The proximate cause of the dulled minds was, of course, the people's own lack of comprehension. But since the narrator believes that God knew that Isaiah's words would fall on deaf ears, and that God had sent Isaiah anyway because God could accomplish God's will even with people's resistance, the narrator describes God as telling Isaiah to have the effect which Isaiah did, in fact, have. In resistance to the truth which Isaiah preached, minds became more dull, ears were stopped, eyes were shut and people became even less able to turn and be healed. In other words, the narrator pictures God foretelling Isaiah's failure, or, more accurately, the people's failure to listen and learn from Isaiah.

In response to this painful commission Isaiah cries out, "How long?" How long will the people be unresponsive? God tells Isaiah that a great deal of suffering will precede the people's change of heart. The cities will be laid waste and the land will be deserted.

"Then why send Isaiah?" one might well ask, since the people are not going to listen?

Again, God's desire to save rather than to punish is the answer. For after all of the devastation a stump will remain standing (Is 6:13). This stump represents the remnant which we mentioned earlier. Isaiah's preaching, the people's lack of response, and all the suffering are not all in vain, for "the holy seed is its stump" (Is 6:13b). The stump will not be destroyed but will be the source of new life. Finally people will see with their eyes, hear with their ears, and turn and be healed. Ultimately God will not be thwarted even if no one listens to God's messenger, Isaiah the prophet.

Review Questions

1. How does the call story of Isaiah address the question, "Was Isaiah a true prophet?"
2. What insight is core to all that Isaiah has to say? How was this insight revealed to Isaiah?
3. What does the realization of God's holiness teach Isaiah about himself?
4. What is God's response to Isaiah's realization of his own sinfulness?
5. Why is God pictured as telling Isaiah to dull people's minds?
6. What is represented by the stump? What hope is expressed?

Discussion Questions

1. Why might a prophet be said to "stop the ears" of his audience?
2. Do you sometimes feel resistant to a particular person even when you know that the person is telling you the truth? Explain.
3. Why do you think people like Gandhi and Martin Luther King often die violent deaths?
4. Do you think it is good or bad to have a clear sense of human beings' sinfulness? Explain.

ARTICLE 10

Immanuel

Question: "I know you said that the prophet is not foretelling far-off future events, but isn't Isaiah 7:14–16 foretelling the incarnation and the virginal conception?" (Is 7:1–25)

When Isaiah says to Ahaz, "Therefore the Lord himself will give you a sign. Look, the young woman is with child and shall bear a son, and shall name him Immanuel" (Is 7:14), Isaiah is not foretelling either the incarnation or the virginal conception.

The reason our questioner thinks the passage predicts the fact that God took on flesh and became a human being (the incarnation) and that Mary conceived Jesus through the power of the Holy Spirit (the virginal conception) is that the questioner has heard Isaiah's words associated with these facts in a liturgical setting. Also, the questioner may be familiar with Matthew's gospel and so with Matthew's use of Isaiah's words. After telling the story of the angel's annunciation to Joseph (see Mt 1:20–21) Matthew says, "All this took place to fulfill what had been spoken by the Lord through the prophet: 'Look, the virgin shall conceive and bear a son and they shall call him Emmanuel, which means, "God is with us" ' " (Mt 1:22–23).

So how can we claim that Isaiah was not predicting these far-off future events?

In order to answer this question, let us remember what we have said about the function of a prophet and see if the text supports our claims.

A prophet is addressing a contemporary audience. He is advising his contemporaries what their behavior should be considering the fact that they live in a relationship of covenant love with God. In

APPROXIMATE TIMELINE FOR 1 ISAIAH

742 B.C.	Isaiah receives his call
733 B.C.	Northern kingdom suffers first defeat at the hands of the Assyrians
* 732 B.C.	Syro-Ephramite war at height; King Ahaz and Immanuel prophecy
722–721 B.C.	Samaria, capital of northern kingdom, conquered
715 B.C.	Hezekiah, Ahaz's son, comes to throne (Judah a vassal of Assyria)
714 B.C.	Philistines revolt against Assyria (Egyptians try to get Hezekiah to join but he doesn't)
705 B.C.	Babylonians revolt against Assyria (Egyptians try to get Hezekiah to join; he finally does)
701 B.C.	Sennacherib crushes Hezekiah's revolt; Jerusalem is spared

addition, the prophet is warning the people of the ramifications of failing to live up to the demands of covenant love.

In Isaiah 7 we read that the southern kingdom (i.e. Judah) under King Ahaz fears a political crisis. Two other kingdoms, Aram (Syria) and Israel (the northern kingdom, also called Ephraim), plan to attack Jerusalem. The reason? These two kingdoms want Ahaz to join with them against Assyria. Ahaz does not think joining them is the best way to handle Assyria. Rather than fight Assyria, Ahaz thinks it would be better to pay tribute to Assyria and thus buy protection. What should Ahaz do?

Isaiah believes that Ahaz should trust neither the Syro-Ephraimite alliance nor the Assyrians for protection. Ahaz should trust God. So Isaiah goes to Ahaz and tells him that the Lord God says not to fear these "two smoldering stumps of firebrands" (see Is 7:4). Rather, trust God.

> If you do not stand firm in faith,
> you shall not stand at all (Is 7:9).

Ahaz does not want to take Isaiah's advice. He will not ask for a "sign" (not a miracle, but an event in which God's power and presence is experienced), probably because he has already made up his mind to pay tribute to the Assyrians. So Isaiah says, "Hear then, O house of David! The Lord himself will give you a sign. Look, the young woman is with child and shall bear a son, and shall name him Immanuel. He shall eat curds and honey by the time he knows how to refuse the evil and choose the good. For before the child knows how to refuse the evil and choose the good, the land before whose two kings you are in dread will be deserted (Is 7:16).

Isaiah is reminding Ahaz that he is in a covenant relationship with Yahweh when he addresses him as "house of David." In article 2 we explained how the covenant promise was now understood to be related to King David's line remaining secure. Isaiah reminds Ahaz that God has promised to keep the line secure. A young woman (most probably one of Ahaz's wives) is with child (no mention of a virginal conception). Through this child, a sign of future hope in time of desperation, God is reminding Ahaz that God promised to be with the house of David. That is why the child will be named "Immanuel." The child is a sign of God's keeping the promise to be with God's people.

Isaiah tells Ahaz that because he is not trusting Yahweh the land will be devastated. That is why the child will eat curds and honey. The produce available in times of peace will not be his food. But it is not the Syro-Ephramite war that will destroy Judah (see Is 7:16). Rather the Assyrians are the ones the Lord will use to chasten the people. "On that day the Lord will shave with a razor hired beyond the River—with the King of Assyria—the head and the hair of the feet, and it will take off the beard as well" (Is 7:20).

LEVELS OF MEANING

FOR ISAIAH AND AHAZ
"House of David"—Ahaz's line
"Young woman"—Ahaz's wife
"Immanuel"—God will be with the child

FOR CHRISTIANS:
"House of David"—The Messiah's line
"Young Woman"—Mary
"Immanuel"—God will become a child

So the text does support our claim that Isaiah is speaking to Ahaz about the contemporary situation. The text makes perfect sense in that context.

Why, then, does Matthew use the text as he does? When Matthew speaks of "fulfilling the words of the prophet," he does not mean "fulfill" in the sense of fulfilling a prediction but in the sense of fulfilling a hope. The hope of the house of David that God would remain with them was fulfilled beyond their wildest expectations in Jesus. In order to help explain the significance of the event which took place in Jesus' birth Matthew uses Isaiah's words. However, the words are used to help explain the event; the event is not used to help explain the words. Isaiah was not a person who foretold the incarnation and the virginal conception. Rather, Isaiah was God's messenger who told Ahaz that his trust should be in his God. If Ahaz failed to trust God, the inevitable result would be suffering.

Review Questions

1. What is the "incarnation"?
2. What is the virginal conception?
3. What is the function of a prophet?
4. What political crisis does King Ahaz face?

5. What does Isaiah think Ahaz should do?
6. Of what is Isaiah reminding Ahaz when he addresses him as "house of David"?
7. Why is the fact that Ahaz's line is being carried on important? Why might Ahaz's child be called "Immanuel"?
8. What is in store for the people because Ahaz does not trust God?
9. Why does Matthew use Isaiah's text?

Discussion Questions

1. Do you think Isaiah's advice to Ahaz to trust God could possibly have been wise politically as well as spiritually? Explain.
2. In what ways might the phrase "God is with us" be understood? Is there a difference in the way God was with God's people through David and through Jesus?
3. What does it mean to say that the words are used to help explain the meaning of the event; the event is not used to help explain the meaning of the words?

ARTICLE 11

Isaiah Waits for the Lord

Question: "Why does Isaiah tell his disciples to seal up his message? (Is 8:16) Shouldn't he be proclaiming it far and wide?" (Is 8:1–20)

Isaiah has proclaimed God's (not his) message far and wide, but he has been ignored. Isaiah now feels that it is time to make a written record of what he has said, and then wait for events to unfold, events which Isaiah is sure will confirm the truth of his insights. Perhaps then, in hindsight, the people will listen.

Scripture scholars think that chapter 8 ends a memoir of Isaiah's which began with Isaiah's call (chapter 6) and which, as a whole, reveals Isaiah's preaching and posture before and during the Syro-Ephramite war (733–732 B.C.). As we mentioned, one of the functions of a call story is to affirm and justify the prophet in his role as God's messenger. If a prophet is being ignored, the prophet would feel the need to affirm that the unwelcome message being delivered is really God's message, not the prophet's.

We have already read of God's message as it was given verbally by Isaiah. "Trust God, not political alliances. Syria and Israel will be destroyed, so you needn't fear them. If you don't trust God, you yourselves will be destroyed by the Assyrians. Suffering is not intended to destroy but to save God's people."

However, God spoke through Isaiah not only in Isaiah's words but in Isaiah's whole life. As Isaiah says, he and his children "are signs and portents in Israel from the Lord of hosts" (Is 8:18).

So far we have read references to two of Isaiah's children. In the first, we read that Shear-jashub accompanied Isaiah when Isaiah spoke to Ahaz (see Is 7:3). Shear-jashub means "a remnant shall return." We have already noted that the hope of a remnant is core to Isaiah's message. Some shall return to Yahweh and place their trust in God.

However, this promise of hope also implies another sad truth. Most will not return to Yahweh and trust in God to protect them. Instead they will place their trust in political alliances.

Isaiah's outspoken condemnation of this trust in political alliances will make him an outcast in his own homeland. One gets a real sense that Isaiah's words might have been considered treasonous by others when we read, "For the Lord spoke this to me while his hand was strong upon me, and warned me not to walk in the ways of this people, saying, 'Do not call conspiracy all that this people calls conspiracy, and do not fear what it fears, or be in dread'" (Is 8:11–12). It seems likely that Isaiah's actions were called treasonous by some. Isaiah was becoming an outcast in his own society.

Isaiah's second child is also a "sign and portent" of Isaiah's teaching, which is being ignored. This second son is named Maher-shalal-hash-baz. The name means, "quick spoils, speedy plunder." Like Ahaz's son (Immanuel) Isaiah's son would still be young when Syria and Israel (the northern kingdom) would be defeated by the Assyrians (see Is 8:4). The son's very presence would remind people that God, through his messenger Isaiah, had said that Ahaz should not have paid tribute to Assyria out of fear of the Syro-Ephraimite alliance. Had Ahaz trusted God rather than the Assyrians, he would have found that the two nations threatening him would be destroyed without his becoming a vassal state to Assyria.

Not only Ahaz but most of those in Judah failed to listen to Isaiah, either to his words or to the signs and portents represented by his children's names. So Isaiah withdrew to the circle of his disciples, sealed up his teachings for future reference, and waited for the Lord, putting his hope in God (see Is 8:17).

The fact that Isaiah entrusted his prophetic oracles to a group of followers, to be brought out later, casts light on the type of literature we encounter when we read the book of Isaiah. As we noted before, we are not reading the words of the prophet exactly as they were spoken. Rather we are reading the words in an edited and arranged format, an editing that occurred after events had confirmed the spiritual insights of the prophet.

Isaiah, God's messenger, will not spend the rest of his life in seclusion. Another political crisis will draw him out, and Isaiah will once more try to make God's voice heard in the midst of God's people.

Review Questions

1. Why does Isaiah think it is time to make a written record of God's message?
2. What does Shear-jashub mean? What is the significance of this name?
3. How might Isaiah's actions have been perceived as treasonous?
4. What does Maher-shalal-hash-baz mean? What is the significance of this name?
5. How did Isaiah practice what he preached?

Discussion Questions

1. What is a "sign" in nature? Name some. Do you think there are also "signs" in the spiritual realm? Can you name any?
2. Do you think it was wise or unwise of Isaiah to seal up his prophecy and wait? Explain.
3. Do you think religious leaders should give advice to political leaders? Why or why not? Do you know of times when this was done? Was the advice taken? Explain.

ARTICLE 12

Messianic Prophecies

Question: "How can you possibly maintain that Isaiah did not foretell the incarnation when he says (Is 9:7) that the child is named, 'Wonderful Counselor, Mighty God, Everlasting Father, Prince of Peace'? " (Is 11:1–9)

Once again we must try to understand Isaiah's words in the context in which they were spoken rather than impose on them knowledge which came centuries later.

The context for Isaiah's message of hope is the Assyrian oppression of the northern kingdom. The "land of Zebulun and the land of Naphtali" (Is 9:1) refers to the land first conquered by the Assyrians. By 733 B.C. the king of Assyria had appropriated territory of the northern kingdom and had established three Assyrian provinces. By 721 B.C. the Assyrians will conquer Samaria, the capital of the northern kingdom.

The "great light" which Isaiah sees and wants the people to see is the insight that all is in the hands of Yahweh. People must learn to trust God and live faithfully in covenant love. Isaiah addresses Yahweh when he says:

> You have multiplied the nation,
> you have increased its joy.
> For the yoke of their burden,
> and the bar across their shoulders,
> the rod of their oppressor,
> You have broken as on the day of Midian (Is 9:3–4).

The hope which Isaiah sees is that if only the people will trust God, God will be with the house of David. God will free the people

47

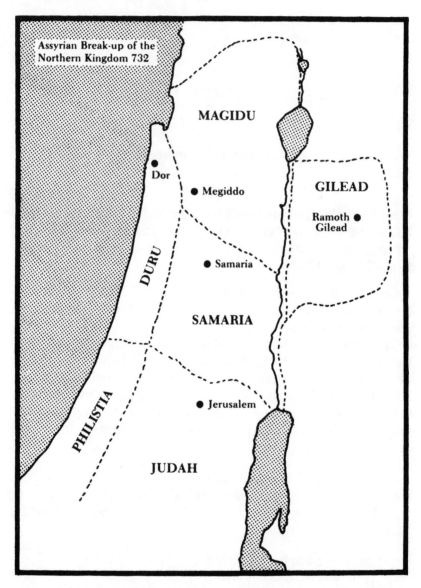

After the attack by northern Israel on Judah in 734–732, Assyria invaded and broke up the northern kingdom into four provinces: Magidu, Duru, Gilead and Samaria. Israel ruled only the latter.

from the yoke of the Assyrians and will reunite them in peace as God had done through King David.

> His authority [i.e. the king in David's line, now Hezekiah] shall
>   grow continually,
>   and there shall be endless peace
>   for the throne of David and his Kingdom.
> He will establish and uphold it
>   with justice and with righteousness
>   from this time onward and forevermore (Is 9:7).

The specific setting for this hymn of hope was the birth of the royal child, Hezekiah, or his ascension to the throne. Either way, the song describes the person through whom God would establish peace and security. This king would be a "wonderful counselor" (Is 7:6) who would not be led astray as Ahaz had been. He would be a "mighty God" (Is 7:6)—that is, God's might would be in him as God's might was in David when David conquered the Philistines. It would not have been unusual to describe a king or future king in terms similar to the way one would describe God, such as "mighty God" or "God's son" (see Ps 2). This kind of description was an expression of faith in God's covenant love since God had promised to be with God's "anointed one," God's "messiah," the king through whom God would rescue the people and establish peace.

The ideal king will be an "everlasting father" (Is 9:16), steadfast in his care and service as Moses had been. He will be a prince of peace because his dependence on Yahweh will result in peace.

This beautiful hymn of hope is one of three songs in Isaiah which are called "messianic prophecies." "Messiah" means "the anointed one." In the Israelite culture, kings, prophets, and priests were anointed as a sign that they were chosen and commissioned by God. So a song about a king in the house of David who will do God's will and so be an instrument of God's protection and peace is a "messianic prophecy."

We have already read and discussed two of these messianic prophecies, the Immanuel prophecy in Isaiah 7:10–14 and this prophecy in Isaiah 9:1–7. The first was urging Ahaz to trust in Yahweh's promise to the house of David. The second is expressing

---

APPROXIMATE TIMELINE FOR 1 ISAIAH

742 B.C. — Isaiah receives his call

* 733 B.C. — Northern kingdom suffers first defeat at the hands of the Assyrians

732 B.C. — Syro-Ephramite war at height; King Ahaz and Immanuel prophecy

722–721 B.C. — Samaria, capital of northern kingdom, conquered

* 715 B.C. — Hezekiah, Ahaz's son, comes to throne (Judah a vassal of Assyria)

714 B.C. — Philistines revolt against Assyria (Egyptians try to get Hezekiah to join but he doesn't)

705 B.C. — Babylonians revolt against Assyria (Egyptians try to get Hezekiah to join; he finally does)

701 B.C. — Sennacherib crushes Hezekiah's revolt; Jerusalem is spared

---

the hope that Hezekiah will be the virtuous king who will rely completely on Yahweh.

The third passage in Isaiah 11:1–9 does not seem to be so distinctly referring to an identifiable person. Perhaps this third message of hope in a messiah is less definite and more universalized precisely because the present king, Hezekiah, was not living up to the hope placed in him. Once more the hoped-for king will be from the house of David (see Is 11:1; Jesse is David's father). He will have those great gifts which past chosen leaders have had, the "wisdom and understanding" of a Solomon, the "might" of a David, the

---

MESSIANIC PROPHECIES

Isaiah 7:10–14
Isaiah 9:1–7
Isaiah 11:1–9

"fear of the Lord" of a Moses. The prophet soars off into the sublime as he describes the kind of peace which God could establish if only people would live in "righteousness" and "faithfulness."

> They shall not hurt or destroy on all my holy mountain;
>   for the earth will be full of the knowledge of the Lord
>   as the waters cover the sea (Is 11:9).

Isaiah's hopes for a messiah of the house of David who would reunite all of Israel and establish peace in the kingdom were not realized in a geopolitical sense. However, after Jesus' resurrection, when the early church began to realize who Jesus had been and what had been accomplished in and through him, these messianic passages were used to help explain these insights about Jesus the Messiah, and the marvelous ways of God. So while Isaiah did not foretell the incarnation, Isaiah's words have been used to explain the significance of the incarnation. The words have taken on a significance that transcends their original context or their original intent.

Review Questions

1. By 733 B.C. what had happened?
2. What is the "great light" which Isaiah sees?
3. What does Isaiah say will happen if only the people will trust Yahweh?
4. Why is it an expression of faith in covenant love to say that the king is "mighty God?"
5. What is a "messianic prophecy"?

6. Why might the third messianic prophecy (Is 11:1–9) be less specific and more universalized?
8. How did these messianic prophecies help explain who Jesus had been?

Discussion Questions

1. Can you think of some expressions in our culture in which the intent of the language and the literal meaning of the words are not exactly the same? Think of words of love, words of praise. Why is "complete exactness" not crucial (or even desirable) in these expressions?
2. Do you think peace is possible? Why or why not?
3. What does it mean to say that Isaiah's hope was not fulfilled in a geopolitical sense? Has it been fulfilled in a spiritual sense? Explain.

ARTICLE 13

The Central Question: What Do Events Say About Our Relationship with God?

Question: "This constant switching back and forth between oracles of hope and oracles of doom is confusing (Is 9–12). Wasn't Isaiah trying to have it both ways by saying both 'You will be destroyed' and 'You will be saved'? "

The oracles of hope and the oracles of doom in Isaiah 9–12 are confusing because they come from different times in Isaiah's ministry and so have different settings. The settings are not always obvious to a modern day reader. So, before we answer the question "Is Isaiah trying to have it both ways? " we will give an overview of the settings within which various oracles were most likely delivered.

We have already discussed the Syro-Ephramite war (735–733 B.C.) as the setting for Isaiah's oracles to Ahaz. At this time in Isaiah's ministry Assyria was a more direct threat to the northern kingdom than it was to the southern kingdom.

We have also already mentioned that Assyria oppressed the northern kingdom for a number of years, finally destroying Samaria in 722 B.C. The Assyrian threat to the northern kingdom as well as the lessons that could be learned from these events by those in the southern kingdom is the setting for oracles such as those in Isaiah 9:7–20.

However, in Isaiah 10 the Assyrian threat is not to the northern kingdom but to Jerusalem itself.

> Shall I not do to Jerusalem and her idols
>   what I have done to Samaria and her images? (Is 10:11).

So, as we continue to read Isaiah it will be helpful to know a little about the threat which Assyria eventually posed to Judah.

In 714 B.C. a Philistine city named Ashdod revolted against Assyria. Hezekiah, then king of Judah, was evidently tempted to join the revolution. We will read of Isaiah's message on this occasion in Isaiah 20.

In 705 B.C. another rebellion against Assyria was launched, this time by Babylonia. Again Hezekiah was tempted to join, and Isaiah counseled against it. Chapters 28–33 of Isaiah date primarily to this time when the Assyrians, under Sennacherib, threatened to destroy Jerusalem itself.

While we can point to some sections of Isaiah which obviously belong to one of these specific historical situations, we cannot always place an oracle in its appropriate setting. Our arrangement is an edited arrangement, rearranged and expanded upon by the prophet's disciples. Some later oracles appear early in the arrangement. Reading this arrangement of oracles from a variety of times and settings will be less confusing if we do not expect the kind of consistent movement of plot which we would find in a narrative.

Instead of asking how each oracle relates to the one which precedes or follows it (there may be no discernible relationship), we would do better to ask. "What is Isaiah telling God's people about their relationship with God? " This is the important question.

With our attention centered on what the oracles say about the relationship between God and God's people, we can address the question, "Is Isaiah trying to have it both ways by preaching both destruction and hope?"

The answer to this question is "no." Both the message of destruction and the message of hope are integral to the truth of covenant love. Destruction or suffering is inevitable if people persist in sin because God is too holy to let sin go on unchecked. However, destruction is never total. God is too loving to abandon God's people. A remnant will turn back to God and be saved.

What Isaiah is trying to make clear is that God is present in events, whether those events be occasions of suffering or of joy.

APPROXIMATE TIMELINE FOR 1 ISAIAH

742 B.C.	Isaiah receives his call
733 B.C.	Northern kingdom suffers first defeat at the hands of the Assyrians
* 732 B.C.	Syro-Ephramite war at its height; King Ahaz and Immanuel prophecy
* 722–721 B.C.	Samaria, capital of northern kingdom, conquered
715 B.C.	Hezekiah, Ahaz's son, comes to throne (Judah a vassal of Assyria)
* 714 B.C.	Philistines revolt against Assyria (Egyptians try to get Hezekiah to join but he doesn't)
* 705 B.C.	Babylonians revolt against Assyria (Egyptians try to get Hezekiah to join; he finally does)
701 B.C.	Sennacherib crushes Hezekiah's revolt; Jerusalem is spared

God is present in the victory of the Assyrians over the Israelites even though the Assyrians are not aware of this. Isaiah makes this clear when he pictures God as saying:

Ah, Assyria, the rod of my anger—
  the club in their hands is my fury!
Against a godless nation I send him,
  and against the people of my wrath I command him,

To take spoil and seize plunder,
  and to tread them down like the mire of the streets.
But this is not what he intends,
  nor does he have this in mind (Is 10:6–7a).

No matter what the event, God is present. Building on this spiritual insight, Isaiah interprets the meaning of current events for his contemporaries. The meaning of events is apparent only when one views them from the context of covenant love. So even though the edited arrangement of oracles sometimes seems disconnected, and even though we are not always able to name with certainty the current event which precipitated the oracle, nevertheless Isaiah's message is clear. Whether the event causes suffering or joy, God is present in the event, and God's purpose is to live in covenant love with God's people.

Review Questions

1. What was the political situation in 735–733 B.C.?
2. What happened in 722 B.C.?
3. What happened in 714 B.C.?
4. What happened in 705–700 B.C.?
5. What is the important question to ask about each oracle?
6. Why is a message of suffering and destruction always integral to covenant love?
7. Why is a message of hope always integral to covenant love?
8. In what way might Assyria's victory over Samaria be within God's providence?
9. What is God's purpose in every event, whether that event be an occasion of suffering or of joy?

Discussion Questions

1. What is the difference between an edited arrangement of individual oracles and a connected narrative such as a novel?
2. Have you ever been involved in an event which caused you suffering, but, in hindsight, you understood that you needed

to go through such an experience to become who you are? Explain.

3. Do you think hardship builds strength? Explain. Do you think luxury builds weakness? Explain.

4. Do you believe God can bring good out of anything? Explain.

ARTICLE 14

Oracles Against the Nations

Question: "These oracles against the nations are confusing too. Was Israel being besieged by all of these nations at the same time? " (Is 13:1–23:8)

The oracles against the nations which appear in Isaiah 13:1–23:8 are also terribly confusing for a person who brings a false expectation to the book and so thinks of the oracles as having been given all at one time or consecutively. As was discussed in Article 13, the book of Isaiah is an edited collection of oracles. Not only do the oracles date to different times in Isaiah's ministry, but some date to times long after Isaiah was dead.

For instance, in chapters 13–14 the oracles are against Babylon. Babylon had not arisen as a threat to the Israelites during Isaiah's ministry. These oracles must date to the time between the late seventh century, the time of Babylonian ascendancy, and 539 B.C., when the Babylonians were defeated by the Persians.

On the other hand, some oracles do date to specific times in Isaiah's ministry. For instance, the oracles against Syria and the northern kingdom in Isaiah 17:1–11 date to the time of the Syro-Ephraimite war which we have already discussed. The oracle in chapter 18 (18:1–7) which describes messengers being sent from Egypt to other countries might well date to 714 B.C. when the Egyptians were trying to get other nations to join with them against the Assyrians. Isaiah, of course, did not think that Judah should join this revolt.

Although some of the oracles can be placed in specific historical situations within or outside Isaiah's ministry, others cannot be dated at all with any real certainty. There are several reasons for

58

WHY ORACLES ARE DIFFICULT TO DATE

- Appear in the work of more than one prophet.
  Appropriate for each setting.

- Cosmic, not specific, references.

---

this. One is that some oracles appear in the work of more than one prophet. For instance, the oracles against Moab in Isaiah 15:1–16:14 are repeated, sometimes almost word for word, in Jeremiah 48:26–43. Moab, a city across the Dead Sea, was an adversary of Judah's through the centuries. So to date the oracles as belonging to the time of Isaiah rather than to the time of Jeremiah (626–580 B.C.) would be difficult since the oracle would have been appropriate in either setting and the present arrangement was edited after Isaiah of Jerusalem was dead.

Sometimes an oracle cannot be dated with any preciseness because its vocabulary makes it cosmic rather than specific in its reference. An example of such cosmic imagery can be found in Isaiah 13:9–16.

> See, the day of the Lord comes,
>   cruel with wrath and fierce anger,
> To make the earth a desolation
>   and to destroy its sinners from it.
> For the stars of the heavens and the constellations
>   will not give their light;
> The sun will be dark at its rising
>   and the moon will not shed its light.
> I will punish the world for its evil,
>   and the wicked for their iniquity;
> I will put an end to the pride of the arrogant,
>   and lay low the insolence of tyrants (Is 13:9–11).

While this oracle has been placed in the context of oracles against Babylon, its vocabulary and scope make it appropriate for any setting where the prophet is warning his audience of coming disaster.

Another oracle which becomes more definite because of its setting is the "taunt song" in Isaiah 14:3–21. Although the prose introduction and conclusion to this song say that the taunt is aimed at the king of Babylon (possibly Nebachadnezzar, who destroyed Jerusalem in 587 B.C.), the poem itself does not name the king. Such a poem, in which those in the netherworld also taunt the fallen king as he arrives, shares much in common with pagan myths from surrounding cultures. Because of its lack of specific reference the unnamed king becomes any king or any powerful being whose might and arrogance signal him out as a person who is headed for a mighty fall. In fact, verses 12–15 in chapter 14 are sometimes used to refer to Lucifer, the fallen angel.

> How you are fallen from heaven,
>   O Day Star, son of dawn!
> How you are cut down to the ground,
>   you who laid the nations low!
> You said in your heart:
>   I will ascend to heaven;
> I will raise my throne
>   above the stars of God (Is 14:12–13)

Because the language of the oracle becomes less specific and more universal it becomes appropriate for a variety of settings.

So once more we must remind ourselves that instead of putting our entire concentration on trying to figure out the connection among oracles in their present arrangement, or even the original historical setting of each, we would do well to concentrate on the theological significance of the oracles. What are the oracles against the nations saying about the relationship between God and God's people?

Two insights seem to be behind these oracles. The first is that political events are not unconnected to God's power and presence in the lives of God's people. No nation is outside of God's power. Nations rise and fall as part of God's provident plan for God's people.

Because God's providence is behind events, people should concentrate on being faithful to their covenant relationship with God and then simply trust God. Fidelity rather than political alliances is what is needed if Judah is to survive.

Review Questions

1. How can you tell that some oracles date to a time after Isaiah of Jerusalem?
2. Give two reasons why some oracles cannot be dated with any degree of certainty.
3. Who is Nebachadnezzar and what did he do?
4. What two insights seem to be behind the oracles against the nations?

Discussion Questions

1. What does it mean to say that the language is "universal" rather than "specific"?
2. Do you believe that God is God of all nations? What are some ramifications of such a belief?
3. Does it change your idea of the Bible or of revelation to know that the same oracles appear in the work of more than one prophet? Explain.

ARTICLE 15

Isaiah: A Sign and Portent to Hezekiah

Question: "Why would God tell Isaiah to walk around town naked? " (Is 20)

In Article 11, when discussing the significance of the names of Isaiah's sons, we noted that Isaiah said, "See, I and the children whom the Lord has given me are signs and portents in Israel from the Lord of hosts, who dwells on Mount Zion" (Is 8:18). The scene in chapter 20, in which Isaiah walks naked through the town, is described as "a sign and portent against Egypt and Ethiopia" (see Is 20:3). To understand why, we need to know something about the political context in which this scene takes place.

In Article 13, when describing the major historical events which act as a backdrop to Isaiah's oracles, we mentioned a revolt against the Assyrians which occurred in 714 B.C. The "sign and portent" inherent in Isaiah's actions in chapter 20 take place in the context of this revolt of 714 B.C.

Shortly before the revolt in question the new king, Hezekiah, had come to the throne in Judah. Hezekiah was the son mentioned earlier in the Immanuel prophecy. Unlike his father Ahaz, Hezekiah was not a weak king. We read in 2 Kings 18 that the narrator considered Hezekiah second only to David as a good king.

Because Hezekiah's father Ahaz had sought protection from the Assyrians during the Syro-Ephramite war, Judah was a vassal of Assyria when Hezekiah ascended to the throne. In order to appease Assyria, Ahaz had allowed an Assyrian altar to be installed in the temple and had been paying a large tribute to Assyria.

Hezekiah, as part of an overall religious reform, had removed Assyrian cult objects from the temple. A political ramification of this religious reform was a growth in nationalism, a growth in the people's desire to throw off the power which the Assyrians exercised over them.

Judah was not the only country which was anxious to rid itself of Assyrian dominance. Egypt of Ethiopia was rallying other countries to join against Assyria. (We noted this when we read Isaiah 18.) The rebellion broke out in a Philistine city named Ashdod. (See the oracle against Philistia in Isaiah 14:28–38.) It is this rebellion of Ashdod that is the setting for Isaiah 20. "In the year that the commander in chief, who was sent by King Sargon of Assyria, came to Ashdod and fought against it and took it . . ." (Is 20:1).

Isaiah is told to walk through the town looking like a person being led out by a conquering army. The reason Isaiah is to portray a prisoner of war is to warn Hezekiah and Judah that they should not be tempted to join the Philistine city in revolt against Assyria, nor should they depend on Egypt for protection against Assyria. Those who were revolting would be conquered. That is why the action is said to be a "sign and portent" against Egypt and Ethiopia; they are leading the revolt.

As things turned out, Hezekiah did not join the revolt of 714 B.C., so Isaiah was, for the time being, successful in persuading Judah to trust Yahweh. However, neither did Assyria invade Egypt. The inhabitants of Egypt were not led away, naked and bound, by the Assyrians. Only the inhabitants of Ashdod itself were conquered.

Even though Egypt was not conquered by the Assyrians, Isaiah's advice was wise advice. Egypt would have been a completely untrustworthy ally, as those in Ashdod discovered. After having revolted with Egypt's encouragement, Ashdod looked in vain to Egypt for help when the Assyrians invaded. No help was forthcoming.

The fact that the Egyptians would prove untrustworthy, however, was not Isaiah's core message. As was true when Ahaz was king, Isaiah's core message to Hezekiah was that Hezekiah should trust God and only God. No political alliance could offer more security than could fidelity to covenant love.

APPROXIMATE TIMELINE FOR 1 ISAIAH

742 B.C. — Isaiah receives his call

733 B.C. — Northern kingdom suffers first
defeat at the hands of the Assyrians

732 B.C. — Syro-Ephramite War at height; King
Ahaz and Immanuel prophecy

722–721 B.C. — Samaria, capital of northern
kingdom, conquered

* 715 B.C. — Hezekiah, Ahaz's son, comes to
throne (Judah a vassal of Assyria)

* 714 B.C. — Philistines revolt against Assyria
(Egyptians try to get Hezekiah to
join but he doesn't)

705 B.C. — Babylonians revolt against Assyria
(Egyptians try to get Hezekiah to
join; he finally does)

701 B.C. — Sennacherib crushes Hezekiah's
revolt; Jerusalem is spared

Review Questions

1. Who is Hezekiah?
2. What was Judah's relationship to Assyria when Hezekiah became king? Why was this Judah's relationship to Assyria?
3. What did Egypt do in 714 B.C.?
4. What is Isaiah's symbolic action supposed to say to Hezekiah and to Judah?
5. What did Hezekiah decide to do?

6. In hindsight did it appear that Hezekiah could have trusted Egypt? Why?
7. What is Isaiah's core message to Hezekiah?

Discussion Questions

1. Can you think of any symbolic actions which people take in our day to try to affect public opinion? (Actions against war? Actions against abortion? Actions against animal experimentation?) Which actions do you think are justified? Which are unjustified? Why?
2. Do you feel sympathetic or unsympathetic toward "symbolic actions"? Is this a way in which you personally might try to influence events? Why or why not?
3. Do you think such symbolic actions have ever succeeded in setting the course of human history? Explain.

ARTICLE 16

Historical Backdrop: 705–701 B.C.

Question: "I don't understand this oracle against Jerusalem (Is 22, 'The Valley of Vision'). Was Jerusalem captured or not? "

The oracle against Jerusalem has caused much debate among scholars for the very reason which the questioner raises. Some of the oracle seems to assume that Jerusalem is not destroyed (see Is 22:1–3, 12–14). Other parts of the oracle seem to assume that Jerusalem is destroyed (see Is 22:4–8). Scholars differ on whether or not this oracle dates to 701 B.C., when Jerusalem was spared, to 587–586 B.C., when Jerusalem was destroyed, or perhaps is an arrangement of oracles from both of these periods.

No matter what the original setting of the oracle, it will be very helpful in understanding this oracle against Jerusalem to know what happened in Hezekiah's reign between 705 and 701 B.C.

As was mentioned earlier, in 705 B.C. another revolt against the Assyrians, still encouraged by the Egyptians, broke out, this time in Babylonia. As more and more nations joined in the revolt, Hezekiah once more found himself sorely tempted to join in. We will read Isaiah's advice on this occasion when we get to Isaiah 28–33. For now, suffice it to say that Isaiah once more urged the king to rely on Yahweh rather than on political alliances. However, this time Isaiah was not successful in persuading the king to stay clear of the revolt.

Hezekiah's decision to join in the revolt against Sennacherib, king of Assyria, proved to be disastrous. One can read of the consequences in 2 Kings 18:13–19:37. In order to punish Hezekiah, Sennacherib invaded Judah and destroyed at least forty-six cities. Hezekiah told Sennacherib that he would pay whatever he was

66

APPROXIMATE TIMELINE FOR 1 ISAIAH

742 B.C. — Isaiah receives his call

733 B.C. — Northern kingdom suffers first defeat at the hands of the Assyrians

732 B.C. — Syro-Ephramite war at height; King Ahaz and Immanuel prophecy

722–721 B.C. — Samaria, capital of northern kingdom, conquered

715 B.C. — Hezekiah, Ahaz's son, comes to throne (Judah a vassal of Assyria)

714 B.C. — Philistines revolt against Assyria (Egyptians try to get Hezekiah to join but he doesn't)

* 705 B.C. — Babylonians revolt against Assyria (Egyptians try to get Hezekiah to join; he finally does)

* 701 B.C. — Sennacherib crushes Hezekiah's revolt; Jerusalem is spared

asked if Sennacherib would withdraw. "The king of Assyria demanded of King Hezekiah of Judah three hundred talents of silver and thirty talents of gold. Hezekiah gave him all the silver that was found in the house of the Lord, and in the treasuries of the king's household. At that time Hezekiah stripped the gold from the doors of the temple of the Lord . . . and from the doorposts that King Hezekiah of Judah had overlaid and gave it to the king of Assyria (2 Kgs 18:15–16).

Despite Hezekiah's capitulation Sennacherib threatened to destroy Jerusalem. We will read of Isaiah's advice at this juncture

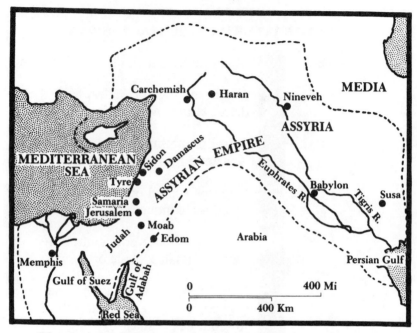

The Assyrian Empire in the 8th and 7th Centuries B.C.

when we get to Isaiah 36–39. As things turned out, Sennacherib did not destroy Jerusalem. The narrator of 2 Kings states: "The angel of the Lord set out and struck down one hundred eighty-five thousand in the camp of the Assyrians; when morning dawned they were all dead bodies. Then King Sennacherib of Assyria left, went home, and lived in Nineveh" (2 Kgs 19:35–36).

The oracle against Jerusalem in Isaiah 22 seems, for the most part, to date from the time of this "miraculous deliverance" in 701 B.C. The people are on the roof tops shouting exultantly (see Is 22:2). Their victory is not because they acquitted themselves well in battle (see Is 22:3). Much of Judah has already been destroyed. In preparation for the battle against Jerusalem the people prepared their weapons (Is 22:8b), checked their water supply, and fortified their walls. However, they failed to turn to Yahweh who, nevertheless, provided the victory (see Is 22:11b).

One would think that the destruction of so much of Judah and the last minute deliverance of Jerusalem would cause the people to reflect on their failures and repent (see Is 22:12). But instead the people are rejoicing as though they had nothing from which to repent.

> Let us eat and drink
>> for tomorrow we die (Is 22:13).

So, instead of rejoicing with his people over their temporary deliverance, Isaiah is in mourning. He mourns the fact that, even when shown that destruction is imminent and that only Yahweh saves, the people still refuse to see the significance of these events in the light of covenant love. The people rejoice over their close call, but fail to learn the lesson which Isaiah believes the close call was meant to teach.

Review Questions

1. Who was Sennacherib?
2. What did Hezekiah decide to do during the revolt of 705 B.C.?
3. What were the ramifications of this decision?
4. According to the account in 2 Kings, why did Sennacherib not destroy Jerusalem?
5. Why did Isaiah fail to rejoice with his people over their temporary deliverance?

Discussion Questions

1. Have you ever had a "close call?" What were your feelings afterward? Did you experience God as present in the events? Explain.
2. When you have something difficult to face, do you ever make the mistake the Israelites made—relying completely on your own preparations and completely forgetting about God? Explain. Is the opposite a good idea: relying completely on God and making no preparations? Explain.
3. What do you think is meant when it is said that "an angel of death" went through the camp?

ARTICLE 17

Isaiah's Apocalypse

Question: "Why, in the middle of total destruction, would one give glory to God? " (Is 24:14–16; see Is 24–27)

One would give glory to God over the destruction of a city if one believed that the city was evil and that right order, God's order, was being established by its destruction. In Isaiah 24:1–27:13, often called the "apocalypse" of Isaiah, the destruction is for just this purpose.

Apocalyptic literature is a kind of literature which promises destruction to oppressors and salvation to the righteous oppressed. The time when this destruction/salvation will occur is often called "the end time." In Isaiah it is called "the day of the Lord." Because apocalyptic literature uses cosmic imagery picturing judgment not only on people but on the earth itself, on the heavens, and in the netherworld, many people read apocalyptic literature as though it were predicting the end of the earth altogether. However, apocalyptic literature, too, is written to a contemporary audience in order to address contemporary problems. Similarities between these characteristics of apocalyptic literature and Isaiah 24–27 will become apparent as we look at the salvific purpose in the destruction described in Isaiah's "apocalypse."

The relationship between the call to praise and the destruction of the city is explicitly stated in chapter 25.

> O Lord, you are my God,
> I will extol you, I will praise your name;
> For you have done wonderful things,
> plans formed of old, faithful and sure.
> For you have made the city a heap

APOCALYPTIC LITERATURE

Promises destruction to oppressors and salvation to the righteous oppressed.

- Written to contemporary audience

- Addresses contemporary problems

- Uses cosmic imagery

- Speaks of "the day of the Lord," or of "the end time," meaning the end of the present suffering

---

> the fortified city a ruin;
> The palace of aliens is a city no more,
>   it will never be rebuilt.
> Therefore strong people will glorify you;
>   cities of ruthless nations will fear you.
> For you have been a refuge to the poor,
>   a refuge to the needy in their distress,
>   a shelter from the rainstorm and a shade from the heat (Is 25:1–4).

The point of view of the speaker is satisfaction at the destruction of the city. Why? Because the city as it had existed was not faithful to Yahweh. It had not been a refuge for the poor and needy. Because the speaker longs for right order he longs for the destruction.

> My soul yearns for you in the night,
>   my spirit within me earnestly seeks you.
> For when your judgments are in the earth,
>   the inhabitants of the world learn righteousness.
> If favor is shown to the wicked,
>   they do not learn righteousness;
> In the land of uprightness they deal perversely
>   and do not see the majesty of the Lord (Is 25:9–10).

In describing destruction the author uses mythological images which draw the whole cosmos into the occurrences which must

precede the establishment of right order. The evil to be defeated is
referred to as "Leviathan the twisting serpent" (see Is 27:1) and as
"the dragon that is in the sea" (see Is 27:1). Not just those on earth
but "the host of heaven in heaven" (see Is 24:21) will be punished.
The sun and moon themselves will be "ashamed" (see Is 24:23).

Salvation as well as destruction is described in cosmic terms. Not
only will the poor and needy on earth find a haven, but death itself
will be defeated.

> Your dead shall live, their corpses shall rise.
>   O dwellers in the dust, awake and sing for joy!
> For your dew is a radiant dew,
>   and the earth will give birth to those long dead (Is 26:19).

When God establishes right order on the earth, God will provide
for all peoples.

> On this mountain the Lord of hosts will make for all peoples
>   a feast of rich food, a feast of well aged wines (Is 25:6).

When right order is established all will recognize Yahweh and will
worship Yahweh. "And on that day a great trumpet will be blown,
and those who were lost in the land of Assyria and those who were
driven out to the land of Egypt will come and worship the Lord on
the holy mountain at Jerusalem" (Is 27:13).

This conclusion to the edited apocalypse may well refer to the
time after the Babylonian exile when the Israelites were being encouraged to return to Jerusalem from other countries. Although
the imagery in apocalyptic literature is so general that it can apply
to any situation of oppression, and the imagery so cosmic that it
encompasses all of creation, nevertheless the call of the prophet is
addressed to his specific historical setting. The prophet expresses
pleasure when destruction comes because only through the destruction of evil can God's power be recognized and God's order be
established.

Review Questions

1. What is the "theme" or "promise" in apocalyptic literature?
2. In apocalyptic literature what phrase is often used to name the time when persecution will stop?
3. What phrase does Isaiah use to refer to this "end time"?
4. In apocalyptic literature why would the speaker rejoice that a city had been destroyed?
5. Give some examples of the use of cosmic imagery in the destruction of evil and the establishment of right order. What is the effect of using cosmic imagery?

Discussion Questions

1. Are you surprised to learn that the phrase "the end time," as it is used in apocalyptic literature, is not referring to a time in your future? Why or why not?
2. Imagine that you are a prisoner of war in the hands of your enemies. Would the message and promise of apocalyptic literature be good news? Explain.
3. Do you think there is spiritual disorder any place but earth? Why or why not?

ARTICLE 18

The Word Is Not Heard

Question: "What does Isaiah mean when he says, 'For it is precept upon precept, precept upon precept, line upon line, line upon line, here a little, there a little' " (Is 28:10; see Is 28:1–33:24)

The lines quoted by our questioner are difficult to understand because they don't make sense. That is the whole point. Isaiah is describing the response of drunken priests and prophets to his teaching. Since they are drunk they do not understand what Isaiah is teaching and so mimic him in meaningless phrases. The line is repeated in 28:13.

> Therefore the word of the Lord will be to them,
>> precept upon precept, precept upon precept,
> Line upon line, line upon line,
>> here a little, there a little (Is 28:13).

The word of the Lord is senseless to those who do not understand it.

What is the "word" which Isaiah is teaching? As was mentioned in Article 16, the bulk of the oracles in Isaiah 28:1–33:24 date to 705–701 B.C. when Hezekiah was king. The Egyptians were encouraging other countries to rebel against Assyria. Hezekiah wanted to join the rebellion. Isaiah warned him not to. Why? Because only God is trustworthy, not the Egyptians. Isaiah says:

> For thus said the Lord God,
>> the Holy One of Israel:
> In returning and rest you shall be saved;
>> in quietness and in trust shall be your strength (Is 30:15).

Instead of listening to Isaiah Hezekiah decided to join the rebellion.

74

O rebellious children, says the Lord,
   who carry out a plan, but not mine;
Who make an alliance, but against my will,
   adding sin to sin,
Who set out to go down to Egypt
   without asking for my counsel,
To take refuge in the protection of Pharaoh,
   and to seek shelter in the shadow of Egypt (Is 30:1–2).

In Isaiah's eyes to seek shelter in the shadow of Egypt rather than in the shadow of Yahweh is complete folly. If one trusts Yahweh one need not fear Assyria. God would take care of Assyria.

Then the Assyrians shall fall by a sword, not of mortals;
   and a sword, not of humans, shall devour him;
he shall flee from the sword,
   and his young men shall be put to forced labor (Is 31:8).

Since the people were not trusting Yahweh, Isaiah saw destruction ahead. After all, the northern kingdom had already been destroyed because of the people's infidelity (see Is 28:1–4). The same fate awaits Judah (see Is 30:8–17).

However, both Isaiah and the editor who arranged these materials did not believe that the destruction would be complete. All through this section oracles of doom are interwoven with oracles of hope and salvation. People would not always ignore God's word, and when they started to hear they would be saved. "Though the Lord may give you the bread of adversity and the water of affliction, yet your teacher will not hide himself anymore, but your eyes shall see your teacher. And when you turn to the right or when you turn to the left, your ears shall hear a word behind you, saying, 'This is the way; walk in it' " (Is 30:20–21).

The reason Isaiah saw hope rather than total destruction for a remnant who would turn to the Lord is that he relied on God's covenant relationship with the people as it was understood in relation to the Davidic dynasty. There will come a day when a king who listens to God's word will reign.

> See, a king will reign in righteousness,
>   and princes rule with justice (Is 32:1).

When this happens there will no longer be drunken priests and prophets muttering meaningless sentences.

> Then the eyes of those who have sight will not be closed,
>   and the ears of those who have hearing will listen.
> The minds of the rash will have good judgment,
>   and the tongues of stammerers will speak readily and distinctly (Is 32:3–4).

When people hear, understand, and respond to God's word they will be saved. God wants to save, and God will save if only the people will trust in Yahweh.

Review Questions

1. What did Hezekiah do against Isaiah's advice?
2. Why does Isaiah think Hezekiah's actions are wrong?
3. What will happen to keep the destruction from being complete?
4. What was the source of Isaiah's hope for the salvation of a remnant?

Discussion Questions

1. Were Hezekiah's actions merely political or was there a moral dimension to his decision?
2. Have you ever had the experience of being completely misunderstood? Explain. Do you think God ever feels this way? When?
3. Has anyone ever said to you, "You're not listening"? Have you ever realized in hindsight that you had not heard? Explain.
4. Why is it that we so often fail to listen and understand? Do you think part of us wants not to hear? Why?

ARTICLE 19

God Saves

Question: "When we get to chapter 36 we are reading a story in which Isaiah is a character rather than the speaker. Who wrote this section?" (Is 36–39)

We don't know who "wrote" chapters 36–39 of the book of Isaiah. We do know that much of these chapters appears in 2 Kings 18:13–20:19, so we can learn a little about this tradition by looking at 2 Kings. We can also learn a little about the intent of the editor who lifted the passage from 2 Kings and placed it here in the book of Isaiah by noticing both what the editor of Isaiah omitted from his source and what he added to it.

2 Kings is part of the Deuteronomic history, a collection which includes the books of Joshua, Judges, 1 and 2 Samuel and 1 and 2 Kings. The collection was assembled during the exile in Babylon, perhaps around 550 B.C. It is called the "Deuteronomic history" because those who assembled its contents evaluated the history of God's people in the light of the book of Deuteronomy.

During the Babylonian exile the people were forced to ask themselves, "Why did God let this defeat and exile happen to us?" The Deuteronomic History was assembled to illustrate the fact that Israel had received exactly what Israel had deserved. God had revealed God's will through Moses and had entered into a covenant with God's people. However, God's people had consistently, all through their history, failed to live in fidelity to God. So the Babylonian exile was deserved. It was the effect of sin. God has never broken God's promise through all of history, and God was not breaking God's promise now. The people must choose God, must choose life.

The collators of the Deuteronomic History inherited a variety of

---

DEUTERONOMIC HISTORY

Includes: Joshua
Judges
1 and 2 Samuel
1 and 2 Kings

Purpose: Assembled around 550 B.C. to respond to the
question: "Why did God let the Babylonians
conquer us?" An evaluation of the history of God's
people in the light of the book of Deuteronomy.

Theme: God is faithful to the covenant. Disobedience results
in suffering. Obedience results in salvation. Israel
has been disobedient.

---

materials in a variety of literary forms. We see the truth of this
statement in the chapters from 2 Kings included in Isaiah, as we
have two accounts that explain why the Assyrian army did not
attack Jerusalem. In one account (2 Kgs 19:8; Is 36:1–37:9a) Sennacherib failed to attack Jerusalem because he heard that the king
of Ethiopia was preparing to attack him. This other battle was more
important. In the second account (2 Kgs 19:35; 37:9b–36) Sennacherib does not attack because an angel of the Lord strikes down
185,000 Assyrian soldiers (see Is 37:36). In the morning the Assyrian troops are all dead. Obviously this second account is a different
kind of writing than the first, a legend which interprets the historical events from a religious perspective, which understands the fact
that Jerusalem was saved as God's work. The Deuteronomic historian included a variety of kinds of writing in the collection because
this variety existed in the sources.

In addition to arranging inherited traditions the Deuteronomic
historian composed speeches and placed them in the mouths of
major characters in order to make the theological significance of
events clear to the reader. We read such a speech, placed on Isaiah's
lips, when we read that Isaiah warned Hezekiah that, although
Jerusalem has been spared from defeat by the Assyrians, it would

not be spared from defeat by the Babylonians (see 2 Kgs 20:16–19; Is 39:5–8). The audience of the Deuteronomic historian knows that fact to be true since the audience is in exile in Babylon.

The editor who included these passages from 2 Kings in the book of Isaiah undoubtedly had several reasons for doing so. One motive was because the chapters form a bridge between 701 B.C., the time of Sennacherib's invasion and Isaiah of Jerusalem's oracles, and 550 B.C., the time of the Babylonian exile, the time of the point of view of the Deuteronomic historian, and the time of Second Isaiah whom we will be reading in Isaiah 40.

In addition to using the material for a bridge between 1 and 2 Isaiah, the editor of Isaiah alters the material for his own purposes. First the editor omits from his account the fact that Hezekiah had paid a huge tribute to Sennacherib (see Article 16). By omitting the fact that Hezekiah had greatly lowered Sennacherib's motive for attack by already giving him what he wanted, the editor of Isaiah shifts the emphasis of the story to God's saving action.

In addition the editor of Isaiah adds Hezekiah's long prayer of thanksgiving after his life has been spared. The prayer sums up the editor's point in including the passages from 2 Kings which described both Jerusalem's and Hezekiah's having been saved from the brink of death.

> Surely it was for my welfare that I had great bitterness;
>> but you have held back my life from the pit of destruction. . . .
> The living, the living, they thank you, as I do this day;
>> fathers make known to children your faithfulness.
> The Lord will save me, and we will sing to stringed instruments
>> all the days of our lives, at the house of the Lord (Is 38:17–20).

God is always faithful to God's promises. God does save.

Review Questions

1. What is the Deuteronomic history?
2. When was this collection assembled?
3. Why is it called the Deuteronomic history?

4. What is the Deuteronomic history teaching?
5. How can we tell that we have two accounts of one event in Isaiah 36:1–37:9a?
6. How does the Deuteronomic history make the theological significance of events clear to the reader?
7. Between what two historical periods does the account from 2 Kings form a bridge?
8. How does the editor of Isaiah alter the material from 2 Kings? For what purpose?
9. What point of view of the author is expressed in Hezekiah's prayer?

Discussion Questions

1. Have you ever been in the situation of the Israelites in exile in Babylon so that you have asked God, "Why me? What does this mean?" Explain. Did you come to an answer that satisfied you? Explain.
2. Have you ever wanted to "defend God"? Explain. In what way is the Deuteronomic historian defending God?
3. In your mind are the two accounts of Jerusalem's being spared contradictory? Why or why not? Why does "literary form" have to be considered in order to answer this question?

ARTICLE 20

Be Consoled, My People

Question: "How could it possibly be considered 'comforting' to be told that people are like grass that 'withers' (see Is 40:16) or that the inhabitants of the earth are no more than 'grasshoppers'?" (See Is 40:22; Is 40–55)

The prophet's purpose in describing humankind as "grass that withers," as well as in claiming that before God "all the nations are as nothing" (see Is 40:17), is not to diminish the people but to exalt God.

As we move into chapter 40 of Isaiah we move to the work of a different prophet in a different historical setting than was Isaiah of Jerusalem. As is always true when reading the words of a prophet, we need to know something of the prophet's audience and that audience's situation to understand exactly what the prophet is saying to his contemporaries.

We do not know the name of the prophet whose commissioning we read in Isaiah 40, who is told to "comfort, oh comfort my people" (Is 40:1), and who asks, "What shall I cry?" (see Is 40:6). However, judging from the content of chapters 40–55 we can conclude that this "Second Isaiah" or "Deutero Isaiah" lived about 550 B.C. and functioned as a prophet to those who were in exile in Babylon.

Second Isaiah addresses his audience directly when he says:

Thus says the Lord,
    your Redeemer, the Holy One of Israel:
For your sake I will send to Babylon
    and break down all the bars (Is 43:14),

81

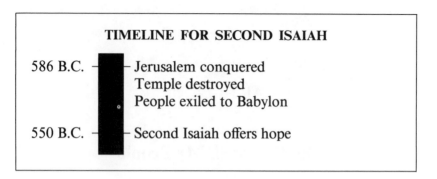

TIMELINE FOR SECOND ISAIAH

586 B.C. ─── ─ Jerusalem conquered
Temple destroyed
People exiled to Babylon

550 B.C. ─── ─ Second Isaiah offers hope

and again when he says:

> Go out from Babylon, flee from Chaldea,
>   declare this with a shout of joy, proclaim it (Is 48:20).

His audience, exiles in Babylon, had suffered a truly traumatic experience. Despite the fact that the people had understood God's covenant promise to David to mean that the kingdom (especially Jerusalem), the house of David, and the temple would never be destroyed, all had been destroyed. In 586 B.C. Jerusalem had been conquered by the Babylonians. The king of the southern kingdom, Zedekiah, had been blinded and taken in bondage to Babylon. His sons and heirs had been killed. All the leaders of Jerusalem were transported to Babylon as well. Those who were left in Jerusalem found their lives in ruins. Their king was gone and their temple was destroyed.

Since the people had linked their understanding of covenant love with the existence of the king, kingdom and temple, they were not only physically devastated by these events, they were spiritually devastated as well. What was the meaning of it all? Were they being punished? Were they still God's people? Did God still love them? Was God in control of events or not?

Second Isaiah offers comfort to God's people in this terrible distress. With the beautiful words:

> Comfort, O comfort *my* people, says *your* God (Is 40:1),

Second Isaiah assures the exiles that they are God's people and that God is their God. Second Isaiah does not deny that the people's sins

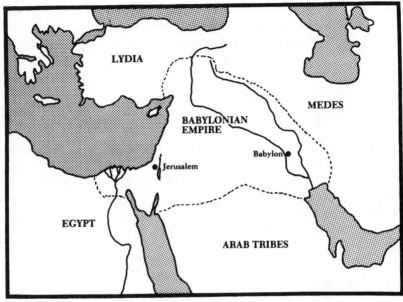

The extent of the Babylonian Empire under Nebuchadnezzar II (605–562 B.C.)

have contributed to their present suffering (see Is 40:2). However, Second Isaiah does not see the Babylonian exile as a time for "I told you so" oracles, oracles which would continue to oppress a people already oppressed. Rather, this was a time to comfort and to offer hope.

> A voice cries out:
> "In the wilderness prepare the way of the Lord,
>   make straight in the desert a highway for our God" (Is 40:3).

Just as God had, at the time of the exodus, made a straight path through the desert for God's people, so would God save them now.

Not only is the covenant still intact, and not only will God save God's people, but God will do new and marvelous things. After all, God is the creator God. Nothing is beyond God's power or outside God's domain. All people are God's creatures. It is in this context that the prophet refers to humankind as grass that withers or as mere grasshoppers. In relation to God's majesty, people, even nations and kings, are as nothing.

Far from diminishing human beings, Second Isaiah wants his audience to know that each person is precious in God's eyes. For this reason, this mighty God, the God of all nations, is compared to a shepherd.

> He will gather the lambs in his arms,
> and carry them in his bosom (Is 40:11).

Second Isaiah wants his audience to know that, despite all the pain and all the mystery which is part of their daily experience, they should nevertheless be comforted. True, God's ways are beyond human comprehension. Still, all could be sure that God loves God's people. God will save God's people, even in Babylon, and God will continue to do wonderful things in their midst.

Review Questions

1. When did Second Isaiah live? Who was his audience?
2. What was Second Isaiah told to do?
3. What had been so traumatic for the Israelites about Babylon's defeat of Jerusalem?
4. Who is Zedekiah? What happened to him?
5. What questions were on the minds of the exiles?
6. Name three comforting ideas which Second Isaiah taught to reassure those in exile.

Discussion Questions

1. Have you ever felt that God was inaccessible? Why would such a feeling be completely devastating?
2. What makes God accessible to you? A person? A particular church building or church community? A Bible? How would God be accessible if all these were destroyed?
3. Is it comforting to you to know that absolutely nothing is impossible for God? Do you believe this?
4. Do you believe that you belong to God? Is this thought comforting or frightening to you? Explain.

ARTICLE 21

"My Servant, Israel"

Question: "Who is this servant in whom God delights?" (Is 42:1; see Is 41:9; 41:22; 42:1–7; 42:8–9; 42:19; 43:10; 49:1–7; 50:4–9; 52:13–53:12)

A great deal of debate among scripture scholars revolves around the answer to the question, "Who is the servant in Second Isaiah?" Debate also revolves around the four passages, or "servant songs," in which the servant is described. We will first define the four "servant songs," and say a few words about the debate over them. We will then try to respond to the question, "Who is the servant?"

The four servant songs in Isaiah appear in Isaiah 42:1–7; 49:1–7; 50:4–9; 52:13–53:12. These songs have been selected out of Second Isaiah because many scholars believe that the poems had an independent existence and were later inserted into Second Isaiah. Evidence for this lies in the fact that if the songs are removed the text runs smoothly, seeming to pick up just where matters were dropped before the song. For instance, the first servant song (Is 42:1–7) seems to be inserted into a trial scene. Nations are called forth to give evidence that their gods are gods.

> Let them bring them,
> > and tell us what is to happen.
> Tell us the former things, what they are,
> > so that we may consider them
> And that we may know their outcome;
> > or declare to us the things to come (Is 41:22).

The trial scene ends when Yahweh declares that only he is God.

> I am the Lord, that is my name;
> > my glory I give to no other,
> > nor my praise to idols.

85

SECOND ISAIAH'S SERVANT SONGS

Isaiah 42:1–7
Isaiah 49:1–7
Isaiah 50:4–9
Isaiah 52:13–53:12

See, the former things have come to pass,
    and new things I now declare;
Before they spring forth,
    I tell you of them (Is 42:8–9).

The servant song appears to be inserted into the trial scene rather than to be an integral part of it.

So some scholars might respond to the question "Who is the servant?" by extracting these four songs from Second Isaiah and analyzing them in themselves. We, however, will take another tact and examine how the identity of the servant is derived from the context in which the poems now appear.

Before the first servant song, the servant is identified as the nation Israel.

But you, Israel, my servant,
    Jacob, whom I have chosen,
    the offspring of Abraham, my friend;
You whom I took from the ends of the earth,
    and called from its farthest corners,
Saying to you, "You are my servant,
    I have chosen you and not cast you off" (Is 41:9).

After the first servant song the servant is again identified as the nation Israel.

You are my witnesses, says the Lord,
    and my servant whom I have chosen,

> So that you may know and believe me
>> and understand that I am he.
> Before me no god was formed
>> nor shall there be any after me (Is 43:10).

However, the wording in the inserted songs causes readers to question whether or not the "servant" can be equated with the nation Israel. One problem is that the servant songs seem to describe an individual rather than a whole community.

> Here is my servant, whom I uphold,
>> my chosen, in whom my soul delights;
> I have put my spirit upon him;
>> he will bring forth justice to the nations (Is 42:1).

In addition to the fact that the servant songs seem to describe an individual rather than a group, the second servant song describes the servant as having a mission *to* Israel.

> And now the Lord says,
>> who formed me in the womb to be his servant,
> To bring Jacob back to him,
>> and that Israel might be gathered to him,
> For I am honored in the sight of the Lord,
>> and my God has become my strength (Is 49:5).

Is the servant the nation Israel or an individual? Is the servant's mission to Israel or by Israel to other nations? Although the wording in Second Isaiah causes us to ask the questions, it is not necessary to solve the dilemma with an either/or response. Because the Israelites understood themselves to be in a relationship of covenant love with Yahweh, the description of the relationship always takes on a very personal tone. We have already noted that in First Isaiah the people as a group are called "daughter Zion" (see Is 1:8). We have seen that when the nation as a whole is offered hope, the hope rests in the birth of an individual child (Is 9:5). We have seen that groups of Israelites are referred to by the name of an individual, the individual who was the father of that tribe (see Is 49:5 just quoted). An individual tribe or the nation itself is often referred to as an individual, so one need not discard the idea that the servant is Israel because the servant is sometimes described as an individual.

Nor need one discard the idea that Israel is the servant because Israel is among the nations who will benefit from the mission of the servant. Israel, although chosen to be a light to all nations, has suffered from blindness herself.

> Who is blind but my servant,
>   or deaf like my messenger whom I send?
> Who is blind like my dedicated one,
>   or blind like the servant of the Lord? (Is 42:19).

The servant in Second Isaiah is the nation Israel. Through the servant songs, whether originally the work of Second Isaiah or inserted later, the prophet (or editor) is helping the nation Israel understand the experience of the exile. What good could possibly be achieved through the experience of the exile? When, in our next article, we look at the mission of the servant Israel, we will begin to answer that question.

Review Questions

1. Why do scholars surmise that the servant songs existed separately from their present context in Second Isaiah?
2. In the context in which the songs now appear, how is the servant identified?
3. Name two problems with equating the servant with Israel.
4. Does the fact that the servant is described as an individual mean that the servant can't be Israel? Explain.
5. Does the fact that the servant has a mission to Israel mean that the servant is not Israel? Explain.

Discussion Questions

1. When you think of who you are, do you think more of what makes you an individual or more of what makes you a member of a family, a church, a nation? Is it possible to know who you

are without considering both individual and community aspects? Explain.

2. Have you ever heard the phrase "wounded healer"? What do you think it means? Do you think that every "healer" is in some way "wounded"? Explain.

3. When you think of "my people," about whom are you thinking? Why?

ARTICLE 22

The Servant's Mission to the Nations

Question: "Surely the servant in Isaiah 52:13–53:12 is Jesus, isn't it?" (Acts 8:34–35; Is 40:2)

A Christian who reads Isaiah 52:13–53:12 can't help but see a "type" or a "model" of Jesus in the song. In fact, the New Testament reveals the fact that Isaiah 53 was used by the early church to explain the significance of Jesus' life, death, and resurrection (see Acts 8:26–39). In Acts we read that Philip, an early Christian evangelizer, came upon a eunuch who was reading this fourth servant song. "The eunuch asked Philip, 'About whom, may I ask you, does the prophet say this, about himself or about someone else?' Then Philip began to speak, and starting with this scripture, he proclaimed to him the good news about Jesus" (Acts 8:34–35).

The eunuch has asked the same question which we addressed in our last article: "Who is the servant?" Instead of being told that the servant was the nation Israel he was told that the servant was Jesus. Why? Because, in trying to come to terms with the meaning of the innocent Jesus' passion, death and resurrection, early Christians had to come to terms with the same mystery with which Second Isaiah was dealing, the mystery of innocent suffering. The early church found the fourth servant song helpful in probing this mystery.

As we read in the very beginning of Second Isaiah the prophet sees the nation as innocently suffering because Israel has suffered beyond what she may have deserved.

> Speak tenderly to Jerusalem, and cry to her
> that she has served her term,
> that her penalty is paid,

> That she has received from the Lord's hand
> double for all her sins (Is 40:2).

Second Isaiah is trying to speak tenderly to God's people, to console them, by trying to help them understand that their suffering means something other than that they are being punished for their sins. Israel's suffering has a positive side to it. God is accomplishing something through Israel's suffering, something which is new and wonderful and is about to happen. By looking carefully at the fourth servant song we will be able to understand what God's wonderful accomplishment through Israel will be, and how this great accomplishment will come about.

The song begins with the announcement that Israel will "prosper," will be "exalted and lifted up" (Is 52:13). God is the speaker. This thought alone would have been wonderful news for the exiles and for those left in devastated Jerusalem. The time of suffering would soon end. The exaltation of Israel would be such that nations would be startled at such a reversal of fortunes (see Is 52:15). Thoughts which had never before occurred to other nations would now be contemplated.

With chapter 53 we hear the voices of these startled kings of nations.

> Who has believed what we have heard?
> And to whom has the arm of the Lord been revealed? (Is 53:1).

What is this startling insight which nations have received, and how have they received it? Isaiah's startling insight is that other nations have been drawn to repentance and union with God because they have observed Israel's undeserved suffering.

To suggest that suffering had any purpose other than punishment was to suggest a startling new idea. But Second Isaiah suggests just that. As the kings say, they had previously looked on someone suffering as having been struck down by God.

> We accounted him stricken,
> struck down by God, and afflicted.

> But he was wounded for our transgressions
>> crushed for our iniquities.
> Upon him was the punishment that made us whole,
>> and by his bruises we are healed (Is 53:4–5).

Two conditions must be present for suffering to have the saving effect which Second Isaiah suggests. The first is that those who suffer must understand the purpose of their suffering and so accept it as something positive in God's plan for God's people. The suffering servant silently accepts his suffering.

> He was oppressed, and he was afflicted,
>> yet he did not open his mouth.
> Like a lamb that is led to the slaughter,
>> and like a sheep that before its shearers is silent,
>> so he did not open his mouth (Is 53:7).

Because those who suffer would make their lives "an offering for sin" (see Is 53:10), they would have a profound effect on those who observed them.

The second necessary condition is that those who observe the sufferers will be led to repentance. Isaiah teaches that the kings of other nations, on viewing the way Israel has accepted undeserved suffering, will realize that Israel is a faithful nation. In contrast, the kings will realize that they, rather than Israel, are sinners. The kings will name their sin and repent.

> All we like sheep have gone astray;
>> we have all turned to our own way,
> And the Lord has laid on him
>> the iniquity of us all (Is 53:6).

Second Isaiah teaches the exiles that God is using them as the instrument of salvation for all nations. They will be exalted, and through their suffering, soon to end, they will be a light for all nations to find their way to God.

Some scripture scholars suggest that the servant songs refer to Second Isaiah himself rather than to the nation as a whole, and that Second Isaiah is finding meaning in the fact that he is personally suffering because his prophetic word has been rejected by his people. Perhaps Second Isaiah, like the great prophet Hosea, came to understand the relationship between Israel and God by seeing himself as a symbol of Israel. Whether Second Isaiah reached his profound insights through personal suffering, through meditating on the meaning of the suffering of the nation, or through a combination of both, he nevertheless reached a profound insight which laid the groundwork for an understanding of Jesus' role in salvation history. Undeserved suffering can be the occasion for great grace for those who suffer as well as for those who observe such suffering. The sufferer can be God's instrument of salvation, and can cause the conversion of those who witness the "servant's" suffering.

Second Isaiah's startling insight is that if the people accepted their suffering and understood it as God's saving action, the nation Israel could become what God wants them to become, a light by which all nations would find their way to God. In being God's instrument of salvation Israel would herself be exalted.

Review Questions

1. Why did the early church find the servant songs helpful in probing the mystery of Jesus' passion, death and resurrection?
2. With what mystery is the fourth servant song dealing?
3. What is Isaiah's startling insight?
4. What two things must be true in order for one's suffering to have a saving effect on another?
5. What is the servant Israel's mission to all nations?
6. How did Second Isaiah's insight lay the groundwork for insights regarding Jesus?

Discussion Questions

1. Do you know anyone who has faced suffering willingly and courageously? Do you know anyone who has faced suffering resentfully and angrily? How did these differences in attitude affect the one suffering? How did they affect you? Explain.
2. Is anyone innocent? Is anyone guilty enough to deserve the

suffering of war? Why do you think the question of an innocent person suffering has engaged every generation?

3. Do you think that suffering would be easier to take if one truly believed that suffering had a positive purpose in God's plan? Why or why not?

ARTICLE 23

Third Isaiah: A Post-Exilic Prophet

Question: "Why would there be any question about whether eunuchs or foreigners could be part of God's people (Is 56:1–8)? After all, God made everyone, so everyone already is part of God's people" (Is 41:2; Is 56–66)

The question being addressed in Isaiah 56:1–8 is whether or not foreigners and eunuchs should be considered part of God's covenant community, whether or not they should be included in temple worship.

The fact that such a question is being addressed tells us something about the context in which this oracle was originally proclaimed.

When we were reading Isaiah 40–55 we were reading oracles which, for the most part, addressed the Israelites in exile in Babylon. The question of who should be allowed to participate in temple worship would have been irrelevant for them because they had no temple. The temple had been destroyed by the Babylonians.

You may have noticed in Second Isaiah that one of the ways in which the people were comforted was that they were told that the time of exile in Babylon would soon be over. Second Isaiah says:

> Who has roused a victor from the east,
>   summoned him to his service?
> He delivers up nations to him
>   and tramples kings underfoot (Is 41:2).

The "victor from the east" is a reference to Cyrus, a Persian, who was conquering surrounding countries during Second Isaiah's

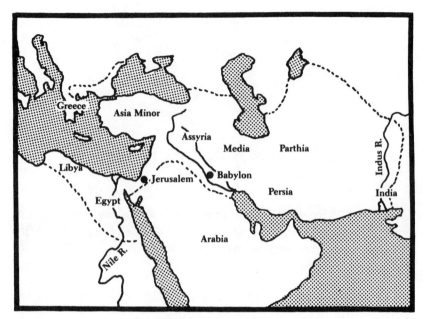

The Persian Empire

ministry. Second Isaiah believed that Cyrus was fulfilling God's purpose in history and would eventually conquer the Babylonians.

Cyrus was an enlightened leader. He respected the religions he found in countries which he conquered. Instead of deporting conquered populations, as had the Babylonians, he let exiles return home. Cyrus did conquer Babylon in 539 B.C. Among the exiles free to return to their homes were the Israelites.

As we read Isaiah 56–66 we are reading an arrangement of oracles addressed to these returned exiles. One way in which we can tell this is that the oracles address questions pertinent to those trying to rebuild their devastated country and trying to integrate into their lives the truths learned through their experience in exile. These chapters are referred to as Third Isaiah.

As you remember, Second Isaiah had tried to console his people by suggesting a salvific purpose for their suffering, a purpose that would embrace all nations, not just the Israelites. Now the Israelites had returned to their own country and had rebuilt their temple.

Should foreigners be included in temple worship? After all, Israel is supposed to be a light to other nations. How should Israel respond when those of other nations follow that light? Third Isaiah teaches that foreigners should be included.

Third Isaiah thinks that eunuchs, too, should now be included in temple worship. Eunuchs had previously been excluded by law (see Deut 23:1). However, Third Isaiah teaches that if eunuchs observe the sabbath and "hold fast" to the covenant (see Is 56:4), they will receive something even better than sons and daughters. They should no longer be excluded from God's covenant community.

These "liberal" teachings would have put Third Isaiah at odds with other prophets and leaders in post-exilic Israel. For instance, the prophet Ezekiel, whose disciples were contemporaneous with Third Isaiah, held an opposite opinion. When addressing the question of who could be admitted to the temple, Ezekiel asserts: "Say to the rebellious house, to the house of Israel: Thus says the Lord God: O house of Israel, let there be an end to all your abominations in admitting foreigners, uncircumcised in heart and flesh, to be in my sanctuary, profaning my temple when you offer to me my food, the fat and the blood. You have broken my covenant with all your abominations" (Ez 44:6–7).

You will notice that Third Isaiah begins and ends with the teaching that foreigners should be included in temple worship.

> All flesh shall come to worship before me,
> says the Lord (Is 66:23).

To begin and end with the same point is to use a structuring device called an "inclusio." Third Isaiah uses two "inclusios," one inside another. The effect is that certain topics are addressed, the central ideas are presented in the middle chapters, 60–62, and then topics already addressed are addressed again, in reverse order, ending where the arrangement began. That is, if "C" is the main focus, the arrangement of the material is ABCBA.

Who is it who arranged these oracles? Because not only the setting but the tone and spiritual outlook differ from Second Isaiah, scripture scholars suggest that Third Isaiah is not the work of Second Isaiah in a new setting, but is the work of a group of disciples who were greatly influenced by First and Second Isaiah and who tried to integrate the vision of First and Second Isaiah into post-exilic Israel.

Review Questions

1. Who is Cyrus? What did he do?
2. How can we tell that chapters 56–66 address a different situation than did Second Isaiah?
3. What is the new setting?
4. What does Third Isaiah teach about foreigners, eunuchs, and temple worship?
5. What should eunuchs who want to be included do to "qualify"?
6. What did Ezekiel teach about foreigners and temple worship?
7. How is Third Isaiah structured?
8. Who was Third Isaiah?

Discussion Questions

1. To what faith community do you belong? Does your faith community exclude anyone? Why? Is this exclusion controversial? Do you agree with it or not?
2. What do you think should "qualify" a person for membership in your faith community?
3. Does your faith community reach out to new members? How are new members integrated?
4. Do churches exist to be exclusive or to evangelize? Explain.

ARTICLE 24

Troubles in the Post-Exilic Community

Question: "The prophet seems very angry when he talks about 'an adulterous wanton race' (see Is 57:3f). Has child sacrifice actually returned?" (Is 57:5; Is 56:11; 58:6–7; 61:6; 63:15; 64:1; 65:5; 66:2; 66:21)

The prophet is indeed very angry, and it does seem that child sacrifice has returned, for Third Isaiah addresses those who "slaughter your children in the valleys under the cliffs of the rocks" (Is 57:5). Evidently a host of idolatrous practices, including child sacrifice, have reappeared in post-exilic Israel.

Third Isaiah believes that the spiritual leadership in Israel after the exile is a disgrace. He refers to the leaders as "blind watchmen" (see Is 56:10) and as "shepherds who know no discretion" (Is 56:11). Third Isaiah feels that such leaders are blind to God's true purpose and are harming the community.

We see these abominable practices delineated not only here but also in chapter 65 (an inclusio). Not only child sacrifice but other practices from Canaanite nature cults were being reintroduced into worship, severely dividing the Israelite community. Actions long outlawed, such as "eating swine flesh," were being practiced (see Is 65:6). Worst of all, those who adulterated true worship considered themselves "holy" (see Is 65:5).

Third Isaiah seems to have felt that too much importance was being given to temple worship. He warns that external actions can become empty ritual rather than true worship when he says that God is not pleased with those who "merely slaughter an ox" (see Is 66:3). Rather, God is pleased with the "humble and contrite in spirit" who "tremble at God's word" (Is 66:2).

99

ISSUES IN POST-EXILIC ISRAEL

- Who should be admitted to temple worship? Gentiles? Eunuchs?
- How important is temple ritual?
- Which is more important: fasting or acting justly?
- Who can be priests?

Third Isaiah's de-emphasis on the importance of temple ritual for its own sake undoubtedly put him at odds with those, like the prophet Haggai, who believed that the hardships experienced by the post-exilic community were due to the fact that they had not made rebuilding the temple and temple worship their primary concern (see Hag 1:7–11).

Third Isaiah attributed the difficult times experienced by the post-exilic community to the fact that they had not made justice their main concern. Third Isaiah makes this clear when he criticizes the way in which people are observing the fast days which had been declared during and after the exile.

> Is not this the fast that I choose,
>   to loose the bonds of injustice,
>   to undo the thongs of the yoke,
> To let the oppressed go free,
>   and to break every yoke?
> Is it not to share your bread with the hungry,
>   and bring the homeless poor into your house;
> When you see the naked to cover them,
>   and not to hide yourself from your own kin? (Is 58:6–7).

To fast and at the same time to be blind to justice is useless. Only when Israel truly fasts and truly worships will God's plan for the Israelites be fulfilled.

Still another belief which Third Isaiah taught would have put him at odds with the religious leaders of his day. This was the belief that the definition of who can be priests should be expanded. In addressing the whole nation Third Isaiah says:

> You shall be called priests of the Lord,
>   you shall be named ministers of our God (Is 61:6).

Such a belief would have directly contradicted the teaching of Ezekiel's disciples, since Ezekiel had insisted that the priesthood be limited to the Zadokite priests, the descendants of Zadok (see Ez 44:16). Not only did Third Isaiah say that other Israelites might be priests, he even suggested that Gentiles might become priests (see Is 66:21).

Beset by all of these internal disputes, the post-exilic community, in addition, had to face political adversaries. The oracle against Edom (see Is 63:1–6), shocking in its gory picture of God's "vindication," expresses clearly the degree of despair experienced by the community facing such continued hardships and divisions.

In fact, Third Isaiah admits to the feeling that God doesn't hear the call of God's people. He asks God:

> Where are your zeal and your might?
>   The yearning of your heart and your compassion?
>   They are withheld from me (Is 63:15).

Third Isaiah expresses more than anger. He sometimes appears near despair. His anger is addressed to the religious leaders of his day who subvert God's purpose by misunderstanding God's will and by practicing a kind of spirituality which ignores justice and God's call to universalism. His despair is addressed to God who, unaccountably, allows God's people to wander off in their own ways. Third Isaiah longs for God to "tear open the heavens and come down" (see Is 64:1) so that God can be truly known by God's people.

Review Questions

1. Name some "abominable practices" which reappeared in post-exilic Israel.

2. Is Third Isaiah completely against temple worship? What is his point?
3. What did the prophet Haggai think about temple worship?
4. To what did Third Isaiah attribute the fact that life was so difficult in the post-exilic community?
5. How did Third Isaiah and Ezekiel differ on the question of who should be priests?
6. In addition to internal disputes, what made life in post-exilic Israel so difficult?
7. At whom does Third Isaiah direct his anger? To whom does Third Isaiah express his despair?

Discussion Questions

1. Do you think we sometimes observe rituals such as going to church and fasting while, at the same time, we neglect the poor? Why is this a danger in every age? Why is it wrong?
2. Have you ever felt near despair? Was anger part of what you felt? At whom did you aim your anger? Your despair?
3. Do you think the differences among the prophets were over core issues? Are we still arguing over the same points today? Explain.

ARTICLE 25

Isaiah's Message of Hope: An Eternal Message

Question: "Chapter 60 sounds more like Second Isaiah than Third Isaiah since it is more hopeful. Is this chapter really Second Isaiah?" (Is 60–62)

Chapter 60 does express the hopes which, in the rest of Third Isaiah, seem to have been frustrated rather than fulfilled. The hopes themselves and the imagery in which they are expressed do come, in large part, from Second Isaiah. In fact Second Isaiah is quoted. Nevertheless, the hopes are applied to a new setting, the post-exilic setting proper to Third Isaiah. In later generations Third Isaiah's use of Second Isaiah finds its way into the New Testament and becomes an expression of hope for generations to come.

Scripture scholars surmise that chapters 60–62 are earlier oracles than some which have preceded them. In chapter 56 the temple had presumably been built. In chapter 60 the call is to rebuild the temple using the timber from Lebanon.

> The glory of Lebanon shall come to you,
>   the cypress, the plane, and the pine
> To beautify the place of my sanctuary;
>   and I will glorify where my feet rest (Is 60:13).

In addressing his post-exilic audience Third Isaiah quotes Second Isaiah:

> Lift up your eyes and look around;
>   they all gather, they come to you.
> Your sons shall come from far away,

103

and your daughters shall be carried on their nurses' arms (Is 60:4;
cf. Is 49:18, 22).

These words not only state the possibility of returning from exile
but they urge people to return. Life in post-exilic Israel was difficult
enough, so that not all who could return wanted to return.

In Third Isaiah foreign nations come to Jerusalem not only to
learn, as they had in First Isaiah, but actually to help rebuild the
city. Third Isaiah's image of nations coming to Jerusalem, bearing
gifts, has become a well-known Christian image.

> A multitude of camels shall cover you,
>   the young camels of Midian and Ephah;
>   all those from Sheba shall come.
> They shall bring gold and frankincense,
>   and shall proclaim the praise of the Lord (Is 60:6).

Matthew picks up on this specific image in his infancy narrative
when he pictures the three wise men bearing gifts of gold and fran-
kincense to the infant Jesus. Matthew is saying, through images,
that the nations have recognized their redeemer.

Another passage in Third Isaiah has taken on special meaning for
Christians, and that is the account of the prophet's call and
commission.

> The spirit of the Lord God is upon me,
>   because the Lord has anointed me;
> He has sent me to bring good news to the oppressed,
>   to bind up the brokenhearted,
> To proclaim liberty to the captives,
>   and release to the prisoners,
> To proclaim the year of the Lord's favor,
>   and the day of vengeance of our God;
>   to comfort all who mourn . . . (Is 61:1–2).

In this passage Third Isaiah is once again using the tradition
inherited from Second Isaiah, this time in the servant song. As in
the first servant song, the prophet has received God's spirit (see Is

42:1) and has been sent on a mission which will result in justice for all (see Is 42:1b).

The "year of the Lord's favor" which is to be proclaimed is a reference to the jubilee year (see Lev 25). The jubilee year was celebrated every forty-nine years. The celebration included, among other things, forgiving others as well as oneself, freeing all who were in bondage, and giving back all property to the Lord so that it could be redistributed equitably. The prophet, in proclaiming a year of the Lord's favor, is proclaiming forgiveness and freedom.

The "day of vengeance" which is also promised is "the day of the Lord" which we have already discussed. In order for God's peace and freedom to come about, God's enemies must be punished. This is good news for the oppressed but not for the oppressors.

Jesus is pictured as using this passage from Isaiah to describe his own mission when Jesus begins his public ministry (see Lk 4:18).

One reason why the images which were used by Third Isaiah to give hope to a discouraged community after the Babylonian exile are reused in a New Testament context is that Third Isaiah himself universalizes the images. In trying to bolster his fellow Israelites Third Isaiah uses language which is appropriate in every age. For instance, in describing the new Jerusalem, full of God's glory, Third Isaiah says:

> The sun shall no longer be your light by day,
>   nor for brightness shall the moon give light to you by night;
> But the Lord will be your everlasting light
>   and your God will be your glory.
> Your sun shall no more go down,
>   or your moon withdraw itself,
> For the Lord will be your everlasting light,
>   and your days of mourning shall be ended (Is 60:19–20).

Such images describe not just the hopes of a beleaguered population trying to rebuild a temple and a city. They describe the ultimate hopes of the entire human race for eternal union with God. We see the same images reappear in the book of Revelation. In describing the new heaven and the new earth the author of Revelation says: "And the city had no need of sun and moon to shine on it, for the glory of God is its light, and its lamp is the lamb. The nations will walk by its light, and the kings of the earth will bring their glory into it. Its gates will never be shut by day—and there will be no night there" (Rev 21:23–25).

The message of hope is much the same from one generation to another. Third Isaiah does use the imagery of Second Isaiah to offer hope to the post-exilic community. Jesus is pictured as using the same imagery to offer hope to his contemporaries. The author of the book of Revelation uses the same images to offer hope to a persecuted audience at the end of the first century A.D. Each generation, in reading Isaiah, Luke, and Revelation, uses the same images to find hope in the situation in which that generation finds itself. The message of hope is always relevant for people in a relationship of covenant love with God because God is love. For this reason Isaiah's images of hope and message of hope are passed down to every generation, and in every generation the prophet's words are "fulfilled."

Review Questions

1. How can we tell that chapters 60–62 are addressed to the post-exilic community? Why do scholars think they are earlier than Isaiah 56?
2. What image from Third Isaiah does Matthew use in his infancy narrative? Why?
3. What is the jubilee year? What is the prophet proclaiming with this reference?
4. What is the "day of vengeance?"
5. How has the account of Third Isaiah's call and commission become part of the Christian tradition?
6. What is the effect of the fact that Third Isaiah uses cosmic imagery rather than specific imagery when expressing the hopes of Israel?
7. How has Third Isaiah's description of the new Jerusalem become part of Christian tradition?
8. Why is the message of hope always relevant to people in a covenant relationship with God?

Discussion Questions

1. What do you understand this phrase to mean: "The words of the prophet are fulfilled"?
2. Why do you think Old Testament images are used to express New Testament concepts? If the image is the same, does that mean that the truth being explored is also the same? Explain.
3. Do you think it is surprising that Jesus and Jesus' disciples used the Old Testament to explain new insights? Why or why not?
4. Are you a hopeful person? On whom do your hopes rest? Explain.

Summation and Transition
from Isaiah to Job

We move now from an example of prophetic literature, Isaiah, to an example of wisdom literature, the book of Job. Several of the concepts which we learned while studying Isaiah will help us in our study of Job.

First, a biblical author, though inspired, is not inspired in the sense that he becomes all-knowing. He lives in a specific time in history and shares with the rest of the human race certain ideas and certain limitations which are simply part of living at that particular time in history. This was true of Isaiah and it is true of the author of Job. We must read biblical authors in the context of their times in history. We must ask, "What is the author saying to his contemporary audience?"

In addition, the book of Isaiah, as we have it, came from the hand of editors. Certain characteristics of the text caused us to ask questions which concerned the history of the text—how it reached its present form—in addition to questions about the intent of the author. The same questions of editor and author will come up in our reading of Job.

When we were reading Isaiah we learned that to understand any book of the Bible we must understand the literary form which the author has chosen to use. To misunderstand the literary form is to misunderstand the intent of the author. When studying Isaiah we learned this concept through looking at such forms as "oracle" and "parable." When we read Job we will be reading different literary forms than we read in Isaiah, but the necessity of understanding these forms and what they say about the intent of the author remains.

Finally, the knowledge we have about the post-exilic period which we gained while reading Third Isaiah will be helpful to us. We already know that this was a period of re-examination, of re-thinking old ways, of coming to new understandings. This intellectual climate is the very climate in which the book of Job was written.

As you read Job for the first time, read it as a whole. Don't read the articles in this book until you have read the biblical text and have jotted down your questions. Hopefully the following articles will respond to the questions which the text raises in your mind.

■ THE BOOK OF JOB ■

ARTICLE 1

God and Satan: A Legend Sets the Stage

Question: "Why would God allow Satan to harm Job? (Job 1:12; 2:3, 6) You would expect God to protect Job." (Ez 14:14, 20)

You would expect God to protect Job. If God is all-loving and all-powerful, you would expect God to make sure that an innocent person wouldn't suffer.

In fact, it is this very expectation that resulted in the belief, common among the Jews, that all suffering was due to sin. If you suffered you must have deserved it. Otherwise God was either not all-powerful or not all-loving.

Despite the fact that most people believed that all suffering was due to sin, the author of the book of Job did not hold such a belief. It was his observation of life that innocent people do sometimes suffer.

In fact, it was to challenge the belief that all suffering is punishment for sin that the author of Job wrote the book in the first place. It must have taken a great deal of courage to challenge the belief because to challenge it seemed to call into question God's love and/or God's power. How might the author do it?

The author of Job probed the mystery of an innocent person's suffering by discussing the problem in the form of a debate: Job and his friends debate the cause and the purpose of Job's suffering. To frame the debate, to set the stage, the author uses a legend, one probably well known to his audience, in which Job suffers, perseveres, and is rewarded in the end.

The question "Why would God allow Satan to harm Job?" is, then, a question about the plot of the legend which the author of Job has used to frame his debate.

113

**STRUCTURE OF DEBATE
IN THE BOOK OF JOB**

Eliphaz's Three Speeches   **Job's Responses**
Chapters 4–5   Chapters 6–7
Chapter 15   Chapters 16–17
Chapter 22   Chapters 23–24

Bildad's Three Speeches   **Job's Responses**
Chapter 8   Chapters 9–10
Chapter 18   Chapter 19
25:1–6; 26:5–14   26:1–4; 27:1–12

Zophar's Three Speeches   **Job's Responses**
Chapter 11   Chapters 12–14
Chapter 20   Chapter 21
24:18–24 ?; 27:13–23 ?   Chapters 29–31

The debate consists of three cycles of arguments. The third cycle presents problems and
various attempts have been made to reconstruct
it. Chapters 32–37 are Elihu's rebuke of Job.

So to answer the question we will need to define "legend." If we
do not know what kind of writing we are reading when we read a
legend, then we will misunderstand the intent of the author.

A legend is an imaginative and symbolic story with an historical
core. It is usually told to exalt a hero for a particular virtue. For
instance, the legend of George Washington and the cherry tree is a
story told to teach honesty, not to teach history.

Evidently during the time of the patriarchs a man named Job
became well known for his goodness (see Ez 14:14, 20). In later
times, if one wanted to refer to a really good person, one would
refer to Job (see Ez 14:14). Job became a figure in a legend, an
imaginative story written not to teach the historical facts of Job's

---

LEGEND

Definition: An imaginative and symbolic story with an
historical core.

Function: Exalts a peson for a particular virtue or
characteristic.

---

life but to teach contemporary generations about the fate of a really
good person.

Details in a legend are imaginative rather than historical. God
did not allow Satan to harm Job in the order of real events, only in
the plot of the legend. So we must reword the question and ask,
"Why does the author of the legend picture God as letting Satan
harm Job?"

For the author, the word "Satan" did not mean the devil as it
probably means to modern readers. As is obvious from the plot, the
"Satan" in Job is not God's sworn enemy. Rather, Satan is one of
the heavenly beings who presents himself before the Lord (see Job
1:16). Satan's function seems to be similar to that of a prosecuting
attorney. He gathers information and uses it to test people's
goodness.

The author of the legend uses the two characters, God and Satan,
to establish a situation which many people would consider impossible: a good man will suffer. The author composes this conversation
to set the stage. Job is suffering, but his suffering is not punishment
for sin. So why is he suffering? The answer which the legend will
eventually give and the answer which the debate itself will give are
not the same. Still, the author of Job appropriates the legend and
uses the beginning of this traditional story to introduce his debate
because he too wants to set the same stage. In Job an innocent
person is suffering. Since this fact is established beyond all doubt
we can now move on to the question at hand: Why would an
innocent person suffer?

Review Questions

1. What was the accepted belief among the Jews about the cause of suffering? Why was this belief held?
2. What did the author of the book of Job observe?
3. What two literary forms does the author use?
4. What is a legend? What is its function?
5. Who is Satan?
6. What situation is established by the conversation between God and Satan?
7. Why does the author of Job use this legend to frame his debate?

Discussion Questions

1. Why was it courageous of the author of the book of Job to write this book?
2. Have you ever had to challenge an accepted belief? Explain. Why is this always a painful thing to do?
3. Why do we need to know what a legend is in order to understand the book of Job?
4. Have you ever observed an innocent person suffering? How did you feel? Did this situation force you to ask any hard questions? What were they?

ARTICLE 2

Do Good People Exist?

Question: "Satan may not be the devil but he certainly is a trouble-maker. Why does he want to harm Job?" (Job 1:9; 2:4–5)

Once again we must remember that we are reading a legend, not an account of an event. So we need to ask why the author pictures Satan as acting in the way he does.

Through Satan the author poses a question which is core to the debate which will soon take place. Satan's question is, "Does Job fear God for nothing?" (Job 1:9)

The word "fear" in this quotation does not mean "to be afraid." Fear is used here as it is other places in wisdom literature to describe the appropriate attitude of awe which one would have who recognizes the right relationship between God and God's people. As the book of Proverbs says, "The fear of the Lord is the beginning of knowledge" (Prov 1:7).

So, to paraphrase, Satan asks God, "Isn't Job righteous for his own benefit, to avoid harsh treatment at your hand?" Satan is pictured as a cynic who believes human beings are incapable of unselfish love of God. God is pictured not as a cynic but as one who believes in human goodness.

Such deep questions as "Could an innocent person suffer?" and "Are human beings capable of unselfish love?" are the kinds of questions which one hears discussed in a body of Old Testament literature called wisdom literature. The wisdom books include Job, Qoheleth (Ecclesiastes), Sirach (Ecclesiasticus), Wisdom, The Song of Songs, Psalms and Proverbs.

All the wisdom books, in the form in which we now have them, date to the time after the Babylonian exile. As we already know

117

WISDOM LITERATURE

Job

Qoheleth (Ecclesiastes)

Sirach (Ecclesiasticus)

Wisdom

The Song of Songs

Psalms

Proverbs

---

from our study of Isaiah, the time after the Babylonian exile was one of re-examination. The expectation that the kingdom, the king and the temple would remain secure forever had proven to be a false expectation. The nation had suffered beyond what they considered "just punishment." A non-Jew, Cyrus, had been God's instrument of salvation in their lives when he conquered the Babylonians and let the Israelites return home. Israel was having to face such questions as "Why did we suffer so? Was it suffering that we deserved?" Why was it a non-Jew who saved us? Are other nations also chosen?"

While the wisdom literature of Israel, in the form in which we now have it, is post-exilic, the roots of wisdom literature are cross-cultural and pre-date the time of the exile. As is true of much of Israel's literature, a kind of writing common to surrounding cultures was appropriated and put to a new use.

In surrounding cultures much of wisdom literature would simply have been about "how to get along successfully in life," and specifically in court circles. The wise person was one whose life was well ordered in every way. Such a person would enjoy food and drink but not be a glutton or a drunkard. He would use money wisely and would have all of his relationships in right order: relationships with parents, spouse, children, neighbors and king.

However, wisdom literature in Israel took on a broader focus because, for the Israelites, all order originates in God who is the real king; all right relationships with people and with the material world flow from being in right relationship with God.

So when God describes Job as "a blameless and upright man who fears God and turns away from evil" (Job 1:8b), God describes Job as a wise man. Since Job is a wise man whose relationships are all in right order, especially his relationship with God, why would Job suffer? This is the question with which the author of Job confronts his audience. "Why is it that not only sinners but good and wise people, people like Job, suffer? Many in the audience would believe that they do not. The fact of suffering alone would convince them that the sufferer was also a sinner.

Review Questions

1. What question does Satan ask?
2. What does "fear God" mean?
3. What attitude toward human beings does Satan reveal? Does God agree? Explain.
4. What books are included in wisdom literature?
5. To what time do these books, in their present form, date?
6. What are some questions which the people were forced to ask after the Babylonian exile? Why were they forced to ask these questions?
7. What was the focus of wisdom literature in countries other than Israel?
8. What was the focus of wisdom literature in Israel? Why?
9. With what question does the author of the book of Job confront his audience?

Discussion Questions

1. Do you believe people are capable of unselfish love? Why do you believe this?

2. Think of a person whom you would call "wise." Why do you think this person is wise?
3. Do you agree that all order in every aspect of life finds its root in a right relationship with God? Why or why not?

ARTICLE 3

Job's Character Change

Question: "Doesn't Job change awfully suddenly? He is accepting in the beginning, but then he begins to curse." (Job 1–3)

Our reader is correct in observing that Job's behavior changes radically from the prose legend which is used in the frame (Job 1–2) to the poetic debate which begins in chapter 3. In the legend Job is accepting, but in the poem he is not.

When we say that the legend is used as a frame, we mean just that. This legend existed independently of the debate and, in addition to picturing Job as an entirely different person than he appears in the debate, proposes a different response to the central question, "Could an innocent person suffer?" When we get to the end of the book of Job we will examine the tension between the message which the legend teaches when it stands alone and the message which the book of Job teaches when it is viewed as a whole.

Since the patient or accepting Job of the legend is not the lamenting and questioning Job of the poem, why did the author of the book of Job use the legend in the first place?

One reason, already discussed, is that the Job of the legend cannot be accused of sin. This Job lived up to God's trust in him. He did not bless God only because it was in his own self-interest. He blessed God even in the face of disaster.

By using a legend which insists on Job's sinlessness the author is able to establish what is called "dramatic irony." Dramatic irony exists when the audience knows something which the characters in the story do not know.

In this case, the audience knows that Job is not a proud man who is unwilling to admit the possibility of sin. (We will read such a

---

WHY THE LEGEND FRAME?

- The Job of the legend cannot be accused of sin.

- Establishes dramatic irony for the debate that follows.

---

charge later.) Rather, Job had offered sacrifice just in case sin had been committed (see Job 1:5).

We also know that Job is not a man who thinks God owes him blessings as a reward for good behavior. Job says, "Shall we receive the good at the hand of God and not receive the bad?" (Job 2:10b). This is in sharp contrast to Job's wife who thinks God should be cursed.

By picturing Job as he is pictured in this legend the author supplies the audience with information which is not shared by Job's friends. Eliphaz, Bildad and Zophar have to judge the situation based on the beliefs which are held by their society. They have no way of knowing, as the audience does, that in God's eyes Job is blameless.

So even though the Job who laments is not the Job of the legend, nevertheless the author of Job had good reason to employ the legend as a frame. There is no need for us to try to make the two Jobs compatible.

Still, even the Job of the debate does not curse God. Rather he curses the day of his birth. He longs for death because life is now sheer pain. Such a cry of pain is called a "lament." We will have occasion to read many laments, not only in the book of Job but also in our study of the Psalms.

Before we leave the Job of the legend we should point out one more way in which the original legend about Job, possibly a patriarch, may have been changed. Notice that in this legend Job is not an Israelite, nor are Job's friends. "Uz," Job's homeland (see Job 1:1), is east of the Jordan. As is often true in wisdom literature, a point of view broader than that of the Israelites is brought into play. While Job is in right relationship with God he is not pictured as an Israelite in covenant relationship with God. Because of this setting Job and his friends will have to rely on reason to search out answers to life's mysteries. They will not be able to reflect on the exodus experience or to draw their conclusions from their knowledge of the way God has revealed God's self to the Israelites.

The author of the book of Job had several reasons to use the legend of Job even though Job's character in the legend does not match the character of the Job in the debate. He uses the Job in the legend to establish the fact that an innocent person is suffering, and the Job in the debate to question, even to demand to know why.

Review Questions

1. How does the Job of the legend differ from the Job of the debate?
2. What is "dramatic irony"? In what way is the book of Job an example of dramatic irony?
3. How does Job's wife's response differ from Job's?
4. Does the Job of the debate curse God? Explain.
5. Is Job an Israelite? How does Job's nationality change the context of the problem of an innocent person suffering? How will Job and his friends have to search out an answer?

Discussion Questions

1. Have you ever met anyone like Job's wife who simply "curses God" in the face of suffering? Is this a helpful response? Why or why not?
2. What is the difference between knowing something from revelation and knowing something from reason? Can you name a conclusion from each source?
3. Are conclusions from revelation and from reason compatible? Explain.

ARTICLE 4

Is All Suffering Deserved?

Question: "Eliphaz's response seems cruel. How could he blame Job for being impatient (Job 4:5) and tell him his suffering is his own fault?" (Job 5:7; Job 4:3; 4:6–8; 4:17; 5:4; 5:8–9; 5:17; 5:27 also discussed)

Eliphaz tries to be gentle, but because his belief is harsh he cannot express it gently. Eliphaz believes that all suffering is due to sin. Job is suffering, so Job must have sinned. In Eliphaz's mind, the only way in which Job could be relieved of his suffering would be if Job admitted and repented of his sin. So Eliphaz, with all good intentions, tries to remind Job of this "truth" which Job seems to have forgotten.

First Eliphaz reminds Job that in the past Job had instructed others in the truth (see Job 4:3). Job had taught confidently and strengthened others in distress. Now Job should remember his past behavior, his "fear of God" which gave him confidence and his "integrity" which gave him hope (see Job 4:6). He shouldn't lose faith just because he is the one who is now in distress.

Eliphaz then clearly states his doctrine of retribution.

> Think now, who that was innocent ever perished?
> Or where were the upright cut off?
> As I have seen, those who plow iniquity
> and sow trouble reap the same (Job 4:7–8).

Notice that Eliphaz not only claims that suffering is deserved but that Eliphaz has gained this wisdom from observation. Eliphaz claims that his experience confirms this belief.

ELIPHAZ'S FIRST ARGUMENT

- Don't change your beliefs based on your own experience.
- Sin is due to suffering. Observation proves this.
- You are suffering. Therefore you sinned. So did your children.
- Repent so that you will be freed from suffering.

At this point the reader knows that Eliphaz is wrong. The frame has clearly established Job's innocence. Moreover, the reader's observation has not confirmed the idea that only the guilty suffer. One would have to fail to observe a great deal to base such a teaching on observation. Eliphaz has lost credibility with the audience.

Eliphaz then goes on to tell of a terribly frightening experience, a vision or a dream accompanied by an awful dread, in which a voice questioned whether any person could be sinless.

> Can mortals be righteous before God?
> Can human beings be pure before their maker? (Job 4:17).

Since all are sinners all will perish.

Again, this argument is Eliphaz's attempt to get Job to admit his sinfulness. Eliphaz does not do this to be cruel. Rather, he believes it is true and that Job must admit it is true before Job will be relieved of his suffering.

Eliphaz then as much as calls Job a fool and points out that a fool's children "are far from safety" (Job 5:4). Since the frame has told us of the destruction of Job's children this remark does strike the reader as cruel.

Next Eliphaz advises Job to seek God.

> As for me, I would seek God
> and to God I would commit my cause.
> He does great things and unsearchable,
> marvelous things without number (Job 5:8–9).

With these words we gain a better understanding of Eliphaz's attitude toward Job and toward life. Eliphaz was evidently disturbed that Job had not turned to God, begging to be relieved of his suffering. Rather Job had merely lamented his ill-fortune.

For Eliphaz, the purpose of turning to God is to be saved from disaster and to be blessed with possessions and good health, the very things which Job has lost. Eliphaz attributes the same motive to Job which Satan attributed to him in the frame. Eliphaz assumes that one turns to God for self-centered motives. One does not "bless God for nothing."

Eliphaz claims that Job should be happy that God has reproved him.

> How happy is the one whom God reproves;
> Therefore do not despise the discipline of the Almighty (Job 5:17).

These words are obviously empty words to Job who knows that the reason behind his suffering is not reproof.

Having uttered his empty "insights," Eliphaz challenges Job. Since Eliphaz bases his conclusions on accepted wisdom, on personal observation and on private revelation (i.e. the dream), how could Job doubt?

> Lo, this we have searched out; so it is!
> This we have heard, and you should know it (Job 5:27).

Eliphaz's beliefs are those which would have been "known" and accepted by the contemporary audience. However, given the frame, not only Job but the audience now knows that Eliphaz's "doctrine" is wrong.

Review Questions

1. What is Eliphaz's belief? Given this belief, what is his conclusion about Job?
2. What is the doctrine of retribution?
3. How does Eliphaz claim to have learned this?
4. Why has Eliphaz lost credibility with the audience?
5. What question frightened Eliphaz in his dream?

6. What does Eliphaz want Job to do? Why?
7. For what reasons does Eliphaz assume one would turn to God?
8. What attitude does Eliphaz think Job should have toward his suffering?

Discussion Questions

1. For what reasons do you think people turn to God? Is it always for self-interest? Explain. Are prayers of petition good? Why or why not?
2. Do you think any person is good enough that suffering is not deserved? Why or why not?
3. Is the idea that all people sin as deeply disturbing to you as it was to Eliphaz? Why or why not?
4. Have you ever, in hindsight, been grateful for hardship? Why or why not?

ARTICLE 5

Job Disillusioned by Friends and God

Question: "Why does Job tell Eliphaz that Eliphaz would 'cast lots over the orphan and bargain over a friend?' " (Job 6:27; Job 6:5; 6:7; 6:10; 6:14; 6:15–21; 6:26–27; 7:11–12; 7:21 also discussed)

Job accuses Eliphaz of such crass and unfeeling behavior because Job has experienced Eliphaz's treatment of him as harsh and uncaring.

Job believes that Eliphaz owes him kindness.

> Those who withhold kindness from a friend
> forsake the fear of the Almighty (Job 6:14).

Yet Eliphaz's response was anything but kind. Eliphaz not only failed to take account of the extent of Job's suffering but added to it by saying things which Job knows are not true.

Job feels he has every reason to cry out in pain. One doesn't complain when there is nothing to complain about—the ass doesn't bray over its grass or the ox over its fodder (see Job 6:5), but Job must cry out because of the severity of his suffering. He shouldn't be criticized for speaking truthfully about his experience.

Eliphaz's empty arguments in no way nourish Job in his time of distress. They are "tasteless," like "loathsome" food (see Job 6:7).

So Job laments once more, but this time his lament is a cry to God. He longs to die. Yet even in the pain that leads to death Job cannot "repent" of something he knows he did not do. He longs for extinction with the sure self-knowledge that he has not separated himself from God.

128

JOB'S RESPONSE TO ELIPHAZ

- I have every reason to lament!
- Eliphaz, you should help me, not accuse me!
- Eliphaz, you have no evidence for your conclusion!
- God, how could you treat me like this? I don't deserve it!

> This would be my consolation,
>> I would even exalt in unrelenting pain;
>> for I have not denied the words of the Holy One (Job 6:10).

This advice to believe he deserved his suffering and to repent in order to be relieved from it is worthless. The friends who could give such advice are as unreliable as a stream that dries up. A caravan that goes to such a stream for drink would end up dead (see Job 6:15–21). Just so, Job had hoped for "drink" from his friends, but he has been sorely disappointed.

After all, Eliphaz has no way to prove his conclusion. He has simply assumed that Job must have sinned because he is suffering. Eliphaz has completely ignored Job's claim of innocence, has acted as though Job's words were no more than "wind" (see Job 6:26).

It is at this point that Job accuses Eliphaz of being so unfeeling that he would cast lots over an orphan or bargain over a friend (see Job 6:27).

Job's disillusionment is not only with his friends but with God. He had believed that his good fortune was reward for good behavior. Now, with his undeserved suffering, he knows that belief was wrong. Job is obviously close to God because he feels free to speak honestly.

> Therefore I will not restrain my mouth.
>> I will speak in the anguish of my spirit;
>> I will complain in the bitterness of my soul (Job 7:11).

Job feels that God is treating him as though he represented cosmic evil, as though he were a dragon of the deep (see Job 7:12).

Surely one little human being couldn't deserve such constant vigilance, such constant suffering.

Job had always believed God was loving. This belief is still present, a presumption behind his terrible doubts and questions. Job tells God that even if he had sinned he doesn't deserve the suffering he is now experiencing. He is too insignificant to do God any serious harm. God should forgive, not stalk and punish (see Job 7:21). Job is so sure that God is loving that he imagines God would be looking for him after he died. But then it would be too late. Why? Because neither Job nor the author of Job has any knowledge of or belief in a life after death. If God is to do right by Job, God must do it before Job dies, for after death Job "shall not be" (see Job 7:21).

It is no wonder that Job lashes out at his friends. He needs kindness but receives only platitudes which Job knows, from experience, are not true.

Review Questions

1. How did Eliphaz fail Job as a friend?
2. Why won't Job repent?
3. What would be Job's consolation in death?
4. Is Job close to God? How can you tell?
5. What complaint does Job make to God about God's behavior?
6. Why does Job think that God must do right by Job soon?

Discussion Questions

1. What does it mean to say that "those who withhold kindness from a friend forsake the fear of the Almighty"? Do you agree? Why or why not?
2. Do you think people who suffer should suffer silently or do you think they have every right to complain? Explain.
3. Does your belief in life after death play a role in your sense that God is a just God? Why or why not?

ARTICLE 6

Bildad Defends God's Justice

Question: "How could Bildad believe that God had killed all Job's children as a punishment for sin? If God would do something like that, then God isn't loving." (Job 8:3–4; Job 8:6; 8:8; 8:14 also discussed)

This question cuts to the core of the problem at hand. Bildad, in defending God's justice, pictures God as unloving. However, Bildad does not seem to realize that this is the effect of his argument. The author of Job does realize the ramifications of this line of thought, and that is why he is bringing it under scrutiny through his debate.

The questioner is accurate in stating that Bildad presumes that Job's children are dead because they were sinners.

> Does God pervert justice?
> Or does the Almighty pervert the right?
> If your children sinned against him,
> he delivered them into the power of their transgressions (Job 8:3–4).

Bildad has assumed that Job's children were sinners. Why? In order to defend God's justice. After all, the children have been killed. If the children were killed and didn't deserve it, then one must question God's justice. Since God's justice is beyond question, Job's children must have deserved what they got.

In other words, Bildad believes in the same doctrine of retribution which Eliphaz expressed. However, Bildad is such a "black

131

BILDAD'S FIRST ARGUMENT

- God is just. Your children deserved what they got.
- Just repent. You'll be restored.
- This is the wisdom of the generations.
- If you were close to God, as I am, you wouldn't be in this situation.

---

and white" thinker that the argument is more blatantly cruel on his lips.

In fact, Bildad is incapable of understanding Job's situation. He tries to comfort Job by suggesting that if only Job would seek God, God would restore Job to Job's "rightful place" (see Job 8:6). However, even in Job's worst agony Job has never asked God to restore him to his "rightful place." What Job longs for is not his "rightful place," but understanding.

As the audience hears Bildad assure Job that all will be well if only Job turns to God, the audience sees all too clearly the shallowness behind Bildad's thinking and the legitimacy of Job's cry. After all, even if Job were to be restored to health and even if Job were to have another family, the important question which Job has raised still remains. New blessings would not undo the fact that those other children are forever lost.

Bildad's posture is all the more alarming because he claims that his position is the result of closeness to God and reliance upon the wisdom of the ancestors. Bildad warns Job that one generation is not wise enough to search out these mysteries. One must "inquire of bygone generations" (see Job 8:8).

Then Bildad as much as accuses Job of not staying close to God. He compares one who forgets God to papyrus which cannot grow if not in marsh, or reeds which cannot grow if not in water. However, the audience knows that Job was and is very close to God. Again, pat answers are presented in such a way as to undercut them. Not only is traditional wisdom shown to be untrue, but those who espouse such "wisdom" are portrayed as cruel.

In Bildad's view people are either in touch with God or have forgotten God. They are either good or evil. Evil people may flourish for a short time, but only for a short time. There is no more substance in their lives than in a spider's web (see Job 8:14) or in a plant that is uprooted.

Since Job is presently suffering, since his old life has been completely uprooted, this argument too seems accusatory rather than comforting. We know that Job is not evil. If Bildad suggests that Job is evil, then we know that Bildad is wrong.

As Bildad draws his argument to a close we are astounded at his apparent optimism. Bildad seems to think he has been consoling and wise. The audience, however, perceives Bildad as shallow, judgmental, and cruel. Not only does he fail to comfort Job or to offer a helpful insight to Job, he completely fails to even address Job's question. Conventional wisdom is worse than inadequate. Those who act on such "wisdom" become cruel themselves and even picture God as though God too were cruel. The irony is that all this harm is done in an attempt to defend God's justice.

Review Questions

1. Why does Bildad argue that Job's children deserved to die?
2. For what does Job long?
3. Would a return to his "rightful place" solve the problem of Job's suffering? Why or why not?
4. How does Bildad claim to have come by his "insights"?
5. How does Bildad seem to suggest that Job is evil?
6. Why does Bildad end on an optimistic note? Does the audience share this optimism? Why or why not?

Discussion Questions

1. Have you ever been given pat answers to mysterious questions? Explain. Do the answers ever strike you as cruel? Explain.
2. Do you think it is always clear that people are either in touch with God or have forgotten God? Why or why not?
3. Have you ever felt that someone completely failed to listen to you? Explain. Why do you think the other person was unable to hear? Have you ever been unable to hear? Do you know why?

ARTICLE 7

How Does One Charge God?

Question: "Why does Job start talking about God's creative power (Job 9:5–10)? Isn't this off the subject?" (Job 9:1–10:22)

God's creative power is not off the subject, either in the context of Job's response to his "friends" (Job 9:1–10:22) or in the context of wisdom literature as a whole.

Remember that wisdom literature tries to probe mystery with reason. It seeks answers not just in the context of Jewish salvation history but in a broader context. Certainly one way in which God reveals God's self to all people is through creation. By looking at creation, at its magnificence, its vastness, its power, its delicacy, its endless variety, one is led to meditate on the question, "What does all that exists say about the one who created everything?" Job, too, is pictured as meditating on the nature of God by looking at creation.

Before this meditation Job picks up on a question that had been suggested by Eliphaz when he described his frightening dream of the night: "Is anyone just before God?" Eliphaz had meant that no one can be just because everyone sins. However, Job gives the sentence an entirely different meaning. Job's conscience is clear and he believes that he is "just" before God. When Job asks "How can a mortal be just before God?" (Job 9:2b), Job is asking how a person who feels mistreated by God can be justified. What recourse is there?

It is at this point that Job talks about the might and power which God the creator must have. After all, the one with whom Job finds himself in contention can remove mountains, can shake the very foundations of the earth, can even undo the course of nature by

134

JOB'S RESPONSE TO BILDAD

- How can I find justice?
- How can I argue with the one who created and ordered the entire universe?
- Can God be summoned?
- Would God listen?
- Perhaps God is neither just nor loving. How can I charge God?

---

telling the sun not to rise (see Job 9:5–9). Job knows that God is the one

> who does great things beyond understanding,
> and marvelous things without number (Job 9:10).

However, Job's meditation on God's power and transcendence is not a hymn of praise. Rather Job feels that he is in a hopeless situation because he has what he sees as a just complaint against a God who is so great that he decides the order of creation itself. Notice the words Job uses in describing this creative God. God "removes" and "overturns" mountains, "shakes" the earth, "commands" the sun, "tramples" the waves (see Job 9:5–8). Ironically the creator Lord is described more as one who undoes order by his command rather than as one who establishes it. Against such a God, what chance has Job, even if his complaint is just? If God "snatches away, who can stop him?" (Job 9:12a).

Because Job is not equal to the one whom he wishes to accuse, he is at a loss to know what to do. The fact that God has already snatched away Job's family, property, and health makes Job think that God is not one to listen. Because Job believes in his own innocence, he interprets his undeserved suffering as an expression of God's arbitrary anger. Since God is already angry, and for no apparent reason, there is no hope in "summoning" God (see Job 9:16). Even were God to respond to such a summons Job does not believe that God would listen to him. Otherwise Job's suffering would already have been relieved. So Job is overcome with a feeling of hopelessness.

> It is all one, therefore I say,
>   he destroys both the blameless and the wicked.
> When disaster brings sudden death,
>   he mocks at the calamity of the innocent . . .
>   if it is not he, who then is it? (Job 9:22–24)

Job's experience has so shattered his previous idea of God as just and loving that he is forced to the opposite extreme. Perhaps God is neither just nor loving.

As Job realizes that he has what amounts to a charge against God, Job also realizes that there is no way to have this charge heard. He is accusing God to God. As Job says, "There is no umpire between us." There is no arbitrator who could judge both Job and God because God is the one who establishes the existence of everyone and everything in the first place. No one can bring suit against God even if his cause is just.

So, as we see, Job's meditation on God the creator is not in the least "off the subject." If the creator creates order, order is whatever that creator says it is. So Job, even if innocent, is left without recourse. Job has no where to turn.

Review Questions

1. Why is a meditation on creation frequently a theme in wisdom literature?
2. What does Job mean when he asks, "Can anyone be just before God?"
3. What is the point behind Job's meditation on God's power in nature?
4. How does Job interpret his undeserved suffering?
5. Why does Job think that God is not listening?
6. Why is it that one cannot bring a charge against God?

Discussion Questions

1. Do you feel the power and presence of God in nature? Is this always a pleasant experience? Explain.
2. Have you ever felt that God is not listening? What causes such feelings? Do you know of any helpful way to get beyond this feeling?
3. Have you ever wanted to argue with God? Have you done it? How? Do you think this is a good or a bad thing to do? Why?

ARTICLE 8

Is God Good?

Question: "Does Job admit guilt or not? When he says, 'You do not acquit me of my iniquity,' it sounds as though he does, but then he continues as though he thinks he is innocent." (Job 10:14b; Job 10:3b; 10:9–12; 10:14–15; 10:21–22 also discussed)

Job never admits guilt in the sense that he admits he purposefully chose to do something wrong. Job's conscience is clear. Certainly the audience is to remain sure that Job is innocent. That fact was established in the frame when God described Job as "blameless and upright" (see Job 1:8). The whole point of the debate is lost if Job is guilty of sin, because then the old pat answers would fit the case. Job would be suffering because he had sinned.

However, Job is at such a complete loss to explain why a just and loving God would inflict such suffering on an innocent man that he suggests every conceivable theory as a cause. Among these theories is the possibility that guilt and innocence have nothing to do with conscious choice. The creator God can establish order in any way God chooses and can assign guilt to anyone God chooses. It is against such an arbitrary standard that Job has no recourse.

> If I sin, you watch me,
>   and do not acquit me of my iniquity.
> If I am wicked, woe to me!
>   If I am righteous, I cannot lift up my head,
> For I am filled with disgrace
>   and look upon my affliction (Job 10:14–15).

Before such arbitrary standards guilt and innocence are indistinguishable. It makes no difference how one acts. The righteous as well as the sinner are "filled with disgrace."

138

Because Job's righteous behavior has ended in disgrace, he has lost any sense that he might know God. Again his present disillusionment appears before a backdrop of a "good God" whom Job used to know. When Job remembers how God used to be, he reminds God that God had fashioned Job as a potter does clay (Job 10:9), as a cheese-maker does cheese (Job 10:10), and as a tailor does clothes (Job 10:11). In a poignant moment Job remembers that the good God was loving.

> You have granted me life and steadfast love,
>   and your care has preserved my spirit (Job 10:12).

It is impossible for Job to understand how this loving God could have let him suffer as he is suffering now. It is this total perplexity that causes Job to cast around for any explanation at all. Perhaps God has a warped mind. Perhaps it seems good to God

> To despise the work of your hands,
>   and favor the schemes of the wicked (Job 10:3b).

Perhaps God isn't all knowing. After all, God doesn't have eyes of flesh and cannot see as humans see. Perhaps God's lack of knowledge has caused God to make a mistake.

Perhaps God never was loving and only formed Job for the pleasure of destroying him. Perhaps the whole time God was planning and waiting for the time when God would search out Job's "guilt," an unknown arbitrary "guilt," for the purpose of destroying him.

Since Job can find no answer to the "why" of his suffering, he asks another "why?" "Why was I ever born?" (see Job 10:18). Death as an infant would have been much preferable to this life of intense and constant suffering.

Instead of calling on this arbitrary and attacking God to save him, Job begs this God to leave him. Only if God leaves him will Job have a little peace before he dies.

Again Job's words make it clear that he expects no life after death. He will go:

... never to return,
    to the land of gloom and deep darkness.
The land of gloom and chaos,
    where light is like darkness (Job 10:21–22).

The fact that this debate was written before a belief in life after death had developed heightens the mystery. The author cannot find a way out of his dilemma by suggesting that rewards and punishments are doled out after death. The answer for which the author has Job search must address the human condition on earth, not in heaven. Just why is it that a loving God would allow an innocent person to suffer so much during his life on earth?

Review Questions

1. Does Job admit that he deserves his suffering?
2. How could guilt and innocence have nothing to do with conscious choice?
3. Name three theories which Job suggests to explain God's behavior.
4. Why does Job ask God to leave him?

Discussion Questions

1. Do you believe God is all-knowing? Has any experience ever caused you to doubt it? Explain.
2. Do you believe God formed you as a potter forms clay? Is this a comforting thought? Why or why not?
3. Have you ever wished that God would leave you alone? Explain. Do you think it is all right to express such feelings? Why or why not?

ARTICLE 9

Zophar Defends God's Wisdom

Question: "Does Zophar add anything to the friends' argument? Chapter 11 seems to be just more of the same." (Job 11)

Zophar's argument includes many of the same points which we heard from Eliphaz and Bildad. However, as Zophar presents his ideas of God's "wisdom," he reveals himself to be even less sympathetic and even more shallow and arrogant than did the others.

First Zophar seems outraged that Job should have searched for answers in the first place. He describes Job's heartfelt questions as "babble," and Job's soul-searching challenges to the traditional wisdom as "mocking" (see Job 11:3). Neither of these charges is accurate, as the audience knows well.

Next Zophar states Job's position as though there were no way on earth it could be anything but completely false.

Ridicules Job

> For you say, "My conduct is pure,
>   and I am clean in God's sight" (Job 11:4).

However, the audience knows that Job's claim is basically true.

So when Zophar launches off on a defense of God's wisdom, he is already thoroughly discredited in the eyes of the audience. We are poised to find fault with him, and find fault with him we do.

Zophar proceeds to add to our impression that he is unsympathetic by telling Job that all of his sufferings are too little to make up for his guilt. Job deserves worse than he has received (see Job 11:6b). Zophar adds to our impression that he lacks wisdom by

141

ZOPHAR'S FIRST ARGUMENT

- Who are you to ask questions?
- You are obviously a sinner!
- You deserve worse than you got!
- I'll pass God's wisdom on to you: God has to punish to remain just.
- Repent!

---

assuming that his understanding of the order of things is identical to God's wisdom. He wishes that God would speak to Job so Job could know wisdom (Job 11:5). But since God can't, Zophar will, in God's place.

In expounding on God's wisdom, Zophar falls into the same trap in which Eliphaz and Bildad found themselves. Those who defend the doctrine of retribution inevitably picture God as unloving and human beings as deserving nothing but suffering. It is as though God in God's wisdom can do nothing but punish because human beings are nothing but wicked.

> If he [God] passes through and imprisons,
>   and assembles for judgment,
>   who can hinder him?
> For he knows those who are worthless;
>   when he sees iniquity, will he not consider it? (Job 11:10–11).

The reader is well aware that God's "wisdom," which truly is "higher than the heavens," "longer than the earth," and "broader than the sea" (see Job 11:8–9), has been reduced to untrue platitudes on the lips of Zophar.

With such an introduction the twice-heard plea that Job should simply repent so that he can regain his material prosperity and the respect of his friends sounds outrageous. Once more Job's questions have been completely ignored. Job has not asked how he could regain goods and friends. He has asked a much more pro-

found question. What does an innocent person's suffering say ✳
about the nature of God?

Why is it that all the friends have completely failed to see, much
less address, the problem? It is because the doctrine of retribution,
once accepted and applied, hides the problem. The possibility of an
innocent person's suffering doesn't exist because the suffering is in
itself proof that the person is not innocent.

The fact that this rock-bound argument inflicts blindness on
those who espouse it is illustrated once more as Zophar brings his
argument to a close. Zophar has interpreted Job's longing for death
as proof of Job's wickedness, since it is the wicked who see no
escape other than to hope for death (see Job 11:20).

Zophar's argument is substantially the same as those of his
friends. However, the effect that such a point of view has on the one
who holds it is most clearly exemplified in Zophar. Zophar, who
tries to defend God's "wisdom," is the opposite of a wise man.
Zophar lacks wisdom in every relationship: his relationship with
Job, with God, and even with himself.

Review Questions

1. How does Zophar discredit himself in the eyes of the audience?
2. How does Zophar show that he equates God's wisdom with his
   understanding of God's wisdom?
3. In what trap do those who defend the doctrine of retribution
   inevitably find themselves?
4. What question is Job asking?
5. Why have all three friends failed to comprehend the problem?

Discussion Questions

1. Do you find the words, "It was God's will," comforting or outrageous when spoken at a time of tragedy? Explain.
2. Have you ever met a person who assumes that his or her under-

standing is identical to God's? Why do you think people make this mistake?

3. Have you ever observed that self-righteous people are sometimes cruel? Can you give any examples? Why do you think this is true?

ARTICLE 10

Job Defends Truth

Question: "Why does Job tell his friends that God will rebuke them for their defense of God?" (Job 13:10; see Job 13–14)

Job believes that God would be displeased with the friends' defense because the defense rings false. Job believes that God is a God who loves truth. Job challenges his friends:

> Will you speak falsely for God,
>   and speak deceitfully for him?
> Will you show partiality toward him,
>   will you plead the case for God?
> Will it be well for you when he searches you out?
>   Or can you deceive him as one person deceives another?
> He will surely rebuke you if in secret you show partiality (Job
>   13:7–10).

Job charges his friends with intellectual dishonesty. In order to defend God they are ignoring truth and giving answers with no more substance than "ashes" or "clay" (see Job 13:12).

Job is so sure that God loves truth that he believes he might save rather than destroy himself by challenging his friends, even by challenging God. Far from thinking that his behavior speaks to his wickedness, Job thinks that his behavior speaks to his innocence. Who would want to plead his case before God if he thought himself guilty? Job says:

> . . . but I will defend my ways to his face.
> This will be my salvation,
>   that the godless shall not come before him (Job 13:15–16).

Job believes he can defend himself before God and live because God, who loves truth, will acknowledge that Job is in the right. Job knows he will be "vindicated" (see Job 13:18).

145

JOB'S RESPONSE TO ZOPHAR

- You are intellectually dishonest.
- God would not be pleased with a defense that rings false.
- God loves truth. God will be pleased with my defense.
- God, answer me!
- God will vindicate me someday, even if it's after I'm dead.

Job then stops addressing his friends and addresses God directly. He wants to present his case but can only do so if God agrees not to overwhelm Job with power or dread. If God will do this, then Job is willing to be either the defendant or the plaintiff.

> Then call, and I will answer;
>   or let me speak, and you reply to me (Job 13:22).

When God fails to respond to this plan, Job is forced to speak first. Again Job challenges God to tell him what he has done wrong, to explain why God is treating Job as an enemy (see Job 13:23–24). Job longs, even demands, to have God explain God's actions. Still God remains silent.

The mystery of Job's suffering would not be quite as mysterious if he believed in life after death. Job even fantasizes of that possibility. After all, a tree, cut down, might sprout a shoot and live again. The same is not true of humans. Once they are dead they are dead. They will not "rise again"; they will not be "roused from sleep" (see Job 14:12).

Job would find his sufferings more endurable were there any chance that God would summon him. Again we see that Job can't stop trusting God's love, even in the face of his terrible suffering. He imagines that God will someday "long for the work of his hands" (see Job 14:15) and so call Job. Job would surely answer.

However, the opportunity to vindicate himself before God in a court of law or the chance that God might yet call him even after he is dead is fantasy, not reality. Neither idea gives Job reason to hope because Job, unlike his friends, insists on naming what he knows to be true from experience, even though it does give the lie to what he had previously believed, even if it does throw him into mystery.

Job's courage in naming the truth he has experienced is a courage his friends lack. In fact, although the friends think they are defending God through their arguments, in fact they are defending their own security. They are afraid to give up the answers they have because they have no better answers with which to replace them. That is why they "whitewash with lies," why they are, in Job's estimation, "worthless physicians" (see Job 13:4).

Job's friends want him to be silent because they believe his argument is an affront against God. Job thinks his friends should be silent for the very same reason. Job believes that silence is the only wisdom which his friends have at their disposal (see Job 13:5). Job, on the other hand, will continue to speak out because, at the very least, Job's words are true.

Review Questions

1. Why does Job believe that God would be displeased with the friends' defense of God?
2. Why does Job think God will be pleased with Job's behavior?
3. What challenge does Job offer God?
4. About what possibility, which Job considers impossible, does he fantasize?
5. Name a kind of courage which Job has and his friends lack.
6. Why do Job's friends "whitewash with lies"?

Discussion Questions

1. Were you taught that it is good to question what you have been taught? Explain.
2. When people are afraid to question, what do you think causes their fear?
3. Do you ever picture God as "longing" for you? Explain. What does such a fantasy say about one's idea of God?
4. At a time of judgment do you picture God as accusing you or defending you? Explain.

ARTICLE 11

My Redeemer Lives!

Question: "What does Job mean when he says that he knows that his redeemer lives? (Job 19:25–26) It sounds as though he believes in life after death." (Job 9:33–35; 14:13; 16:18–19; 19:23–24; 19:25–27; 30:23)

Job never does come to a belief in life after death. We have noted his lack of belief in a resurrection all along. He will continue to reveal his belief that humans, like all living creatures, die once and for all as the debate progresses (see Job 30:23).

However, many Christians who bring to this passage a belief in the resurrected Christ as redeemer project their own beliefs onto Job's words. In order to understand what Job meant by these words, we will have to look at them in context.

As we noted in Article 7, Job had longed for an "umpire," an "arbitrator" who could decide the case between himself and God (Job 9:33–35). Job believed he was innocent and that there must be, someplace, someone who would testify to his innocence.

Again, in Article 10 we noticed that Job fantasized a good and loving God looking for him after he has died (Job 14:13). This same sense that Job would one day be vindicated appeared in chapter 16.

> On earth do not cover my blood;
>> let my outcry find no resting place.
> Even now, in fact, my witness is in heaven,
>> and he that vouches for me is on high (Job 16:18–19).

Scholars debate who this imagined "witness" might be. Is it a member of the heavenly court, like Satan in the opening frame, who would, after Job's death, testify that he had not deserved his suffering? Or is it God himself, the good God in whom Job had so firmly believed before his suffering began? Either way, Job imagines that even after his death a voice will speak the truth on his behalf so that he is justified before God and before his friends.

This passage in chapter 19, in which Job expresses a belief that his redeemer lives, seems to be revealing much the same hope for vindication after death.

> For I know that my redeemer lives,
>   and that at the last he will stand upon the earth;
> And after my skin has been thus destroyed,
>   then in my flesh I shall see God,
> Whom I shall see on my side,
>   and my eyes shall behold, and not another.
> My heart faints within me! (Job 19:25–27).

Despite all his terrible suffering—not just in losing his health, his children, his property, and his reputation, but also in losing his unquestioned belief in a loving God—Job just can't stop hoping. This passage represents a triumph of hope.

Job doesn't hope to avoid death. In fact he wants his claim to innocence written down so that it will survive him (see Job 19:23–24). Job is sure that he will die. However, Job can't stop hoping that perhaps, even after his death, God will stand on earth and clear Job's reputation with his friends. Job imagines that even were he already dead, God would somehow make him conscious of the fact that he has been vindicated.

With this jubilant affirmation of faith Job completely rejects the doctrine of retribution, to which his friends still hold fast. Job does not lose faith in himself and begin to see his suffering as punishment for sin. On the other hand, and most remarkably, Job finally does not lose faith in God. True, God is acting in a mysterious way. True, God has not answered Job's pleas and charges. God has, so far, remained silent. But despite all this, Job does not give up on God. Job believes that sometime, somewhere, somehow God will justify Job. In justifying Job, God will justify God. Job does not know how his vindication will take place, but Job believes that it

---

JOB'S BASIS FOR HOPE

- Not the doctrine of retribution.
- Not his own rights or goodness.
- Not life after death.
- God's nature: God's goodness; in justifying Job, God will justify God.

---

will. Job knows that his redeemer lives and will finally speak on Job's behalf.

Review Questions

1. Why might it appear to a Christian reader that Job had come to a belief in life after death?
2. What persistent longing and belief does Job have even in the face of his suffering?
3. Who might Job's imagined "witness" be?
4. What will Job's "redeemer" do for him?
5. Does Job lose faith in himself? Explain.
6. Does Job lose faith in God? Explain.

Discussion Questions

1. Have you projected a Christian understanding on Job's words, "I know that my redeemer lives"? Do you agree that the meaning of the words on your lips and on Job's lips is not the same? Why or why not?
2. Have you or anyone you know achieved a "triumph or hope"? Explain.
3. What does it mean to say that in justifying Job God would also justify God?
4. Have you ever thought that God needed to "justify" God's self? Explain. Do you still feel the same way? Why or why not?

ARTICLE 12

"Your Judge Lives!"

Question: "Why does Job warn his friends that they should be afraid of God's judgment? (Job 19:29) After all, it isn't their fault that they don't know Job is innocent." (Job 21:7–9; 19:3; 19:13–17; 19:21–22; 21:19–21)

Job believes that his friends are at fault because they have pre-judged him, they have failed to listen to him, they have failed to be honest observers of life, and they have failed to treat him with compassion. Because Job has made his leap of faith in a God who will bring about justice sometime in the future, he believes that his friends will be held accountable for their behavior.

It should be true that Job's friends do not know whether Job is guilty or innocent. However, despite all that Job has said, the friends have judged him guilty. Why? Because the friends are holding on tenaciously to a belief which they can't bring themselves to question even in the face of evidence to the contrary. Not one second's consideration has been given to the possibility that Job might be speaking the truth. All the friends seem capable of doing is to throw doctrine at Job, not to offer him compassion. Job charges them with this fault when he says:

> These ten times you have cast reproach upon me,
> are you not ashamed to wrong me? (Job 19:3).

When people remain adamantly in the wrong, despite evidence to the contrary, one must ask why. The author of Job forces his audience to ask why Job's friends won't give the slightest consideration to the possibility that Job is speaking the truth. After all, as Job points out, even observation of the ways of the world brings

151

JOB FINDS FAULT WITH HIS FRIENDS

- You have pre-judged me.
- You haven't listened.
- You aren't honest observers of life.
- You haven't treated me with compassion.

---

their doctrine into question. Anyone can see that it is simply untrue that the good prosper and the wicked don't. Job asks:

> Why do the wicked live on,
>   reach old age, and grow mighty in power?
> Their children are established in their presence,
>   and their offspring before their eyes.
> Their houses are safe from fear,
>   and no rod of God is upon them (Job 21:7–9).

The friends would respond that the wicked man's children will suffer. But how would that right anything? Once dead, what difference would it make to a wicked man if his children did suffer since he would know nothing about it? (see Job 21:19–21). The friends' doctrine of retribution just won't stand up. Any honest observer would be forced to question it.

But even if the friends' theory were correct, which it obviously isn't, they still have acted cruelly toward Job. If Job has done wrong, then Job has done wrong. But what right would that give the friends to treat him without pity? Job has lost his children, his acquaintances are having nothing to do with him, his relatives keep their distance, his servants do not respond to his call, and his wife finds him loathsome (see Job 19:13–17). Given all of this rejection, how could Job's friends possibly heap abuse rather than compassion on his head? Job pleads with his friends:

> Have pity on me, have pity on me, you my friends,
>   for the hand of God has touched me!
> Why do you, like God, pursue me,
>   never satisfied with my flesh? (Job 19:21–22).

Job's hard-won belief that there is a loving God who will, sometime in the future, right wrongs gives him reason to believe not only that he will be vindicated but that his friends will be exposed for the uncompassionate and intellectually dishonest people whom they have revealed themselves to be. The idea of God's final judgment has become a comfort to Job, but Job thinks his friends should find the thought disturbing. They should indeed fear God's judgment.

Review Questions

1. Name four ways in which Job thinks his friends are at fault.
2. Why haven't Job's friends considered the possibility that he is right?
3. If Job's friends couldn't believe him, what other evidence, available to all, should have caused them to question?
4. Why does the idea that a wicked man's children would suffer for his sins not help Job?
5. Had Job sinned, would his friends' behavior be justified?
6. Why does Job think his friends should be fearful?

Discussion Questions

1. Do you regard lack of sympathy for a person who is at fault a sin? Why or why not?
2. How do you picture God treating the self-righteous and judgmental? Why do you think this?
3. Do you think children do suffer for their parents' faults? Do you regard this as God's will? Explain.

ARTICLE 13

Eliphaz: The Opposite of a Wise Person

Question: "Why does Eliphaz accuse Job of neglecting the poor? Isn't this a new charge without any evidence?" (Job 22:6–9; 22:23; 27:3–5)

This is a new charge without any evidence, and the whole speech goes to show what can happen to a sincerely religious person who thinks that God's actions cannot be other than what he has come to understand and believe them to be.

The fact is that Job is of a moral caliber completely outside Eliphaz's comprehension. In addition, God's ways are obviously not limited to Eliphaz's understanding of God's ways. Because Eliphaz is narrow-minded, because he ignores evidence available to each person from observation and experience, and because he is incapable of examining his own beliefs in the light of his friend's experience, Eliphaz changes from a person who tries to be kind (although unsuccessfully) to a person who condemns and accuses without any basis in fact at all.

When Eliphaz begins his speech he asks a number of rhetorical questions. For Eliphaz the answers are obvious. The answers are "no." But for the reader the answers are also obvious, and the answers are "yes." This is true because of the dramatic irony which has been established by the legend which acts as a frame for the debate. In the frame God was very proud of Job. So, in answer to Eliphaz's question as to whether or not a mortal can be of "pleasure" to God, the answer is "yes." Job was and is of "pleasure" to God. In answer to Eliphaz's question "Is it for your piety that he reproves you?" (Job 22:4), the audience is also inclined to say "yes," although the audience would disagree with the word "re-

---

ELIPHAZ GROWS WORSE

- He cannot perceive or understand Job's integrity.
- He cannot separate God's ways from his understanding of God's ways.
- He cannot re-examine a cherished belief.
- He resorts to blindness, anger, and false accusations.

---

prove." It was because of Job's piety that the Advocate wanted to test Job. The Advocate believed that a human being could only act lovingly toward God for his own benefit. God had a higher opinion of Job. We see now that Eliphaz agrees with the Advocate, but that Job is living up to God's high opinion of him.

That Eliphaz sees a self-serving motive as the only possible motive is evident in his final plea to Job to repent.

> If you return to the Almighty
>   you will be restored (Job 22:23).

That Job values an honest relationship with God over reward is evident when he says:

> As long as my breath is in me
>   and the spirit of God is in my nostrils,
> My lips will not speak falsehood,
>   and my tongue will not utter deceit.
> Far be it from me to say that you are right;
>   until I die I will not put away my integrity from me (Job 27:3–5).

In addition to Eliphaz's being unable to understand Job's integrity, he is unable to separate God's ways from his understanding of God's ways. It is this inability which causes him to grow from insensitivity and blindness to completely false accusations.

Eliphaz illustrates a danger which is only too real among narrow-minded, "religious" people. Instead of letting experience force him to re-examine a cherished belief, he allows the cherished belief to define his reality, a reality which exists nowhere but in his own mind.

For Eliphaz the cherished belief is that only the wicked suffer. Job is obviously suffering; therefore Job must be among the wicked. Originally Eliphaz had attributed Job's "sin" only to his unwillingness to acknowledge that his suffering was indeed due to his sinfulness. But as Job persists in claiming his innocence and in accusing God of inflicting unmerited suffering upon him, Eliphaz decides that Job is such a wicked person that he must have committed every sin which was in his power to commit. He must have failed to clothe the naked, to give drink to the thirsty, to give bread to the hungry, to protect the widow and to help the orphan (see Job 22:6–9).

As our questioner noted, Eliphaz has absolutely no evidence for a single one of these charges. He has arrived at his conclusions through inverted logic. He believes in a cause and effect relationship between sin and suffering. He sees the effect—suffering—so he claims the cause—sin. This is the inverse of the way a "wise" person would reason. As we noted before, "wisdom" allows experience and observation to challenge belief. Eliphaz has ignored Job's experience and has failed to observe what any person could observe. Eliphaz has come to represent the opposite of a "wise" man.

Review Questions

1. How does Eliphaz change? Why does he change?
2. What answer does Eliphaz expect to his rhetorical questions? Would the audience agree? Explain.
3. For Eliphaz what is the motive for turning to God?
4. What does Job value most?
5. How does Eliphaz form his idea of reality? Why is this dangerous?
6. How did Eliphaz arrive at his conclusion of Job's sinfulness?
7. How does Eliphaz differ from a wise person?

Discussion Questions

1. Have you ever completely misjudged someone? Do you know how this occurred? Explain.

2. Have you ever been completely misjudged? Do you know how this occurred? Explain.
3. Can you give any example, either in your experience or in someone else's, in which pre-judgments and cherished beliefs formed your/their idea of reality, an idea that later proved to be wrong? Explain.
4. Do you have any suggestions on how to help yourself or someone else avoid this mistake? Explain.

ARTICLE 14

A Corrupt Text or a Dire Warning?

Question: "In Job 27:13–23 isn't Job contradicting what he said before? It sounds as though he now says that the wicked do suffer where before he said they don't." (Job 21:7–33; 22:1–27:21)

Many scholars would agree with the observation of this reader. Job's description of the ways in which the wicked suffer does seem to contradict Job's earlier claim that anyone can see that the wicked don't suffer (see Job 21:7–33). There are two possible ways to respond to the question. One is to agree that the words cannot be Job's and so to conclude that the text is corrupt. Another is to suggest an interpretation for the words as they now stand in the canonical text.

When we began reading chapter 22 we began reading what we would expect to be the third cycle of speeches. So we would expect to hear from each of Job's friends once. However, this third cycle (see Job 22:1–27:21), while it does assign a third speech to Eliphaz, shows Bildad giving only a short, truncated speech and Zophar giving no speech at all. Why is this? Are some of the words attributed to Job misplaced? Should Job's speech on the unhappy fate of the wicked be attributed instead to Zophar?

While scholars agree that chapters 25–27 seem to be corrupt, they do not agree on how the text might be rearranged into what might have been its original sequence.

If taken as expressing Job's own belief, it certainly is difficult to attribute Job's speech on the evil which will befall the wicked to Job. Not only has Job maintained the opposite, but he has further contradicted contemporary orthodoxy by claiming that God, in addition to failing to punish the wicked, fails to protect the poor

158

and innocent from the wicked. In fact, the wicked do, and succeed in doing, the very things which Eliphaz accused Job of doing. They mistreat the widow and orphan, they abuse the poor, and they steal other people's crops (see Job 24:3–6).

> From the city the dying groan,
>> and the throat of the wounded cries for help;
>> yet God pays no attention to their prayer (Job 24:12).

How could Job now turn around and claim that the wicked are punished? Must we simply admit that the words should be attributed to Zophar?

Scholars suggest a possible reason for attributing the words to Job. As we noted in Article 12, Job has warned his "friends" that they should fear God's judgment. Just before this speech on the lot of the wicked Job says:

> May my enemy be like the wicked,
>> and may my opponent be like the unrighteous (Job 27:7).

Job's friends, as illustrated in Eliphaz's last speech, full of completely untrue accusations, have become Job's enemies. Their treatment of him has put them among the wicked.

Perhaps Job is simply reminding these newly revealed enemies that according to their own beliefs they will soon be suffering the lot of the wicked. Job points out to his oppressors:

> This is the portion of the wicked with God
>> and the heritage that oppressors receive from the Almighty (Job
>> 27:13).

If the beliefs of Job's friends are true, then the friends can expect their children to be mutilated by the sword, to face hunger, pestilence and premature death. Whatever wealth they accumulate will not stay with them but will be divided up by the innocent, and they too will be overtaken by terrors (see Job 27:14–20).

Are the words Job's or Zophar's? Since there is other evidence that the text is corrupt, and perhaps incomplete, one cannot answer the question with certainty. If the words are Job's, they do not represent a change of mind or heart on Job's part. Job has thoroughly rejected the idea of retributive justice as an explanation for the mysterious ways of God. However, since the friends have not rejected this belief, they should beware. Their treatment of Job has placed them among the wicked. Whatever they believe the lot of the wicked to be, they should think of as their own lot.

Review Questions

1. What evidence is there that the third cycle of speeches is not complete?
2. What two orthodox beliefs about the wicked has Job contradicted?
3. Why might Job's words on the suffering of the wicked be attributed to Zophar instead of Job?
4. Is there any way of understanding Job's words on the suffering of the wicked so that they don't contradict his earlier statements?

Discussion Questions

1. How do you balance the belief that "the Lord is our shepherd; there is nothing we should fear" with the knowledge that crime is rampant?
2. Even though scholars agree that a text might be corrupt, they still accept the fact that it is canonical. Why do you think this is?
3. Do you think Job's friends could fairly be called wicked? Why or why not?

ARTICLE 15

Only God Knows Wisdom

Question: "Is this poem about wisdom in chapter 28 a continuation of Job's speech? All the vehemence seems gone." (Job 28)

The poem about wisdom is not a continuation of Job's speech. Rather the voice behind the poem seems to be that of a narrator who, by expressing his views on wisdom, not only comments on what has already occurred in the debate between Job and his friends, but prepares the reader for what is yet to come.

The attitude of the narrator of the poem is the attitude neither of Job nor of Job's friends. First we will look carefully at the thoughts on wisdom which the poem reflects. Then we will see how these thoughts comment on the rest of the book of Job.

The narrator of the poem on wisdom does not think that wisdom is accessible to human beings. The refrain of the poem expresses this idea clearly.

> But where shall wisdom be found?
> And where is the place of understanding? (Job 28:12, 20).

The poem begins by contrasting wisdom to precious metals such as silver, gold, iron and copper, all of which are accessible to miners (see Job 28:1–6). Wisdom is not found under mountains or at the source of rivers. Even were one able to fly like birds of prey and like falcons, one still would not be able to find wisdom (see Job 28:7–11). Mortals cannot find wisdom in the "land of the living" (Job 28:13) or in the land of the dead (see Job 28:14). Neither can mortals buy wisdom. Wisdom is far more valuable than any precious stone (see Job 28:19).

Only God understands wisdom. Only God knows the way to wisdom (see Job 28:23). When God made the world, God sought out wisdom and used it in ordering the universe.

> Then he saw it and declared it;
>> he established it and searched it out.
> And he said to humankind.
>> "Truly, the fear of the Lord, that is wisdom;
>> and to depart from evil is understanding (Job 28:27–28).

In other words, the narrator of this poem on wisdom believes that while humans cannot know wisdom, which is completely beyond their comprehension, they can know how God would have them act. God would have people recognize their proper place in the created order and in relation to God and so have "fear of the Lord" (see Job 28:28). One who lives in right relationship with God would also avoid evil.

The words which God is pictured as using to describe how people might approach, if not understand, wisdom are the identical words which God was pictured as using to describe Job in the frame. God said of Job, "There is no one like him on the earth, a blameless and upright man who fears God and turns away from evil" (Job 1:8).

While the poem's words never directly refer to Job, Job's friends, or the problem about whether or not an innocent person might suffer, its position in the debate allows the poem to function as a comment on the debate thus far.

If wisdom is inaccessible to humans, so that humans should simply "fear the Lord" and "avoid evil," how should we view Job's friends? Obviously Job's friends fail in every regard. They have not realized that their understanding of God's ways is not identical to God's actual ways. In failing to recognize the limits of human knowledge, they have put too much credence in the theory of retributive justice and so have drawn untrue conclusions about Job. They have failed to avoid evil because they have truly misjudged and mistreated a person whom they should have treated with compassion.

Using the same yardstick, how are we to view Job's plight and Job's behavior? Job did originally act as a wise man should act.

However this behavior did not spare him suffering. Although Job doesn't claim wisdom as his friends did, nor does he teach retributive justice as his friends did, he still seems someplace deep in his bones to believe that there is a cause and effect relationship between good behavior and freedom from suffering. Otherwise he would not be accusing God of being his enemy and demanding to be vindicated. Were there no connection, vindication would not be an issue.

When it comes right down to it, in wanting to judge God as having mistreated him Job is falling into the same trap that his friends fell into in relation to him. Just as the friends cannot know Job's guilt or innocence, and so should not judge him, so Job cannot know wisdom, and so should not judge God. Human beings do not have access to the wisdom which would be necessary to judge God.

In addition to commenting on the past debate, this poem on wisdom prepares us for what is yet to come in the book of Job.

Since the author of the book of Job has chosen a debate as his literary form, how are we to know with which character in the debate the author agrees? As we have just seen, even though Job is innocent he doesn't seem to represent the author's point of view. Notice that in this poem on wisdom, God speaks. God says what relationship humans can have to wisdom. This is the narrative technique which the author will use to end his debate. God will speak on God's behalf. It is when God speaks that we are hearing the author's point of view.

Review Questions

1. What is the refrain of the poem on wisdom? What belief does it express?
2. To whom is wisdom accessible?
3. Even though humans cannot know wisdom, what can they know?
4. How does the poem on wisdom comment on Job's friends?
5. How does the poem on wisdom comment on Job?
6. Why can't human beings judge God?

7. In the poem, who says what relationship humans can have to wisdom?
8. How does the poem on wisdom prepare us for the end of the debate?
9. How will the author express the author's point of view?

Discussion Questions

1. Do you believe human beings have access to wisdom? Why or why not?
2. Do you believe that the spiritual order is, to some extent, revealed in the natural order? Can you give some examples?
3. Are you willing to live with the answer, "It is a mystery"? Explain. Do you think this is often necessary? Why or why not?
4. Are you ever tempted to judge God? To tell God what God should do? Can you give some examples?

ARTICLE 16

The Importance of Honor

Question: "Isn't Job too concerned with what others think of him? (Job 29:1–30:15) If he knows he is right with God, why does he feel he must be respected by people?" (Job 29–31)

The person who asked this question reflects a value system which would be difficult to live up to in any culture, but more difficult in Job's culture than in ours. One of the many differences between our American culture and the Mediterranean culture some four hundred years before Christ is that our culture puts a great stress on individualism and the priority of one's individual conscience. Job's culture put a great emphasis on honor in the eyes of society, and on the public acknowledgment of that honor in the behavior of others. In chapters 29–31 of Job we get a clear picture of how important that honor was to Job, how the loss of that honor, or shame, is causing Job terrible distress, and how, through an "oath of innocence," Job tries to regain his honor not only before God but before other people.

First Job recalls in precise detail the life of honor which had been his. Job was a person of great dignity. When he "took his seat in the square" at the gate of the city where business was carried on, the young men simply withdrew out of respect. Older people stood in Job's presence, and even the nobles and princes refrained from speaking (see Job 29:7–10).

Job earned these marks of respect by living an exemplary life, a life diametrically opposite from the life which Eliphaz has earlier accused him of living. Job had taken care of the poor, of orphans, and of widows. He had been helpful to the blind, the lame, the needy, and the stranger. Job had presumed that such a life would be

165

CULTURES IN CONTRAST

In the United States: • Be your own person.
• Follow your own conscience.
• Don't worry about the opinion of others.

In Job's world: • Act honorably.
• Avoid shame.
• The measure of your honor is in others' behavior toward you.

---

rewarded with years of health and continued respect. Job had lived as chief in his society, and possessed the honor which was all-important to his sense of well-being (see Job 29:12–25).

How all that has changed! Now, in Job's new condition, he lives with shame instead of honor. People who never did possess honor now treat Job with scorn. They mock him, spit at him, and physically torment him (see Job 30:1–15).

Once more Job complains to God that this treatment is unfair. Why is it that since he never ignored the cry of one in need, God now ignores him when he is in need? Again we see that despite Job's lack of belief in the doctrine of retribution he still acts as though God is bound by this logic. Since Job led a good life, God is being cruel to treat him as he has been treated. Where is God? Why doesn't God answer Job's charge? (Job 30:20–23).

Since God still does not answer Job, Job seeks to restore his honor by taking an "oath of innocence." Such an oath was used when, due to lack of witnesses, an accused person had no other way to clear his name. In such an oath the accused denies whatever has been the charge and then calls down a curse on himself should he be lying. In this way the case is turned over to God. If the curse is not carried out the person is presumed innocent.

Since the charge against Job is non-specific, Job denies all the sins which a man in his high estate would have had the opportunity to commit. In doing so, Job once more reveals the fact that he does indeed have a very high moral standard.

For instance, Job's first denial has to do with his internal state rather than his actions. Job had made a "covenant" with his eyes not to "look upon a virgin" (see Job 31:1). This disclaimer reminds us of Jesus' later teaching that "everyone who looks at a woman with lust has already committed adultery with her in his heart" (Mt 5:28). Job claims that he has practiced no dishonesty. Were God to weigh him in a just balance, God would know his integrity (see Job 31:1–7).

In fact, Job's virtue seems to extend beyond what society would ask of him. In Job's society just treatment of others would not include just treatment of slaves, since slaves were property. Job holds the enlightened view that because slaves too are God's children they should be treated justly, and Job has done just that (see Job 31:13–15).

Job even realizes that he should treat his enemies kindly. He never rejoiced at the ruin of an enemy or called down a curse upon those who hated him (see Job 31:29–30). Again, this reminds us of Jesus' teaching, "You have heard that it was said, 'You shall love your neighbor and hate your enemy.' But I say to you, love your enemies and pray for those who persecute you" (Mt 5:43–44).

Once more Job longs for God to write an indictment against him because he is sure God that will tell the truth and vindicate him (See Job 31:35–37).

> Oh that I had the indictment written by my adversary!
>> Surely I would carry it on my shoulder;
>> I would bind it on me like a crown;
> I would give him an account of all my steps;
>> like a prince I would approach him (Job 31:35–37).

Job's oath of innocence contains Job's last words in the debate with his friends. The friends cannot bring witnesses to contradict Job, so, in terms of the vindication of his honor, Job can do no more. His oath prevails unless the curses which he has called down upon himself occur. However, this vindication is not enough for

Job. In a culture where honor is all-important Job believes that God should support Job's claim that he did not deserve to lose honor in the eyes of his friends and fellow townspeople.

Review Questions

1. On what did the Mediterranean culture place a great emphasis?
2. How had Job been treated before his tragedies?
3. How has Job been treated during his time of suffering?
4. Even though Job has dismissed the doctrine of retribution, what does he still expect from God?
5. What is an oath of innocence?
6. How does Job's oath of innocence reveal that he has a high moral standard?
7. In what way does Job's virtue extend beyond what society would ask of him?
8. Why, given the circumstances, does Job's oath of innocence prevail?

Discussion Questions

1. Which is more important to you, your knowledge that you yourself believe you have done right or your knowledge that an external authority agrees you have done right?
2. Do we use shame as a punishment in our culture? Can you think of any examples?
3. Does an oath of innocence hold any weight in our culture? Why or why not?
4. Do you think gospel teachings are sometimes counter-cultural? Can you give some examples?

ARTICLE 17

Elihu Speaks: An Insertion or a Parody?

Question: "Who is this Elihu? He seems to have come out of nowhere and simply repeats what Job's friends have already said." (Job 32:1–37:24)

Scholars debate whether the four speeches of Elihu are the work of a later writer (our questioner seems to be leaning toward this point of view) or whether they were originally an integral part of the book of Job. Those who view the speeches as a later addition point out that the words on Elihu's lips do not compare to the words attributed to other characters in their poetic beauty. Nor is Elihu mentioned anywhere else in the poem, either in the prologue or in the epilogue. Perhaps a later author, having carefully studied the work of his predecessor, felt that the contribution which wisdom could make to the debate was not well represented by the three friends. So the later writer tried to remedy the situation by introducing a "wiser" and "more persuasive" character.

If Elihu's speeches are the work of a later writer who wanted to present wisdom in a better light, one can only conclude that this later author did not succeed. In fact Elihu is an unattractive character who adds little to the debate. Elihu is such an unattractive person that some critics think the speeches are the work of the original author and are meant to be a parody of a much too wordy, self-proclaimed "wise" man who is too young and too angry to add significantly to the debate. Traditional wisdom becomes less, not more, persuasive as we listen to Elihu's arguments.

In the short narrative introduction to Elihu's speeches we are told that Elihu is angry—angry at Job "because he justified himself

169

ELIHU'S CHARACTERISTICS

- Pre-judges Job
- Very wordy
- Cruel to Job
- Arrogant
- Lacks wisdom

---

rather than God," and angry at the friends because "they had found no answer" (see Job 32:2–3). Does Elihu find a better answer?

For the most part Elihu repeats the platitudes of his friends. The doctrine of retributive justice is restated as Elihu says:

> For according to their deeds he [God] will repay them,
> and according to their ways he will make it befall them (Job 34:11).

However, Elihu does suggest, as did Job, that a mediator working on Job's behalf might be part of the order of things (see Job 33:23–28). But Elihu's mediator would not simply declare a person in the right as would Job's, but would lead a person to repentance. Then that person would say to others:

> I have sinned and perverted what was right,
> and it was not paid back to me (Job 33:27).

In fact, Elihu's most interesting and thoughtful point involves God's power to forgive. Elihu presents Job with the following argument:

> For has anyone said to God,
> "I have endured punishment; I will not offend anymore;
> Teach me what I do not see;
> If I have done iniquity, I will do it no more"?
> Will he then pay back to suit you,
> because you reject it?

For you must choose, and not I;
   therefore declare what you know (Job 34:31–33).

Job has blamed God for treating Job in a way which Job did not
deserve. When God forgives, God is treating a person in a way
which the person does not deserve. Would Job therefore deny God
the right to forgive? If Job accepts God's lack of meting out "just
retribution" on the side of forgiveness, why does Job claim his own
treatment is unjust?

Despite this argument, though, Elihu too assumes that Job is
guilty. Because Job refuses to understand his sufferings as the way
in which God is speaking, and because Job refuses to repent, Elihu
completely loses patience with him. Elihu claims that the wise
would say:

Would that Job were tried to the limit,
   because his answers are those of the wicked.
For he adds rebellion to his sin;
   he claps his hands among us,
   and multiplies his words against God (Job 34:36–37).

In addition to his verbosity, his lack of any real wisdom, and his
cruelty, Elihu is either an ineffective spokesperson for wisdom or a
parody of a wise man because of his insufferable arrogance. As the
debate has progressed the stage has been set for God to speak.
However, before God speaks a brash young man who doesn't speak
well has the absolute gall to say that he speaks "on God's behalf"
(see Job 36:2). The reader wearies of Elihu long before Elihu concludes his remarks. Elihu seems to describe one like himself when
he says that God does not "regard any who are wise in their own
conceit" (see Job 37:24). The reader has little regard for Elihu, who
is wise only in his own conceit.

Review Questions

1. What evidence is there that Elihu's speeches are a later
   insertion?
2. How might Elihu's speeches be understood as the work of the
   original author of the book of Job?

3. At whom is Elihu angry? Why is Elihu angry?
4. How does Elihu agree with Job's friends?
5. What idea does Elihu suggest that is similar to Job's thinking? Is Elihu's idea identical to Job's? Explain.
6. What is Elihu's most thoughtful point?
7. What is Elihu's worst fault?

Discussion Questions

1. Do you think Elihu's speeches are the work of the original author of Job or are a later insertion? Why?
2. Are you more willing to accept undeserved blessings than undeserved sufferings? Why do you think it is that we ask "Why me Lord?" more often when faced with undeserved suffering?
3. Have you ever known anyone who claims or assumes that he or she speaks "on God's behalf"? Is such a claim ever true? Explain.

ARTICLE 18

God "Answers" Job

Question: "God never really answers Job, does God?" (Job 38:1–41:34)

It is true that God responds to Job with questions rather than "answers." However, it is also true that through those questions God responds to Job in such a way that Job's situation is completely changed. Job receives an "answer." In this article we will see what is taught through God's "answer out of the whirlwind" (see Job 38:1). In our next article we will see how God's appearance and words change Job.

First, and perhaps most importantly, we must ask what is being taught by the *fact* that God appears. After all, Job has longed for some response. Job has felt that God had become his enemy, mistreating him and not speaking. Of course, Job hoped that when God spoke God would tell Job's "friends" and all others before whom he had lost honor that Job's suffering was not punishment for sin.

While God does not say what Job had hoped God would say, God does come to Job and speak to him. By the very fact that God comes and speaks, God is pictured as one who has listened all along, who has never been absent from Job, and who has waited patiently until Job has said all that Job wanted to say. By the very fact that God comes and speaks, God is pictured as one who does love Job, as one who does want to be known and loved by Job.

Why, then, is the response couched in endless questions rather than clear answers? Why does God ask Job where Job was when God created the world in the first place, when God established the

---

GOD "ANSWERS" JOB

- God has listened.
- God knows and loves Job.
- The answer to Job's question is beyond Job's comprehension.
- There is an order, and therefore a reason behind everything, including Job's suffering.
- God is proud of God's creation, including Job.

---

order evident in creation? Can Job command the elements of nature? Can Job provide for the needs of the animals?

To the question "Where were you?" Job could only respond, "I don't know." To the question "Can you order all of creation?" Job could only respond, "No."

Two clear "answers" are implicit in God's questions. The first is that God cannot give a direct answer to Job's question about the meaning of Job's suffering because the answer itself would be beyond Job's comprehension. Job had been acting as though he understood the whole order of creation and the reason for everything right up until the time when he began to suffer. Then, because Job's suffering did not fit into the order as he understood it, he demanded an explanation. Job then acted as though he understood the whole order of creation except for this one thing—the reason behind the fact that good and evil do not meet respectively with reward and punishment. Through God's many questions God is making it clear to Job that there are a myriad of things which Job does not understand. The whole order of creation is completely beyond Job's comprehension.

A second implicit teaching in God's questions to Job is the fact that although Job does not understand the order of creation, nor can Job control it, still there is an order which God, who created the order, does understand and can control. So while Job might not understand nor be able to control the respective fates of the good and the bad person, nevertheless Job can rest assured that God does understand each person's situation, and no person is outside of God's "providence," God's order. Just as order exists in the world of the stars and in the world of the animals, so order exists in the world of people.

The thought here is one similar to the idea taught by Jesus when he says, "If God so clothes the grass of the field, which is alive today and tomorrow is thrown into the oven, will he not much more clothe you—you of little faith?" (Mt 6:30).

Similarly, God asks Job:

> Who has cut a channel for the torrents of rain,
>   and a way for the thunderbolt,
> To bring rain on a land where no one lives,
>   on the desert which is empty of human life,
> To satisfy the waste and desolate land,
>   and to make the ground put forth grass? (Job 38:25–27).

God orders and takes care of all God's creation, even places where there are no human beings. God takes care of creatures which humans might consider frightening in their strength like Behemoth (a hippopotamus?) or dangerous and chaotic like Leviathan, the mythical sea monster (Job 40:15–41:26). Although humans do not see the purpose or the order represented by these places and creatures, God their creator does, and God is proud of them.

So while God responds to Job with questions rather than answers, inherent in those questions are answers which Job desperately needed to hear. God has as much as said, "Job, I do love you and I have listened. You and all your experiences are part of the order of my creation. The reason I don't explain that order to you is because it is completely beyond your comprehension. Nevertheless, I am proud of all my creatures, and I am especially proud of you."

Review Questions

1. What is taught by the fact that God comes and speaks?
2. What two clear "answers" are implicit in God's questions?

3. What is the relevance of God saying that God sends rain where no human lives and God cares for exotic animals?
4. What is the relevance of God saying that God is proud of all God created?

Discussion Questions

1. Do you think of yourself as one who pretty much understands the order of the world or as one who understands very little? Why do you think this?
2. Why do you think God created a hippopotamus? What does this creature reveal about God?
3. Do you view the world as though all that has been created exists for human beings? Why or why not? Do you think our society lives as though this were our belief? Why or why not?

ARTICLE 19

Job's Change of Heart

Question: "Why does Job 'despise' himself and 'repent'? Has he come to believe he had sinned after all?" (Job 42:6; see Job 29:9; 29:21; 29:25; 40:4–5; 42:3; 42:5–7)

Job does not repent in the sense that he admits he had sinned and that his sin had been the cause of his suffering. However, God's appearance to Job does bring about a great change in Job. Job "repents" in the sense that he experiences a change of mind and heart.

Job responds to God's questions twice. In his first response Job says:

> See, I am of small account;
>> what shall I answer you?
>> I lay my hand on my mouth.
> I have spoken once, and I will not answer;
>> twice, but will proceed no further (Job 40:4–5).

We have read the expression, "laid their hands on their mouths," earlier in Job when Job was describing the manner in which he had been treated at the city gate (see Job 29:9). Job was describing the deep respect with which the young men, the nobles and the princes of the town treated him. They "listened" to Job and "waited," and "kept silence" for Job's counsel. Job acted as their "chief," as their "king" (see Job 29:21, 25). Now for the first time Job is in the presence of one for whom he has waited, one for whose counsel Job has longed. Job acts as one should act in the presence of the Almighty.

In Job's second response to God Job says:

JOB'S CHANGE OF HEART

- He no longer demands.
- He trusts God's love even though he does not understand his suffering.

> Therefore I have uttered what I did not understand,
> > things too wonderful for me, which I did not know. . . .
> I had heard of you by the hearing of the ear,
> > but now my eyes see you;
> Therefore I despise myself,
> > and repent in dust and ashes (Job 42:36)

Notice that Job does not ask God why he had suffered. Nor does Job ask God to return Job to his former state. Once Job experiences the presence of God it is no longer necessary for Job to question God. Two of Job's questions have already been answered. The answer to the question "Are you my enemy?" and to the question "Why do you remain silent?" have been answered by the fact that God came to Job. God loves Job and is present to Job. What else does Job need to know?

So Job "repents" not because he had claimed innocence. Job was right to do that. Job had been speaking the truth. Job had also been right when he warned his friends that they should not warp the truth to defend their own theories about God and the way God acts. In fact, God himself says that Job, rather than the friends, had spoken what was "right" of God (see Job 42:7).

Job "repents" because he had failed to recognize the proper order between the creature and the creator and so had demanded an explanation from God of God's behavior. Job's repentance is illustrated by the very fact that he no longer questions God but has learned to trust God's love even though he cannot understand the reason for everything God does.

However, the author of the book of Job is not teaching that, when confronted with mystery, one should not question. The ques-

---

THE VALUE OF QUESTIONING

- Enables Job to grow beyond a mistaken belief.
- Spares Job from acting with prejudice and cruelty, as did his friends.
- Helps Job grow in clarity of thought.
- Helps Job maintain his integrity.
- Helps Job develop courage and strength.

---

tioning was not in itself a sin. On the contrary, the author encourages questioning and pictures God as encouraging it. Through questions Job broke out of the trap of a belief in retributive justice, a belief which, as we observed in Job's friends, could lead one to misjudge both God and fellow human beings, and to act with blindness and cruelty. Through questioning Job grew in his own clarity of thought. He maintained his integrity and developed a strength built on that integrity. As is often true, Job's laments did not begin and end in despair but moved from despair to faith.

In fact the freedom to question inherited belief in the light of present experience is a freedom upon which wisdom literature depends. One cannot become wise if one never questions. God is pictured as encouraging the questioning. That is why God lets the debate go on so long before God appears. God wanted to give Job time to break out of his old belief system, to work through the challenges offered by his orthodox friends, to lament the loss of his old security, both materially and spiritually, and to find within himself a constant, rock-bottom faith in a loving God despite his suffering.

Job's questioning led him to his core desire to be in right relationship with God. Satan had been wrong. Job's desire to be in right relationship with God did not rest on his desire for reward. What Job needed and wanted was the relationship itself.

Wisdom literature encourages people to listen to the inherited tradition but to integrate it into their own experience. As we noted Job says:

> I had heard of you by the hearing of the ear,
>   but now my eyes have seen you (Job 42:5).

Job's personal experience of the presence of the living God has solved Job's problem. He "repents" in that he no longer feels he must have an answer. He no longer has to question God because he now knows God to the extent that he is able, and he trusts God's love and providence in those things which are beyond his ability to understand.

Review Questions

1. In what sense does Job "repent"?
2. What is meant by the phrase, "I lay my hand on my mouth?"
3. Why does Job not ask God what Job had previously demanded to know?
4. In what two ways was Job right all along?
5. In what way had Job failed?
6. Does the author disapprove of one's questioning God? Explain.
7. What does Job accomplish through his questions? How is God pictured as encouraging the questioning?
8. What is Job's core desire?
9. Why is questioning integral to wisdom literature?

Discussion Questions

1. Have you ever had a complete change of mind and heart? If so, what brought about this change?
2. Have you ever felt that God "answered" you? In what form did this "answer" arrive?
3. Do you encourage others—students, children, friends—to ask the hard questions, or are you uncomfortable with this? Do you know why you feel as you do?
4. Have you reached the point in your relationship with God or with another person where "trust" is the only way to proceed? Why is this sometimes the only "answer"?

ARTICLE 20

A Happy Ending: A Courageous Step Toward Truth

Question: "Doesn't it undercut the whole point of the book of Job to have Job return to prosperity? It makes it seem as if Job's suffering was a test, and that after Job repented his goods were returned as a reward. So, in the end, the friends were right." (Job 42:7–17)

The author of the book of Job loves to hold truths in tension with each other. By ending his agonizing debate with the second half of the traditional legend with which he began, the author has given his audience a traditional and expected "happy ending," but an ending that does not mask the inadequacy of such a "happy ending" when accepted as an answer to the mystery of human suffering.

The author takes pains to assure the reader that this happy ending does not mean that Job was wrong and his friends were right. God is pictured as stating exactly the opposite, twice. God not only expresses his anger at the friends for not speaking "rightly" of God as did God's servant, Job, but God directs the friends to ask Job to intercede for them so that they might be forgiven (see Job 42:7–8).

However, the fact that the friends are roundly condemned does not mean that everything they said was false, just as the fact that Job is commended does not mean that everything Job said was true. Some of what the friends said is true, such as the fact that God's awesome power and pervading presence are visible in the order of creation. God reaffirms this part of the friends' traditional wisdom by saying much the same thing. And some of what Job said was false, such as the idea that God had become Job's enemy and owed Job an explanation of God's ways.

The reason Job is affirmed and the friends condemned is that Job understood that a right relationship with God has to be based on

181

the truth. The friends denied truth known from experience to maintain their inherited beliefs. For this they must seek forgiveness not only from God but from Job whom they harmed immeasurably by their blind cruelty. The epilogue doesn't lead the reader to believe that the friends were right.

Why, then, does the author picture Job returning to prosperity after, and only after, Job intercedes for his friends? (Job 42:10) Is the author reaffirming the old belief that material prosperity is the reward of virtuous behavior?

It does seem that the old legend, used as a frame around the debate, reaffirms the idea preached by the friends and rejected by Job (and the author of Job) that Job's suffering was a test which he passed and so is now being rewarded. The old legend embodied the beliefs of the people, and that is what the people did believe.

By ending the debate with this legend the author is not affirming the teaching in the legend. Rather, because the debate has already undercut this teaching, the author is demonstrating that this easy answer, which has been accepted for years, which everyone still wants to believe because it is simple and happy, promotes virtue, warns against evil, and seems right, is woefully inadequate. One cannot forget what one has learned in the debate merely because one hears a conventional happy ending. Such is the stuff of stories, but life does not always follow the script.

We must remember that the audience of the book of Job would be resistant to the truth which the author is teaching. It is not terribly satisfying to be forced to admit that one's belief system is inadequate. It is even less satisfying when one is forced to give up a treasured belief and replace it, not with a better answer, but with a mystery.

A better answer might have been that there is life after death, so one cannot judge the fate of the good person and the evil person simply from the perspective of life on earth. The author of Job could not suggest this answer because he did not know it. A better answer might have been that an innocent person's suffering can be redemptive just as Jesus' suffering was redemptive. Again, the author could not suggest this answer because he did not know it. A belief in life after death preceded Jesus by only about two hundred years, and a belief in the redemptive value of suffering became clear only after the resurrection.

A PROCESS OF REVELATION

Coming to Knowledge by Reflecting on Experience

Question: Why do we suffer?

Understanding

Account:	Adam and Eve	We suffer because we sin.
Date:	1000 B.C.	
Experience:	We experience suffering	

Account:	Ezekiel	People don't suffer for their parents' sins but for their own. No innocent person is to be found.
Date:	593–571 B.C.	
Experience:	Is each of us personally responsible for whatever destruction comes?	

Account:	Second Isaiah	This is a terribly painful mystery. An individual or a community might suffer to save the sinner.
Date:	540 B.C.	
Experience:	Why are we in exile in Babylon?	

Account:	Job	Innocent people do suffer. There must be a reason since there is a reason for everything. The reason isn't a test or punishment.
Date:	400 B.C.	
Experience:	Innocent people do suffer	

Date:	30 A.D.	A totally innocent person has suffered. Why? What was its effect?
Event:	Jesus is crucified and dies, and many experience the presence of the risen Christ	

Account:	Paul to Colossians	Christ's suffering redeemed us. We are honored to share in his suffering, to participate in the process of redemption.
Date:	62 A.D.	
Experience:	Paul in captivity in Rome	

One can only stand in awe at the courage, faith and intellectual integrity of the author of the book of Job. Although he could not offer a completely satisfying answer to the question he raised, he nevertheless had the courage to discard that part of traditional wisdom which experience had taught him could not be true.

The author of the book of Job acts as a wise man himself. He listens carefully to inherited wisdom, he takes into account what can be learned from experience, and he acknowledges the limitations of a human being's ability to come to complete knowledge of God. Nevertheless, he affirms his faith in the fact that God is powerful, present, and loving. With such a faith one has the courage to ask the hard questions and to live with partial answers. One can assert that suffering is not always a punishment, that it has some other purpose in the order of creation even though one does not know what that purpose is. Even in the face of mystery one can still go on living and loving, just as Job did. Mystery need not entirely deny us our happy ending, but neither should we forget that we do live in mystery. After reading the book of Job the audience is no longer satisfied with the traditional happy ending. Like Job and the author of Job the audience now has both the need and the permission to question.

Review Questions

1. What is the conventional and expected ending of the legend frame? How is the ending in tension with the debate which precedes it?
2. Does the happy ending mean that the author is saying that Job's friends were right after all? How do you know?
3. Were the friends completely wrong? Explain. Was Job completely right? Explain.
4. Why is Job affirmed?
5. For what do the friends need to seek forgiveness?
6. What does the legend standing alone seem to teach? By ending the debate with the legend what is the author teaching?
7. What "better answers" could the author of Job not give? Why?

8. How does the author of the book of Job model a wise man?
9. What could the author of Job assert about suffering?

Discussion Questions

1. Since the author of Job could not give a complete answer to the question he raised, do you think it was all right for him to raise the question in the first place? Explain.
2. Does your family, your school, your religious tradition give you permission to question? Explain. Why is this permission so important?
3. What is the most valuable insight you received from reading Job? Why is this insight valuable to you?

Summation and Transition from Job to Proverbs

As we move from Job to Proverbs we move from one example of wisdom literature to another. The two books do have some similar characteristics.

The questions raised in Job were questions raised by experience. The advice given in Proverbs is advice based on experience.

The path to knowledge in Job was the path of reason. Proverbs, too, addresses the question, "What is the reasonable thing to do?"

The ideas of right and wrong behavior which we saw in Job are the ideas of right and wrong behavior contained in Proverbs: One must be honest. One must treat others kindly and fairly, especially the poor.

However, the agonizing problems raised in Job are not addressed in Proverbs. As you read Proverbs you will notice that some proverbs sound as though they could have been said by Eliphaz. Proverbs does not probe the reasons for the exceptions to the rule. The book does not ask why a just and conscientious person might suffer. Rather, Proverbs gives good advice that holds true most of the time. Usually wise choices lead to prosperity.

For the first time in our study I cannot claim that it is terribly important that you read the proverbs in order as you would a novel. Individual proverbs do stand alone, out of context, in a way that passages from Isaiah and Job do not. Nevertheless, the articles which follow assume that you have read Proverbs in its edited order. So, once more, I urge you to read the proverbs in the order in which they appear, jotting down your questions as you read. While Proverbs does not have a plot, it is still useful to have a sense of the book as a whole.

THE BOOK OF PROVERBS

ARTICLE 1

"Instructions" Attributed to Solomon

Question: "Did Solomon write all these proverbs?" (Prov 1:1)

Despite the fact that the book of Proverbs begins, "The proverbs of Solomon, son of David, king of Israel," Solomon did not write all the proverbs. That sentence is an attribution, not a claim of authorship.

It was not unusual in biblical times to attribute a collection of traditional material which had actually developed over centuries to an esteemed figure of the past. Such an attribution added authority to the collection.

We know that King Solomon had a reputation for wisdom. You may be familiar with the story in 1 Kings 3:3–15 in which the Lord invites Solomon to ask for anything he wishes and Solomon asks for "an understanding mind to govern your people, able to discern good and evil" (1 Kgs 3:9). God answers Solomon's prayer. "God gave Solomon very great wisdom and discernment, and breadth of understanding as vast as the sand on the seashore. . . . He composed three thousand proverbs, and his songs numbered a thousand and five" (1 Kgs 4:29–32). It is no wonder that among the Israelites' ancestors, Solomon is the one to whom the book of Proverbs was attributed.

In fact, the book which begins, "The proverbs of Solomon," is actually a collection of materials which reached the form it now has after the Babylonian exile. As you read the book you will be able to distinguish some of the sections either because the literary form of the writing changes or because a new introduction is included. For instance, chapter 10 begins, "The proverbs of Solomon," chapter

189

OUTLINE OF BOOK OF PROVERBS

Chapters 1–9	The Proverbs of Solomon, Son of David
Chapters 10–22:16	The Proverbs of Solomon
Chapters 22:17–24:22	The Words of the Wise
Chapters 24:23–34	Also the Sayings of the Wise
Chapters 25–29	More Proverbs of Solomon, Copied by the Men of Hezekiah, King of Judah
Chapter 30	The Words of Agur, Son of Jakeh
Chapter 31:1–9	The Words of Lemuel, King of Massa
Chapter 31:10–31	An Acrostic Poem on the Good Wife

22 begins, "Sayings of the wise," chapter 25 begins, "These are other proverbs of Solomon that the officials of King Hezekiah of Judah copied," and chapter 30 begins, "The words of Agur, son of Jakeh."

In addition, as you begin to read the book of Proverbs you are not actually reading proverbs. A proverb is a short, pithy, two-line saying, which expresses a truth learned from experience in a striking way. We will define the form further when we get to chapter 10, "The Proverbs of Solomon."

In the book of Proverbs, "The Proverbs of Solomon" are prefaced by a collection made up of another literary form, an "instruction."

Israel appropriated the "instruction" from the Egyptians who had employed them for centuries to teach scribes. While the word "instruction" referred to the purpose of the writing rather than to its form, instructions had a regular form. The word "instruction," when used to name a literary form, refers to a poem in which a teacher is passing sage advice to his "son" (student). The advice is practical in nature. The student is exhorted to consider the consequences of his actions and to choose the way of the wise. The first

---

AN INSTRUCTION

A poem in which a teacher is passing on sage advice to his "son" (student).

A PROVERB

A short pithy saying which expresses a truth learned from experience in a striking way.

---

section of the book of Proverbs (Prov 1:1–9:18) consists primarily of instructions.

While the setting for Egyptian instructions was clearly a formal school setting, the same is not true for Israel's instructions. Israel's instructions are certainly appropriate for a school setting and an upper class audience, but they are equally appropriate for a family setting and a wider, less privileged audience. The reader of Israelite's wisdom is exhorted:

> Hear, my child, your father's instruction,
>   and do not reject your mother's teaching (Prov 1:8).

Perhaps the familial tone of Israel's instructions is due to the fact that the development of Israel's wisdom literature began in the tribal setting and then moved to the monarchical setting. In fact, scholars try to date the origin of individual units of the book of Proverbs by determining whether the imagery employed presumes a tribal or a monarchical setting.

WAYS TO DATE PROVERBS

- Does the imagery presume a tribal setting or a monarchical setting?
- How well integrated are Israel's religious traditions?

A second dating method is to see how the practical advice of wisdom literature is integrated into the specific religious tradition of the Israelites. While Israel appropriated literature from surrounding cultures, Israel always adapted that literature to its own experience and ways of understanding the unique relationship which Israel understood itself to have with Yahweh.

One way in which the editor of the book of Proverbs integrates wisdom's sayings into Israel's religious tradition is to attribute the collection to Solomon. As we know from Solomon's request to God, Solomon understood that wisdom is ultimately a gift from God.

Review Questions

1. What does the word "attribution" mean?
2. Why were the proverbs attributed to Solomon?
3. At what point did the book of Proverbs reach its present form?
4. How can one distinguish various sections in the collection?
5. What is a proverb?
6. What is an instruction?
7. How does the setting for Israel's instructions differ from the setting for Egyptian instructions?
8. Name two ways in which scholars date individual proverbs.

Discussion Questions

1. In your mind is there any difference between knowledge and wisdom? If so, what is the difference?
2. Do you think of wisdom as a gift from God or as an acquired characteristic? Explain.
3. Do you know anyone you consider wise who is young? If so, why do you consider this person wise?

ARTICLE 2

Israel's Integration of "Secular" Advice

Question: "Why is 'fear of the Lord' said to be 'the beginning of knowledge'? (Prov 1:7) I think God wants us to love God, not fear God."

You may remember when we first met Job that he was described by God as "a blameless and upright man who fears God and turns away from evil" (see Job 1:8). At that time we mentioned that "fear of the Lord" should not be understood as "afraid of" so much as "in awe of."

The phrase "fear of the Lord" occurs often in the book of Proverbs and represents, in a phrase, the way in which the Israelites integrated what might be understood as purely secular advice into their religious tradition.

The advice given in the book of Proverbs is often of such a practical nature that many fail to see why it is in the Bible. Couldn't a person who never even thought about God come to many of the same conclusions? After all, much of the advice is common sense for anyone who wants to stay out of trouble: don't get mixed up with prostitutes, don't use money carelessly, don't run with a bad crowd, don't be rude and obnoxious, don't break your promises, don't be a slob. What is revelatory about any of this?

While it is true that a person who never even thought about God might come to the same conclusions, it is not true that such conclusions have no relationship to one's relationship with God. For the Israelites, who understood themselves to be in a covenant relationship with God, no choice, obviously ethical or not, could be outside of the context of covenant love.

193

Why? Because God, who created all, created an orderly universe. You may remember that we noticed wisdom literature's interest in the order of creation while reading Job. If one observes creation, one perceives order. The wise person will observe creation, reflect on the ramifications of his or her own behavior, and discern that there is an order that undergirds all.

Part of that order is the specific place of human beings in the created order. To recognize one's true limitations as a creature before the creator is to have "fear of the Lord." And for the Israelites:

> The fear of the Lord is the beginning of wisdom
> and the knowledge of the Holy One is insight (Prov 9:10).

Once a person recognizes God as creator and one's own place in creation, this recognition becomes the moral undergirding for all other choices. The way one treats money, time, drink, even other people is all a reflection of one's understanding of the order of things as created by God.

So while wisdom literature does rest on the premise that reason and observation are necessary in order to discover wisdom, it does not teach that only reason and observation are necessary to possess wisdom. Even in relational matters where human beings have choice, one must have "fear of the Lord" and recognize God's presence in the outcome of events.

This limitation to a person's being able to determine his own fate even in relationships is clearly evident in Proverbs. For instance, while the book constantly warns against involving oneself with prostitutes and advises fidelity to one's wife, nevertheless the author asserts:

> House and wealth are inherited from parents,
> but a prudent wife is from the Lord (Prov 19:14).

We see the same acknowledgment that God is finally in charge in the teaching against revenge:

Do not say, "I will repay evil";
wait for the Lord, and he will help you (Prov 20:22).

While human beings may choose the way of the wise or the way of
the fool, the choice of the human being is not the sole determiner of
the eventual outcome:

The human mind may devise many plans,
but it is the purpose of the Lord that will be established (Prov
19:21).

The thorough integration of what might be considered secular
advice within Israel's understanding of God's role in the universe is
embodied in the phrase "fear of the Lord." Only when one is in awe
of God and God's order will one make wise choices in the ethical
and secular areas of one's life.

Review Questions

1. What does "fear of the Lord" mean?
2. In what context did Israel put "practical" advice?
3. What conclusion might one draw from observing creation?
4. What is the moral undergirding for all other choices?
5. Does wisdom literature suggest that reason and observation
   alone will lead to wisdom? Explain.
6. Can a human being secure his or her fate through careful human
   choice? Explain.

Discussion Questions

1. Is there any choice you have which you think has no connection
   at all with your relationship with God? Explain. How do you
   think the editor of Proverbs would answer this question?
   Explain.

2. Do you sense God's presence in nature? Explain. What do you learn about your relationship with God by observing nature?
3. When you think about the order of the created world and our place in that order, what do you believe our place to be? Do you think the human race has had a proper sense of "place" in the created order? Why or why not?

ARTICLE 3

The Prophetic Voice of Wisdom Personified

Question: "Who says, 'How long, O simple ones, will you love being simple?' in Proverbs 1:22? Is it a prophet?" (Prov 1:20–33)

While the speaker in Proverbs 1:20–33 is not a prophet, but rather is wisdom personified, nevertheless the voice has much in common with prophecy.

The speaker's voice is identified as that of wisdom in verse 20.

> Wisdom cries out in the street,
> in the square she raises her voice.
> At the busiest corner she cries out;
> at the entrance of the city gates she speaks (Prov 1:20–21).

Personification is the literary technique of speaking of something which is not a person as though it were a person. We saw the prophet Isaiah use personification when he referred to the nation, Israel, and the city, Jerusalem, as though they were individual people. We saw the nation personified as a male person in the suffering servant songs of Isaiah (see Is 52:13–53:12), and the city personified as a woman in the expression "daughter Zion" (see Is 52:2b).

While personification is common in the prophets, one might still ask why wisdom is personified as a woman. A variety of explanations are offered. One is that the book of Proverbs is written by males, primarily to other males. This is evident in the constant warnings against prostitutes as well as the admonitions to practice fidelity to one's wife. Since wisdom is presented as that which is most desirable in life, a woman is an apt metaphor for wisdom from a male point of view.

197

WISDOM'S SPEECH AND PROPHETIC LITERATURE

- Both use personification.
- Both proclaim the message to the entire population.
- Both call for conversion.
- Both warn of dire consequences if the call is ignored.

Other scholars suggest less psychologically based reasons. The Hebrew word for wisdom is a feminine word, and perhaps this fact alone is enough of an explanation for the personification of wisdom as female. Still other scholars posit a background to wisdom personified which predates monotheism and includes a goddess of wisdom. Perhaps wisdom personified is a "descendant" of such a goddess. Whatever the root, wisdom is personified as a woman both here and in Proverbs 8:1–36.

A second characteristic of prophetic literature which is present in wisdom's speech is the public proclamation of the message to the entire population. Notice that the word which wisdom proclaims is proclaimed in the street where everyone has access to it (see Prov 1:20), as well as at the entrance of the city gates where the upper class carried on business (see Prov 1:21). You may remember that we saw this same social setting in Job and in Isaiah (see Is 58:1). Wisdom is not relegated only to the upper classes in Israel.

Still a third similarity between wisdom's speech and prophetic literature is the call to turn away from sin before dire consequences become inevitable.

How long, O simple ones, will you love being simple?
   How long will scoffers delight in their scoffing
   and fools hate knowledge?
Give heed to my reproof (Prov 1:22–23).

Because the call to conversion, the call to heed the words of wisdom, is ignored, the fool will face destruction.

For waywardness kills the simple,
  and the complacency of fools destroys them.
But those who listen to me will be secure
  and will live at ease without dread of disaster (Prov 1:32–33).

Since we have just finished reading Job it is difficult to read these words of wisdom without realizing that they are not always true. The author of the book of Job confronted us with this fact with great power and clarity. But the author of Job had a different purpose than did the editor of Proverbs. While the author of Job questioned the idea of an order which assures retributive justice, the editor of Proverbs does not. In Proverbs we read the lessons drawn from experience which usually hold one in good stead. The book contains good and persuasive advice, not law. The way of wisdom is much more likely to lead to a life of comfort and happiness than is the way of folly. Wisdom should be the object of "man's" desire, and, as such, wisdom is personified as a woman.

Review Questions

1. What is "personification"?
2. Give three possible reasons why wisdom is personified as a woman.
3. Name three similarities between wisdom's speech and prophetic literature.
4. What difference in purpose is there between the author of the book of Job and the editor of the book of Proverbs?

Discussion Questions

1. If you were personifying wisdom, would you personify it as a man or as a woman? Why?
2. Do you think wisdom is available to all in our society? Is it more available to one class than another? Explain.
3. Is practical advice which is usually true but not always true worth giving? Why or why not? If it is not always true, do you think it should be in the Bible? Why or why not?

ARTICLE 4

A Choice That Leads to Death

Question: "Why are there so many warnings against adultery?"
(Prov 5:1–14; 6:20–35; 7:5–27)

Three separate levels of meaning can be understood in the repeated warnings against adultery.

First and most obvious is that adultery could literally lead directly to one's death. We read about the dire consequences of adultery in the book of Deuteronomy: "If there is a young woman, a virgin already engaged to be married, and a man meets her in the town and lies with her, you shall bring both of them to the gate of that town and stone them to death . . . the man because he violated his neighbor's wife" (Deut 22:23–24). So the consequences explained to the adulterer—you will lose your reputation, your wealth, and even your life—are no exaggeration.

In marked contrast to the horrifying death of the adulterer is the wonderful life of one who remains faithful to his wife. A faithful marriage is described as drinking "flowing water from your own well" (see Prov 5:16), as a life full of intoxicating joy.

> May her breasts satisfy you at all times;
>> may you be intoxicated always by her love (Prov 5:19).

As one continues to read Proverbs, as wisdom is personified as a woman, and as the fool's way is more and more identified with the adulterer, one begins to see the invitation of the faithful wife as a metaphor for the invitation of wisdom herself. What is true of the faithful wife is also true of wisdom. She offers the same security which wisdom offers. Those who choose her will walk on their way

200

LEVELS OF MEANING IN THE WARNINGS AGAINST ADULTERY

Literal level:
- The act of adultery can result in the death penalty.

Metaphorical level:
- Adultery symbolizes the way of folly. To choose the way of folly leads to unhappiness.
- Adultery symbolizes idolatry. To choose idolatry is to choose spiritual death.

---

securely, they will sit down and not be afraid, and they will lie down to sweet sleep (see Prov 3:23–25).

So, on the metaphorical level, a warning against adultery is a warning against choosing the seductions of evil over the way of Lady Wisdom.

A third level of meaning in the repeated warnings against adultery might be a warning against idolatry. In Canaanite religious practice, sexual relations with priestesses was not unusual. Israelites were, of course, forbidden to involve themselves in religious practices which honored other gods. To sleep with a cult prostitute would have involved a double infidelity, to both wife and God.

Scholars suggest that the woman who entices the young man to adultery in Proverbs 7 is a priestess because she says:

> I had to offer sacrifices,
>   and today I have paid my vows;
> So now I have come out to meet you,
>   to seek you eagerly, and I have found you (Prov 7:14–15).

Scholars suggest that the woman is equating the sexual encounter with her religious duty. She seems to be a cult prostitute who is soliciting business. To choose to involve oneself with her would surely be to choose death, both physically and spiritually.

Her house is made up of ways to the nether world,
   leading down into the chambers of death (Prov 7:27).

Perhaps this same idea of the death offered by cult prostitutes is present in the invitation by personified Folly to her banquet (see Prov 9:13–18). Like wisdom, Folly has built her house in the "high places of the town," perhaps a reference to Canaanite worship. She urges the simple to come in and drink her "stolen water" (see Prov 9:17), an image in sharp contrast to drinking the "flowing water from your own well" which described marital fidelity (see Prov 5:15). Those who respond to folly's invitation meet death.

   ... her guests are in the depth of Sheol (Prov 9:18b).

As you continue to read Proverbs you will continue to read warnings against adultery (see Prov 22:14; 23:27–28). The warnings are repeated over and over because they warn against behavior that has such a serious consequence that it can never be undone. To choose adultery is to turn away from wife, wisdom and God. To choose adultery is to choose death.

Review Questions

1. Literally, why was adultery a life-threatening choice?
2. What metaphor can be seen in the invitation of the faithful wife? Explain why this metaphor is implied.
3. What second level of meaning can be found in the warnings against adultery?
4. What third level of meaning is present in these warnings? What evidence in the text suggests this interpretation?
5. What in the invitation of personified Folly suggests Canaanite cult worship?
6. What three choices are made when one chooses adultery?

Discussion Questions

1. On the literal level, why is adultery such a destructive choice for individuals and for society?
2. Why do you think adultery is so often a metaphor for idolatry?
3. Can you think of a better metaphor for idolatry? Explain.

ARTICLE 5

Wisdom: God's First Creation

Question: "Aren't Wisdom's claims in chapter 8 terribly grandiose? Wisdom seems to present herself almost as another god." (Prov 8)

Wisdom does claim a great deal for herself in chapter 8, but she does not claim to be another god. Rather, she claims that she was first to be created and that she accompanied and helped God in all that was created after her.

> The Lord created me at the beginning of his work,
> the first of his acts of long ago (Prov 8:22).
> When he marked out the foundations of the earth
> then I was beside him like a master worker;
> And I was daily his delight,
> rejoicing before him always (Prov 8:29b–30).

Once again we see the idea that wisdom can be discerned in the order of creation. If one carefully observes all that God has created, one can learn something about the God who did the creating. Such observation leads one to believe that God loved order and used order when God made everything else, when God put the parts of creation in right relationship with each other.

> When he established the heavens, I was there,
> when he drew a circle on the face of the deep,
> When he made firm the skies above,
> when he established the fountains of the deep (Prov 8:27–28).

Just as God used wisdom to establish the order of nature, so God uses wisdom to establish the order of nations.

WISDOM REVEALS GOD'S ORDER

- In creation
- In the relations among nations
- In personal relationships

The fruits of living in right relationship with Wisdom are:

- A relationship of love with Wisdom herself
- Enduring wealth and prosperity

> By me kings reign,
>   and rulers decree what is just;
> By me rulers rule,
>   and nobles, all who govern rightly (Prov 8:15–16).

Wisdom calls to all to heed her words so this right order in relationships will be established. Notice that, as in chapter 1, Wisdom personified speaks both in the streets (Prov 8:2) and at the city gates (Prov 8:3) so that her message is accessible to all, not just to a privileged few. All the words from Wisdom's mouth are "righteous" (see Prov 8:8), in sharp contrast to the words in the mouth of the adulteress. They are "straight" and "right" (see Prov 8:9). To listen to wisdom is to establish right order in one's personal life.

Wisdom promises a great reward to those who heed her voice, a personal relationship of love.

> I love those who love me,
>   and those who seek me diligently find me. . . .
> I walk in the way of righteousness,
>   along the paths of justice (Prov 8:17–20)

This passage reminds us of the "right relationship" of covenant love to which the prophets constantly called the people. When the people were faithful to covenant love they were full of justice and righteousness, but when they were not they acted the whore (see Is 1:21).

In addition to a relationship of love, wisdom promises "enduring wealth and prosperity" (see Prov 8:18, 20). This seems an ironic promise since wisdom has just claimed that she is much preferable to riches (see Prov 8:11, 19). We will see something of an inconsistent attitude toward wealth throughout Proverbs, a topic which we will discuss in a later article.

Wisdom offers her "good advice" and "sound wisdom" (see Prov 8:14) to all so that people may attain "knowledge," "discretion," and "fear of the Lord." If all would heed her word, then people would find that happiness which their creator intended them to have.

> Happy is the one who listens to me,
>   watching daily at my gates,
>   waiting beside my doors.
> For whoever finds me finds life
>   and obtains favor from the Lord (Prov 8:34–35).

By personifying wisdom the author is not claiming that wisdom is herself a god. Rather, wisdom represents a characteristic of God which every person has the opportunity to observe in nature and learn from experience. God intended right order in creation, among nations and in relationships. To discern this order and to choose to live within it is to find wisdom.

Review Questions

1. What two things does wisdom claim?
2. What conclusions would one who observes creation draw?
3. What order, in addition to the order of nature, does God establish?
4. To whom is wisdom's message available? Why?
5. What two rewards does wisdom promise to those who heed her voice?
6. What would a person who found wisdom choose to do?

Discussion Questions

1. Do you think there is a "right order" in creation, in national relationships and in personal relationships which can be discovered and followed? Why or why not?
2. When you look at life in the United States, do you see order or disorder? Explain.
3. Do you regard "happiness" as a goal? An attainable goal? Why or why not?

ARTICLE 6

The Figures of Speech Used in Proverbs

Question: "Are we reading a completely different source when we start chapter 10? These seem to be all two-liners with no particular relationship to each other."

Chapters 10:1–22:16 constitute the longest section of the book of Proverbs. It consists of three hundred and seventy-five proverbs which, if they are arranged in a particular order, is an order which scholars have not yet been able to discover.

As we mentioned in Article 1, the transition from the first section of Proverbs to the second is noticeable not only because of its introduction, "The Proverbs of Solomon" (see Prov 10:1), but because we change literary forms. We move from the "instruction" to the "proverb."

In Article 1 we defined a proverb as "a short, pithy, two-line saying which expresses a truth learned from experience in a striking way." Proverbs are "striking" primarily because of their use of "parallelism" and various other "figures of speech."

We defined parallelism when we were reading Isaiah. Parallelism is the structural technique employed in Hebrew poetry in which a unit of thought is the predominant characteristic of a poetic line rather than the number of syllables or the placement of accent as is often true in our poetry.

In Proverbs you will read three basic kinds of parallelism. The first, which we discussed when reading Isaiah, is synonymous parallelism, so named because the second poetic line repeats the thought in the first poetic line. An example of synonymous parallelism appears in Proverbs 14:19:

PARALLELISM

Synonymous Parallelism:	The second poetic line repeats the thought of the first poetic line.
Antithetic Parallelism:	The second poetic line contrasts to the first, expressing the opposite thought.
Synthetic Parallelism:	The second poetic line expands on the thought of the first line.

> The evil bow down before the good,
>> the wicked at the gates of the righteous (Prov 14:19).

A second kind of parallelism predominant in this section of Proverbs is antithetic parallelism. In antithetic parallelism the second line of the proverb is in contrast to the first, expressing the opposite thought. The word "but" often introduces the contrasting thought.

> A wise child makes a glad father,
>> but a foolish child is a mother's grief (Prov 10:1).

The third kind of parallelism is synthetic parallelism. In synthetic parallelism the second line neither repeats nor contrasts with the first line. Rather, it expands upon it.

FIGURES OF SPEECH

Metonymy: The real meaning is expressed through a word closely associated with that meaning

Synecdoche: A part of the whole is used to refer to the whole.

Scoffers do not like to be rebuked;
   they will not go to the wise (Prov 14:12).

While these three kinds of parallelism do not describe the form of every proverb they do describe the form of most. The striking quality of proverbs is often due to these various arrangements of the units of thought.

In addition to using parallelism, proverbs employ other "figures of speech." When we depart from the normal meaning or construction of language in order to achieve an effect, we call such a departure a "figure of speech." The kinds of parallelism which we have just described are a departure from the normal construction of language and are one kind of figure of speech. So is the personification which we saw in Wisdom's two speeches earlier in Proverbs. Other figures of speech used regularly in Proverbs are metonymy and synecdoche.

Metonymy is a figure of speech in which the real meaning is expressed through a word closely associated with that meaning. We use metonymy when we say, "The white house said," but mean, "The president said." An example is:

The fruit of the righteous is a tree of life (Prov 12:30).

"The fruit" of the righteous means "the result" of virtuous living.

Closely associated to metonymy is synecdoche. In each the meaning is expressed through another word, but in synecdoche a part of a whole is used to refer to the whole, or the whole is used to refer to only a part. All through Proverbs you will hear a person referred to by a part rather than a whole, by "lips," or "mouth," of "tongue," as, for example:

The lips of the righteous feed many (Prov 10:21).

The literary technique most prevalent in Proverbs is the use of alliteration. In alliteration an initial consonant is repeated, such as "the poverty of the poor" (see Prov 10:15b), "reject a rebuke" (see Prov 10:17b), or "lying lips" (see Prov 10:18). "Lying lips" employs both alliteration and synecdoche and is certainly a more striking phrase than "a person who lies."

You may find analyzing such figures of speech annoying at first. Many students do. However, understanding these figures of speech should aid you in understanding the literary form "proverb," and in understanding the ways in which proverbs convey meaning so strikingly. After all:

> A scoffer seeks wisdom in vain,
>> but knowledge is easy for one who understands (Prov 10:6).

Review Questions

1. What is the order behind the arrangement of Proverbs in chapters 10–22?
2. What characteristics of Proverbs makes them "striking"?
3. What is parallelism?
4. Name and define three kinds of parallelism.
5. What is a "figure of speech"?
6. What is metonymy?
7. What is synecdoche?
8. What literary technique is most prevalent in Proverbs? Define it.

Discussion Questions

1. Do you see any value in being able to name the figures of speech you find in poetry? Why or why not?
2. Which saying do you prefer: "A stitch in time saves nine" or "A stitch in time saves eight"? Why?
3. Have you ever tried to write proverbs? In what way would understanding figures of speech help you write?

ARTICLE 7

Wealth: A Blessing or a Temptation?

Question: "Did the people's attitude toward wealth change? Sometimes it seems to be thought of as God's reward for doing good, but at other times it's presented as a temptation."

Israel's attitude toward wealth became more nuanced over the years. The root insight behind the change seems to have been the growing realization that God made and loves the poor.

> The rich and the poor have this in common:
> the Lord is the maker of them all (Prov 22:2).

Because the poor belong to God, those who can help them should. To help is a way to please God.

> Whoever is kind to the poor lends to the Lord,
> and will be repaid in full (Prov 19:17).

We know from our study of Isaiah that the prophets called the people to treat the poor well (see Is 1:16–17). In Job too we saw that Job prided himself on having been generous to the poor (see Job 21:16–23). In fact, generosity to the poor is a demand of covenant love. If one ignores the needs of the poor, one fails in one's own relationship with God.

The idea that wealth is a sign of God's blessing is not compatible with the idea that God loves the poor and wants them to receive help. So with the realization of God's love for the poor came a growing awareness that lack of wealth is not always a sign of the

---

CONFLICTING BELIEFS

- Wealth is a sign of God's love.
- God loves the poor and wants those with wealth to share with the poor.

---

lack of God's blessing. The author of Job made this clear when he pictured the innocent Job losing all his possessions. What, then, should be one's attitude toward wealth?

Proverbs teaches that wealth should not be a goal in itself, achieved at the sacrifice of that right order in relationships with God and others which is wisdom's goal. "Fear of the Lord" is far more valuable than wealth.

> Better is a little with fear of the Lord
>   than a great fortune with anxiety (Prov 15:16, NAB)

Also more important than wealth is one's integrity.

> Better the poor walking in integrity
>   than one perverse of speech who is a fool (Prov 19:1).

It would be more important to remain loyal and honest in one's relationships with others than to sacrifice these for wealth.

> What is desirable in a person is loyalty,
>   and it is better to be poor than a liar (Prov 19:22).

You will notice that some of the proverbs in this collection are repeated in later collections, proverbs on wealth among them. Chapter 28 both repeats and adds to the collection of proverbs on wealth. Wealth is seen not only as a gift from God but as the result of hard work.

> Anyone who tills the land will have plenty of bread,
> but one who follows worthless pursuits will have plenty of
> poverty (Prov 28:19).

If a person pursues wealth with dishonest means he will be punished by losing his wealth.

> One who augments wealth by exhorbitant interest
> gathers it for another who is kind to the poor (Prov 28:8).

But if a person uses wealth to help the poor that person will remain wealthy.

> Whoever gives to the poor will lack for nothing,
> but one who turns a blind eye will get many a curse (Prov 28:27).

As we see, even as Proverbs reflects an understanding that the poor are not necessarily in God's disfavor, nevertheless reward through material blessings is constantly presented as the result of doing what is right.

The people's attitude toward wealth did change in the sense that it became nuanced. Wealth is still considered a blessing but it should not be pursued at all costs. Poverty may not be a sign of God's disfavor but it certainly is not to be desired. The pursuit of wealth may be a temptation, but wealth itself is a blessing, the gift of a loving God to a person who works hard and lives with integrity.

Review Questions

1. What root insight nuanced Israel's attitude toward wealth?
2. What conclusion about human behavior follows from the realization that God loves the poor?
3. What is incompatible about realizing that God loves the poor and at the same time claiming that wealth is a sign of God's blessing?
4. What attitude toward wealth is taught in Proverbs?

5. What should one do with one's wealth?
6. Did the Israelites stop considering wealth a blessing? Explain.

Discussion Questions

1. Do you regard wealth as a blessing or a temptation? Explain.
2. What do you think God expects of a wealthy person?
3. Do you think some people have a vocation to be wealthy? Why or why not?
4. Can you see any good reason for choosing to be poor? Why or why not?

ARTICLE 8

Proverbs: Practical Advice, Not Law

Question: "Was offering a bribe considered a legitimate thing to do in Israel? Several proverbs seem to condone it." (Prov 17:8–9; 18:16; 21:14)

The reader is correct in noting that several proverbs seem to give the impression that offering bribes was a legitimate way to operate. However, Israel did not approve of accepting bribes. Rather than approval, these proverbs reflect pragmatism. We will see this pragmatic attitude in Proverbs in several additional areas, such as offering surety on a loan and using the rod to reinforce a lesson.

First, the question of bribes. The fact of the matter is that bribes sometimes work. This fact is reflected in proverbs such as:

> A bribe is like a magic stone in the eyes of those who give it;
> wherever they turn they prosper (Prov 17:8).

> A gift opens doors;
> it give access to the great (Prov 18:16).

Even though these proverbs acknowledge that bribes often work, there is still nowhere in Proverbs any suggestion that one should accept a bribe. In fact, the opposite is true.

> The wicked accept a concealed bribe
> to pervert the ways of justice (Prov 17:23).

The book of Proverbs also reflects practicality in the attitude expressed toward offering surety on a loan, that is, promising to pay another person's loan should that person be unable to do it. We saw

---

AREAS OF PRAGMATISM IN PROVERBS

- *Bribes:* Bribes do work but still you shouldn't accept one

- *Surety on loans:* It is not wise to offer surety on a loan. You might get left holding the bag.

- *Discipline:* Children need discipline. It might help a child to "beat some sense" into him.

---

an instruction against this in Proverbs 6:1–5. Additional proverbs which contain this warning are sprinkled throughout the book (see Prov 11:15; 17:18; 20:16; 22:26). Why is there constant warning against such behavior? Not because it is immoral but because it is chancy. Experience proves that people who need to borrow money are often unable to repay it. To back up such a borrower is to put oneself in financial jeopardy, and this is not a wise thing to do.

Still a third area in which Proverbs reflects practicality more than any other concern is in the area of the use of the "rod" to discipline children. In chapter 13 we read:

> Those who spare the rod hate their children
> but those who love them are diligent to discipline them (Prov 13:24).

In other sections of Proverbs this idea is repeated:

> Do not withhold discipline from your children;
>   if you beat them with a rod, they will not die.
> If you beat them with the rod
>   you will save their lives from Sheol (Prov 23:13–14).

Unfortunately these passages are used by some to support what our society has come to regard as abusive treatment of children. The society from which these proverbs came obviously did not consider physical punishment abusive. There is no suggestion that the rod should be used in anger. The motive behind the beating is to "beat some sense" into the child, to help the child, not to hurt the child.

The question which our society asks, given our knowledge of psychology, knowledge which the original audience did not have, is: "Is this advice still good advice in the sense that it is practical?" Does it work? Is the rod the most effective means to discipline a child for the child's own good? Our society would say no. But that judgment is based on knowledge which the Israelites simply did not have.

When one makes observations about the practical way to handle a given situation, one is doing only that. The purpose is not to claim divine revelation, not to lay down a law which can never be broken. Rather it is simply to say, "This is what works most often." Because the practical thing to do doesn't always work, and a given incident might call for a different response, the proverbs sometimes give opposite advice on the same subject. In one obvious example the two proverbs appear next to each other.

> Do not answer fools according to their folly,
>   or you will be a fool yourself.
> Answer fools according to their folly,
>   or they will be wise in their own eyes (Prov 26:4–5).

Obviously when one is dealing with a fool, there is no one way to respond which will always be best. Sometimes one response proves to be the wisest; sometimes the opposite response proves to be the wisest. In some instances, whatever works is wise.

The fact that Proverbs offers practical advice, not law, says something about the tone and purpose of the book. The book of Proverbs was meant to educate, to help people learn how to think, to help them make decisions about present behavior in the light of tradition, in the light of what was known from experience. But the wise person would take into account not only the inherited tradition but the specific circumstances of the present situation before deciding on the wise course of action. The wise person is flexible and reflective. The wise person notices what works.

Review Questions

1. Did Israel oppose offering bribes? Explain. What does Proverbs acknowledge about bribes?
2. Why does Proverbs warn against taking surety on a loan?
3. For what motive did Proverbs teach that one might use the "rod"?
4. What question would our society ask regarding the use of the rod? Why would we ask this question and the Israelites did not?
5. What is the difference between practical advice and law?
6. Why does Proverbs sometimes give opposite advice?
7. What was the purpose of the Book of Proverbs?
8. What, in addition to inherited tradition, would a wise person consider?

Discussion Questions

1. Do you think it is all right to use a wrong means to achieve a good end? Why or why not?
2. Do you think Proverbs should be used to support the use of physical punishment as a means of discipline? Why or why not?
3. Do you think practical advice has any place in the Bible? Explain.

ARTICLE 9

Two Ways: Compared and Contrasted

Question: "The book of Proverbs seems to be always comparing and contrasting. Why is this?" (Prov 11:13; 12:16; 15:18; 15:32; 16:23; 16:27; 18:6; 18:21)

It is true that the book of Proverbs relys heavily on comparing—drawing analogies—and contrasting—putting things in antithetical relationships. The reason lies in the structure of the proverb itself, in the purpose of the book, and in its theme.

We have already discussed the structure of individual proverbs, the fact that ideas are put in synonymous or antithetical relationship to each other. The similarities and differences between thoughts are expressed partially by their placement, their juxtaposition to each other. This is a poetic device and a very effective one.

Such a form, in which people are constantly led to see similarities and differences, is most appropriate if one's desire is to teach another how to think as well as how to retain what has been learned. The ability to observe the world around us, to draw analogies, to see similarities and differences, and to draw conclusions based on what has been learned and observed is crucial to education in any time or place. The proverb form promotes one's ability to retain information and to think, to apply the information to new settings.

Most importantly, however, is the theme of the book of Proverbs: there is a wise way which the wise person will choose. Since the book is urging people to choose the way of wisdom, the opposite way, the way of the foolish, is also clearly described. This basic division between the way of the wise and the way of the foolish is further broken down into specific areas of wise and foolish behavior. We have already seen examples of this in the way of the faithful

219

THE VALUE OF COMPARING AND CONTRASTING

- Helps sharpen the mind.
- Helps retention.
- Helps one discern the way of the wise from the way of the fool.

  - Cool vs. hot tempers.
  - Careful vs. careless speech.

---

husband vs. the way of the adulterer, the invitation to the banquet of wisdom vs. the invitation to the banquet of folly. As we continue to read Proverbs we see the contrast between the way of the cool-tempered and the way of the hot-tempered as well as the contrast between the way of those who use speech for good and the way of those who use speech for harm.

The wise person does not fly off the handle. Sprinkled throughout the collections of proverbs are admonitions not to lose one's temper.

> Fools show their anger at once,
>   but the prudent ignore an insult (Prov 12:16).

> Those who are hot-tempered stir up strife,
>   but those who are slow to anger, calm contention (Prov 15:18).

The reason that expressed rage is the act of a fool is because of its effect. Hot tempers destroy right relationships; they destroy order. The way of wisdom always leads to establishing order, not destroying it.

A second subdivision of the way of the wise and the way of the foolish has to do with the way a person uses speech. Speech can be used for good or for ill.

When used as it should be used, speech is used for another's good, to comfort and to teach.

Pleasant words are like a honeycomb,
    sweetness to the soul and health to the body (Prov 16:24).

The mind of the wise makes their speech judicious,
    and adds persuasiveness to their lips (Prov 16:23).

A wise person benefits from hearing the truth.

Those who ignore instruction despise themselves,
    but those who heed admonition gain understanding (Prov 15:32).

However, speech can also be misused, to harm others rather than to help them.

A fool's lips bring strife
    and a fool's mouth invites a flogging (Prov 18:6).

A gossip goes about telling secrets,
    but one who is trustworthy in spirit keeps a confidence (Prov 11:13).

Scoundrels concoct evil,
    and their speech is like a scorching fire (Prov 16:27).

The fruit of the abuse of speech is strife, ruined reputations, loss of one's personal integrity, and the evil disruption of right relationships.

Death and life are in the power of the tongue,
    and those who live it will eat its fruits (Prov 18:21).

The wise person understands the power of speech and always uses it to promote, not destroy, right relationships.

The belief that a right way does exist and can be discovered and chosen is core to wisdom literature. This belief rests on the Israelites' concept of God. God is love and has established an order which reflects God's loving purpose. The wise human being will discover this order and choose to live within it.

However, the way of the foolish also exists. One way to learn to distinguish between the way of the wise and the way of the foolish is to compare and contrast them. For this reason, the book of Proverbs is always doing just that.

Review Questions

1. What is the difference between "comparing" and "contrasting"?
2. What is a synonymous relationship? An antithetical relationship?
3. What two advantages does the structure of a proverb have if one's desire is to teach?
4. What is the theme of the book of Proverbs?
5. Name three sub-divisions of the way of the wise vs. the way of the foolish.
6. Why is expressing rage often the act of a fool?
7. How can speech be used by the wise? By the foolish?
8. What idea is core to a belief that wise and foolish ways exist?

Discussion Questions

1. Do you have a good memory? What helps you retain something? What sorts of things do you have difficulty remembering? Do you know why?
2. Do you believe that there is a right and a wrong way that can be discovered and followed? Explain.
3. Do you think anger is ever effectively expressed? Why or why not?
4. Do you agree that the tongue has immense power for good or evil? Explain.

ARTICLE 10

Proverbs' Attitude Toward Kings

Question: "Doesn't Proverbs treat the king almost like a god when it says that no judgment he pronounces is false? (Prov 16:10) Or are they just recognizing the king's authority, acknowledging that what he says goes?" (Prov 16:12; 16:9; 16:15; 17:17; 18:5; 19:5; 19:12; 20:1; 20:28)

The person who asked this question has read Proverbs 16:10 as it appears in the New American Bible translation.

> The king's lips are an oracle;
> no judgment he pronounces is false (Prov 16:10; NAB).

The same proverb in the New Revised Standard Version is:

> Inspired decisions are on the lips of a king;
> his mouth does not sin in judgment (Prov 16:10).

This second translation reflects more accurately the attitude toward the king expressed in Proverbs. While an ideal king is described, one who is inspired and so does God's will, Proverbs certainly never suggests that the king or others in positions of authority are above God's order. Kings and judges too must obey God.

In Proverbs a king's authority rests on God's authority, on the king's acting within the right order which God has established. Because the king's authority rests on his respecting God's order, it is an "abomination" for a king to do otherwise.

PROVERBS' ATTITUDE TOWARD KINGS

- An ideal king seeks to do God's will.
- A king's authority rests on God's authority. The king too must live within God's order.
- Kings have power. The wise person stays in the king's good graces.

> It is an abomination to kings to do evil
>> for the throne is established by righteousness (Prov 16:12).

> Loyalty and faithfulness preserve the king,
>> and his throne is upheld by righteousness (Prov 20:28).

A king's throne is secure only if the king obeys God. To do otherwise is to undermine the king's authority, for the throne is upheld by "righteousness."

While Proverbs maintains that kings too must obey God, it also acknowledges a king's power and the fact that one does well to stay in the king's good graces.

> In the light of a king's face there is life,
>> and his favor is like the clouds that bring the spring rain (Prov 16:15).

> A king's anger is like the growling of a lion,
>> but his favor is like dew on the grass (Prov 19:12; see also Prov 20:2).

Proverbs, always practical, acknowledges that one must stay in the king's good graces to prosper.

However one should not desire to please a king so much that one would give false witness. The same right moral order applies to all. Kings as well as subjects must tell the truth.

False speech is not becoming to a fool,
    still less is false speech to a ruler (Prov 17:7).

A false witness will not go unpunished,
    and a liar will not escape (Prov 19:5; see also 19:9,19:28; 21:28).

Just as witnesses, whether a king or not, must be truthful, so must judges. To have the power of a judge and to use it dishonestly is to act outside of God's order.

One who justifies the wicked and one who condemns the righteous
    are both alike an abomination to the Lord (Prov 17:15).

It is not right to be partial to the guilty
    or to subvert the innocent in judgment (Prov 18:5).

In fact, when all is said and done, the king is in exactly the same relationship to God and God's order as is everyone else. God establishes order, and all human endeavors, whether a king's, a noble's, a rich person's, or a poor person's, must conform to that order. It is God's will which prevails.

The human mind plans the way,
    but the Lord directs the steps (Prov 16:9).

So too with kings:

The king's heart is a stream of water in the hand of the Lord;
    he turns it wherever he will (Prov 21:1).

Proverb's attitude toward kings shows clearly what scripture scholars call the "Yahwehization" of Proverbs. Concrete advice about currying favor with the king because of the king's authority could have been written in any culture. Israel's earliest proverbs on the subject of kings may well date to around the time of Solomon and may differ little from the proverbs of other nations who also had kings. However in Israel's tradition such practical advice becomes integrated into the Israelite's understanding of Yahweh. It is

Yahweh and not the king who is the final judge, the final establisher of order. Only if the king too acknowledges Yahweh's place in the order of things will the king be considered wise.

Review Questions

1. What attitude does Proverbs express toward kings?
2. What practical attitude toward kings is expressed in Proverbs?
3. Is a king's or a judge's relationship to law any different from anyone else's? Explain.
4. What does the "Yahwehization" of Proverbs mean?
5. Under what conditions would a king be considered wise?

Discussion Questions

1. Do you think that anyone, such as the president or the CIA, should be above the law? Why or why not?
2. Do you think it is ever right to disobey a law? Explain.
3. What is the difference between civil law and moral law? Are they the same? Do they overlap? Do you feel more bound by one than another? Explain.

ARTICLE 11

Israel's Wisdom: Appropriated Yet Unique

Question: "Is this King Hezekiah in Proverbs 25:1 the same Hezekiah we read about in Isaiah? Are Amen-em-ope (Prov 22:19), Agur (Prov 30:1), and Lemuel (Prov 31:1) also kings of Israel?" (Prov 22:17–30:9)

The Hezekiah referred to in Proverbs 25:1 is the same Hezekiah we read about in Isaiah, the Hezekiah who was Ahaz's son and who trusted Yahweh (715–688 B.C.). However, the others are not kings of Israel.

The word Amen-em-ope is a name in the title of an Egyptian instruction, *The Teaching of Amen-em-ope,* upon which this collection of "the sayings of the wise" is based. Agur and Lemuel are unknown. Whether they are historical or fictional, they are not Israelites. Some translations say they are from Massa (see NAB), a location east of Edom. (Translations differ because "massa" can also mean "oracle.")

As was mentioned in an earlier article, the attribution of proverbs to a particular person reveals a "seam" in the book of Proverbs. It marks the place where two separate collections have been combined. We will now look at three of these collections as individual units.

The first collection, Proverbs 22:17–24:22 is clearly based on the Egyptian work, *The Teaching of Amen-em-ope.* The New American Bible translation has made this connection explicit by translating a corrupt text:

DIVISIONS AND SOURCES

Proverbs 22:17–24:22: "The Words of the Wise." Based on the Egyptian, *The Teaching of Amen-em-ope.*

Proverbs 23:12–24:22: Based also on *The Words of Ahiquar.*

Proverbs 25:1–29:27: "More Proverbs of Solomon, Copied by the Men of Hezekiah, King of Judah." Based on an Egyptian instruction for the king and his subjects.

> I make known to you the words of Amen-em-ope.
> Have I not written for you the "thirty,"
>   with counsels and knowledge (Prov 22:19–20; NAB).

The same passage in the Revised Standard Version reads:

> I have made them known to you today—yes, to you.
> Have I not written for you thirty sayings (Prov 22:19–20)?

The Teaching of Amen-em-ope used the instruction form with which we are familiar from Proverbs 1–9. It was divided into thirty chapters, presumably the basis for the reference to "thirty" sayings in Proverbs 22:20. The purpose of *The Teaching of Amen-em-ope* was to teach an upper class how to conduct itself successfully. As is always true when Israel appropriates the literature of other cultures, the Israelites broadened the purpose by integrating it into their concept of their relationship with Yahweh. The purpose of the collection, once it had been incorporated into Israel's wisdom literature, was "so that you may trust in the Lord" (Prov 22:19).

Within this context are ideas which are also present in *The Teaching of Amen-em-ope* and with which we are familiar from earlier proverbs: You must not mistreat the poor. Don't involve yourself with a person who can't control his temper. Act with proper respect when you are in the king's presence. Don't let wealth become a goal in itself.

In Proverbs 23:12 what appears to be another introductory verse is inserted.

> Apply your mind to instruction
> and your ear to words of knowledge (Prov 23:12).

Scholars suggest that this introduction is present because a new source, *The Words of Ahiquar,* is at the base of much of what follows. This popular mixture of narrative and proverbs may well date to the seventh century B.C. and was appropriated not only by Israel but by many other nations as well. Again, the source is integrated into the Israelites' religious tradition. While Ahiquar warns his son to fear the king, Proverbs 24:21 warns:

> My child, fear the Lord and the king (Prov 24:21).

The section of Proverbs which is said to have been passed on by "officials of King Hezekiah" (Prov 25:1–29:27) has much in common with what has preceded it. It begins with what scholars believe to be an instruction for the king and his subjects based on an Egyptian model (see Prov 25:1–28). It then proceeds on to topics with which we are already familiar: the foolish person (Prov 26:1–12), the lazy person (Prov 26:13–16), and the person who uses speech for evil (Prov 26:17–28). As the collection continues the proverbs are no longer grouped around a theme. Still the themes themselves are familiar to us.

The words attributed to Agur (Prov 30:1–9) remind us of passages we read in Job (see Job 26:8; 38:4) in which God's great transcendence is emphasized.

> Who has ascended to heaven and come down?
> Who has gathered the wind in the hollow of the hand?
> Who has wrapped up the waters in a garment?
> Who has established all the ends of the earth (Prov 30:4)?

Wisdom reminds us that, no matter how wise we become, we are still human beings and God is still God. No one can completely master wisdom because wisdom is with God, and complete knowledge of God is simply beyond us.

Nevertheless, Israel, among all the nations, had come to know God in a unique way. It is the integration of the common wisdom of nations into Israel's unique knowledge of Yahweh that makes Israel's wisdom revelation. When we read the wisdom of Israel we are never reading merely secular advice. Rather we are coming to understand how all of life, all right order in one's personal, social, political, and business life, is part and parcel of one's spiritual life. This is true because, as only Israel understood, all order finally rests in Yahweh.

Review Questions

1. To what does the word "Amen-em-ope" refer?
2. What clue about the history of the text is given by the various attributions to particular people?
3. What was the purpose of the Egyptian instruction? How was this purpose changed when Israel appropriated the instruction?
4. What is *The Words of Ahiquar*?
5. In what way do the words attributed to Agur remind us of the book of Job?
6. Why is all this appropriated literature considered revelation?

Discussion Questions

1. If you were going to appropriate some secular story or song to teach a religious insight, which one would you pick? Why?
2. Do you find it at all disillusioning to realize that the sources of Proverbs were literature from other cultures? Why or why not?
3. Has your idea of inspiration changed as you have read Proverbs? Explain.

ARTICLE 12

Numerical Proverbs and Wisdom Literature

Question: "What do these numerical proverbs in Proverbs 30:15–33 have to do with wisdom?"

The numerical proverbs exercise the mind, as do riddles. As we know, one purpose of the Book of Proverbs is to help:

> . . . the discerning acquire skill,
> to understand a proverb and a figure,
> the words of the wise and their riddles (Prov 1:5b–6).

Like riddles, the numerical proverbs help people see what very disparate things have in common.

The numerical proverbs begin with a similar introductory phrase such as:

> Three things are never satisfied,
> four never say, "Enough!" (Prov 30:15b).

> Three things are too wonderful for me,
> four I do not understand (Prov 30:18).

> Under three things the earth trembles,
> under four it cannot bear up (Prov 30:21).

The introductory lines challenge the reader to see that the disparate things which are then named do have something in common, the quality mentioned in the introductory lines.

231

NUMERICAL POEMS AND WISDOM LITERATURE

- Both force us to think, often through analogies.
- Both offer practical advice based on observation and experience.

While the form of the numerical proverbs remains constant, the tone does not. In the five present here (Prov 30:15–16; 30:18–19; 30:21–23; 30:24–28; 30:29–33) we see a variety of tones.

In the first numerical proverb (Prov 30:15–16), in which four things are compared because each is never satisfied but is always craving more, the tone seems to be more than simple observation; it is disapproval. Perhaps this tone is set by the introduction:

> The leech has two daughters;
>   "Give, give" they cry (Prov 30:15).

The lesson in regard to human behavior is that an insatiable desire is not a good thing.

The second numerical proverb (Prov 30:18–19) also moves beyond simple observation, but this time to awe and wonder. Why are things as they are? An eagle in flight, a serpent on a rock, and a ship on the sea are all compared to a man in love with a woman. The juxtaposition of ideas suggests that the man's behavior too should be considered a mystery of nature and not simply a free choice. Why do humans feel and act as they do?

The inserted verse on the behavior of the adulterous woman (Prov 30:10), because of its placement, forces us to ask how the behavior of the adulteress might relate to the proverb above. Is the behavior of a person who can destroy relationships, who can literally unravel the order of society, and who then can eat a meal and claim to have done no wrong, more mysterious than the behavior of the man in love? The reason for each is beyond our understanding.

In the third numerical proverb (Prov 30:21–23) the tone again changes, this time to ironic humor. In an obvious use of hyperbole (exaggeration) the author claims that the earth "trembles" and "cannot bear up" under the behavior of various "low lifes" who have risen above their calling: a slave, a fool, an unloved woman and a maid servant.

In the fourth numerical proverb (Prov 30:24–28) the tone becomes admiration. Wisdom is attributed to four creatures of nature who succeed despite their "handicaps": ants, rock badgers, locusts and lizards. The lesson in regard to human behavior is that we too might well succeed despite any handicaps which we might have.

The tone of the fifth numerical proverb (Prov 30:29–33) is also admiration, but this time for creatures who have a certain "stateliness" about them: the lion, the strutting rooster, the goat and a king. Again we see a note of humor in the juxtaposition of ideas. A king who hears himself compared to a strutting rooster either would feel insulted or would understand that he shouldn't be too in awe of his own splendor.

So, as we see, the numerical proverbs relate to wisdom literature not only in their technique, the fact that they force us to think in analogies, but in their content, for they offer good practical advice based on experience and observation. Were we to take these five numerical proverbs to heart we would avoid greed, arrogance, and pride, we would persevere despite our handicaps, and we would stand in humble awe at the wonders in God's creation. All of these are the attitudes of a wise person.

Review Questions

1. In what way do numerical proverbs exercise the mind?
2. What is the tone and purpose of the proverb about insatiable desire?
3. What is the tone and purpose of the proverb which compares an eagle, a serpent, a ship and a man in love?
4. What is the tone and purpose of the proverb about a slave, a fool, an unloved woman, and a maid servant?
5. What is the tone and purpose of the proverb about the ants, the rock badgers, the locusts and the lizards?
6. What is the tone and purpose of the proverb about the lion, the strutting rooster, the goat and a king?

7. How do the numerical proverbs relate to wisdom literature in both technique and content?

Discussion Questions

1. Did you like the numerical proverbs? Why or why not?
2. Do you like puzzles and riddles? Do you know why? What do you think is their purpose?
3. Did any of these proverbs suggest an idea to you that you have never thought of before? Explain. If so, did the new thought occur to you because of the explicit words of the proverb or because of the juxtaposition of ideas?

ARTICLE 13

The Capable Wife: Wisdom Incarnate

Question: "Why did the editor end the book of Proverbs with this poem about a capable wife? Since nearly all the advice in Proverbs is aimed at men, this ending seems out of place." (Prov 31:10–31)

If one reads the poem on a capable wife simply at the literal level, the topic does seem rather narrow and specific to use as a conclusion to the book of Proverbs. However, in Article 4 we discussed the fact that what was true of the faithful wife was also true of Wisdom herself. This poem on the capable wife in Proverbs 31:10–31 can also be read on two levels. When one reads the poem on the metaphorical level it does seem a fitting summation and conclusion to the book of Proverbs.

The poem represents a different form than we have encountered before, a form not evident in translation. Were we reading this twenty-two-line poem in its original Hebrew, we would see that this is an acrostic poem, a poem in which each succeeding line begins with the next letter in the Hebrew alphabet.

If we read the poem simply at the literal level we see that the capable wife is a perfect example of a person who has listened to wisdom. The capable wife is never lazy. She is a willing worker who rises early to provide for those in her household. She is also a person who responds to the needs of the poor. Because of her industriousness and prudence she need not worry about the future. She is skilled at relationships because "kindness" is on her tongue. She uses speech as it should be used. The capable wife is truly a wise woman. Because she "fears the Lord," all she does prospers.

However, several hints in the poem encourage us to look a little deeper and to see another level of meaning in the poem. Re-

---

LEVELS OF MEANING

Literal: A capable wife is industrious, prudent, kind, and fears the Lord.

Metaphorical: Wisdom is more precious than jewels. She gathers "food" from other nations to "feed" her "children." She "co-creates" with God.

---

member, wisdom has twice previously been personified as a woman in the book of Proverbs. So when we see the capable wife described in words almost identical to those applied to Lady Wisdom, we take note. When wisdom spoke in chapter 8 we heard:

> Wisdom is better than jewels,
> and all that you may desire cannot compare with her (Prov 8:11).

The capable wife, too, is described as "far more precious than jewels" (Prov 31:10).

A second hint that we should read the poem at the metaphorical level is that the capable wife is compared to "ships of the merchant" that bring food from far away. This comparison seems inappropriate except at the metaphorical level, for while a capable wife would not gather her food from foreign lands, wisdom has done just that. As we have noted, Israel has appropriated the wisdom, the "food," from surrounding nations and has "prepared it," integrated it into her own understanding of Yahweh's power and love in order to feed her children.

The capable wife "girds herself with strength" (see Prov 31:17). Wisdom too claims to have "strength" (see Prov 8:14). And just as wisdom personified called out at the city gate (see Prov 8:3), so is she now praised at the city gate (see Prov 31:31).

The capable wife, as she provides for her family is awake before everyone else and spends her time planting and "creating."

> She puts her hands to the distaff,
>   and her hands hold the spindle. . . .
> She makes herself coverings,
>   her clothing is fine linen and purple (Prov 31:19–22).

This "early rising" and constant involvement in "creating" calls to mind the claim which wisdom made earlier, that she alone was present with the Lord when the Lord created the world itself, when the Lord clothed the earth with soil and took daily delight in wisdom, just as the capable wife's husband and children now find her delightful.

> Her children rise up and call her happy;
>   her husband too, and he praises her (Prov 31:28).

Just as the capable wife surpasses all other women, so does wisdom surpass all. Those who choose either "will have no lack of gain" (see Prov 33:11).

The poem on a capable wife is a fitting end for the book of Proverbs, for in it we not only see an example of a life lived in the light of wisdom but we see wisdom herself, in all her glory, claiming to be God's partner in creating order at every level of life: personal, communal, political (at the city gate), and spiritual. However, this time Lady Wisdom appears not as personified wisdom, an abstraction, but as wisdom fully incarnate in every day life, as a wife in a relationship of love. Only when wisdom becomes incarnate in everyday life, in a life lived in the context of Yahweh's love, will people experience the rich fare which wisdom has to offer.

Review Questions

1. What is an acrostic poem?
2. On the literal level why is the capable wife an example of a wise person?
3. What two hints are there that the capable wife might be understood as wisdom personified?

4. What does the capable wife do that wisdom also does?
5. Why is the poem on a capable wife a fitting conclusion to the book of Proverbs?

Discussion Questions

1. Did you think of reading this poem metaphorically before you read this article? Why or why not?
2. Do you agree that the comment about gathering food from foreign lands is a hint to move to the metaphorical level? Why or why not?
3. Did you enjoy your study of Proverbs? Why or why not?
4. Is there some part of your life that you value but still cannot see how it fits into your relationship with God? Do you think the editor of Proverbs would see how it fits? Explain.

Summation and Transition from Proverbs to Psalms

We move now from Proverbs, a collection of material that was used primarily for teaching, to Psalms, a collection of material that was used primarily for worship. Nevertheless, what we have learned while studying Proverbs will help us in our study of Psalms.

We know that the book of Proverbs contains pre-existing collections, and that these collections developed over centuries before they were organized after the Babylonian exile into the form in which we now have them. The same is true of Psalms.

We know that the root of some of the proverbs goes back to a courtly setting where people learned the wise way to behave. In Psalms, too, we will see the effect of the court on the lives and thinking of the people.

As always, knowledge of the literary forms which we will read will be all-important as they will tell us something about the intent of the author. Some forms we will recognize from Proverbs, such as "beatitudes" and "acrostic" poems. Other forms will be new to us.

As with Proverbs, we cannot claim that the psalms must be read in their present edited order to be understood. Psalms, too, can be understood out of the context of the book of Psalms. However, they still need to be placed in the context in which they were originally used in order for their purpose and function to be understood by a modern reader.

Some of the psalms are wisdom psalms. You will be able to recognize them because they will remind you of Proverbs and even of Job. But most of the psalms differ from wisdom literature in form and content. Read the first book of Psalms now, jotting down any questions which occur to you. The articles that follow will respond to some of your questions.

THE BOOK OF PSALMS

ARTICLE 1

The Way of the Lord: Preparation for Worship

Question: "Is the book of Psalms wisdom literature? This first psalm gives the same kind of advice we read in Proverbs." (Ps 1)

Some of the psalms are categorized as wisdom psalms but most are not. The book of Psalms contains a collection of psalms which represent a variety of literary forms. Most scholars categorize the psalms into three major genres: hymns, laments, and psalms of thanksgiving, all of which were probably used during liturgical celebrations. We will have ample opportunity to read and study examples of each of these types of psalms in future articles.

Psalm 1, a wisdom psalm, differs from the majority of psalms in both content and style. Scholars believe that this wisdom psalm was placed at the head of the collection of psalms by a post-exilic compiler. The final compiler arranged the inherited psalms which had been collected over centuries into five books, probably to recall the Torah, or law, which is also arranged in to five books. Book 1, which includes Psalms 1–41, is an early collection, attributed to David. In this collection God is referred to as "Yahweh."

In contrast, Book 2, including Psalms 42–72, uses the word "Elohim" to refer to God. As in the Pentateuch, the tradition which refers to God as Yahweh is a southern tradition. The tradition that refers to God as Elohim is a northern tradition.

Book 3, which includes Psalms 73–89, is thought to have been collected not at court, as was Book 1, but by the temple singers. Book 4, including Psalms 90–106, is thought to be a royal collection, as is Book 5, Psalms 107–150. We will be studying only Book 1 in the ensuing articles.

Some psalms are categorized as wisdom psalms because they resemble wisdom literature in form and/or content. While scholars

243

PSALMS: THREE MAJOR GENRES

- Hymn
- Lament
- Psalm of Thanksgiving

---

do not agree on which psalms belong in the category of "wisdom psalms," the following are at least discussed in this context: Psalms 1, 19, 34, 36, 37, 49, 73, 112, 119, 127, 128.

Psalm 1 resembles wisdom literature in both form and content. The psalm begins, "Happy are those who . . . " This form—sometimes translated "Blessed are those who . . . "—is called a beatitude and is common in wisdom literature. You may remember that we read this form in Proverbs (see Prov 3:13; 8:32–33). Psalm 1 also resembles Proverbs in that it presents two ways, the way of the Lord and the way of the wicked. As in Proverbs, the ramifications of each way are pointed out. Those who choose the way of the Lord prosper, as do trees planted by streams of water. Those who choose the way of the wicked perish.

Why, one might wonder, would the post-exilic compiler of the book of Psalms preface the collection with a wisdom psalm? After all, wisdom literature is didactic in nature and suggests a school or

---

PSALMS: A COLLECTION OF FIVE BOOKS

Book 1   Psalms 1–41

Book 2   Psalms 42–72

Book 3   Psalms 73–89

Book 4   Psalms 90–106

Book 5   Psalms 107–150

PSALMS WHICH AT LEAST SOME SCHOLARS
CATEGORIZE AS WISDOM PSALMS

1	37	119
19	49	127
34	73	128
36	112	

family setting. Most of the psalms are liturgical in nature and suggest a worship setting. What is the compiler trying to say by prefacing the collection with wisdom literature?

By beginning the collection in this way, the editor is saying that the appropriate preparation for worship is a life lived in covenant love. Notice that in describing those who choose the way of the Lord the psalmist says:

> Their delight is in the law of the Lord,
> and on his law they meditate day and night (Ps 1:2).

The "law" refers to the law found in the first five books of the Old Testament, itself called "the law" or the "Torah." This law is the social expression of covenant love. Because God has chosen Israel to be God's people, because God loves Israel, a certain kind of behavior is necessary as an appropriate response, a behavior spelled out in the law.

To approach worship without first living a life of covenant love is wrong. You may remember that in Isaiah we read the same insistence that worship must be preceded by a life lived in covenant love. Isaiah pictures God as saying:

> When you stretch out your hands,
> I will hide my eyes from you;
> Even though you make many prayers,
> I will not listen;
> your hands are full of blood.
> Wash yourselves; make yourselves clean;

remove the evil of your doings from before my eyes;
Cease to do evil,
    learn to do good (Is 1:15–16).

After the Babylonian exile, when the Israelites returned to the holy land, there was a great deal of emphasis put on rebuilding the temple. The second temple was completed in 515 B.C. The book of Psalms was assembled over time, probably between the fourth and second centuries, to be the psalter for community worship in the second temple. By prefacing the psalter with a wisdom poem, the editor once more reminds the people that worship is futile unless the worshiper has first chosen to walk in the way of the Lord.

Review Questions

1. What are the three major genres found in Psalms?
2. In what setting were the psalms used?
3. When was the book of Psalms collated?
4. Into how many books is the collection arranged? Why?
5. Why are some psalms categorized as wisdom psalms?
6. How does Psalm 1 resemble wisdom literature?
7. What is the compiler of Psalms saying by beginning the collection with a wisdom psalm?
8. What must a person do before approaching worship?
9. When was the second temple completed?

Discussion Questions

1. Why do you think it is that both the Old and the New Testaments teach that before you bring your gift to the altar you must be in right relationship with others?
2. Think about how our liturgical song books are collated. What do they have in common with the book of Psalms?
3. What is the difference between a didactic setting and a worship setting? Do you think one is more important than the other? Why or why not?

ARTICLE 2

A Royal Psalm in Its Cultic Setting

Question: "To whom is the Lord speaking in Psalm 2 when the Lord says, 'You are my son; today I have begotten you?' (Ps 2:7) It sounds as if the words are addressed to Jesus, but could that be right?"

To a Christian reader the words of Psalm 2 seem to refer to Jesus. We will understand why this is true after we place the psalm in its original context and try to understand what it meant to people who preceded Jesus.

Psalm 2 belongs to a group of psalms called "royal psalms" because they are about the king. The group includes Psalms 2, 18, 20, 21, 45, 72, 78, 89, 101, 110, 132, and 144. To understand the context for royal psalms we need to review a kind of "covenant theology" which we discussed when reading Isaiah (see Article 2), a theology that interpreted God's covenant love as being expressed through God's choice of David and his line as king, and God's choice of Jerusalem or Zion as God's dwelling place.

The Israelites had understood themselves to be in a relationship of covenant love with Yahweh long before Israel had a king. We see covenant love described at the time of Abraham (1850 B.C.) when God promises Abraham land and descendants. We see covenant love described at the time of Moses (1250 B.C.) when God promises Moses a nation. After Moses the covenant was celebrated through the celebration of the Passover, a feast which reminded the people of God's mighty acts at the time of the exodus.

By the time of David (just before 1000 B.C.), a new understanding of covenant emerged. We read about this idea of covenant love in 2 Samuel 7. In this passage the prophet Nathan is telling David

247

ROYAL PSALMS

Psalms in which the king is the subject/speaker

2	45	101
18	72	110
20	78	132
21	89	144

---

that Yahweh has chosen David and David's line to be his king forever. God is pictured as telling David:

> When your days are fulfilled and you lie down with your ancestors, I will raise up your offspring after you, who shall come forth from your body, and I will establish his kingdom. He shall build a house for my name, and I will establish the throne of his kingdom forever. I will be a father to him, and he shall be a son to me (2 Sam 7:12–14).

As you may know, David's son Solomon did build the first temple in Jerusalem. The ark of the covenant, a sign of God's covenant love for God's people, was brought to the temple. Covenant renewal ceremonies then changed. Instead of celebrating the Passover, the people celebrated their king, God's "son," and their temple, God's dwelling place in Zion.

Psalm 2 was probably used in communal celebrations honoring the king over centuries. It may have been used at a king's coronation, or during the fall festival which recalled and celebrated God's choice of the Davidic line and of Zion.

The psalm begins with the narrator's voice questioning why nations would conspire against "the Lord and his anointed." In a ceremonial setting various lines of the psalm would have been assigned to various participants. A priest might have asked this question. The question presupposes Davidic covenant theology. It is ridiculous to conspire against God's "anointed," the king of Israel,

---

QUESTIONS TO ASK WHEN STUDYING PSALMS

- What is the literary form of this psalm?
- What is the original cultic setting for this psalm?

---

because it is identical to conspiring against God. God laughs at such a ridiculous undertaking.

A person assigned God's part would say, "I have set my king on Zion, my holy hill" (Ps 2:6).

The next voice would be the voice of the king:

> I will tell of the decree of the Lord:
> He said to me, "You are my son;
>   today I have begotten you (Ps 2:7).

So, to answer the question with which we began—"To whom is the Lord speaking when he says these words?"—the Lord is speaking to each and every king of the Davidic line as the king's election is acknowledged and celebrated by the gathered community through the centuries.

The reason that these words, in the ear of a Christian, seem to refer to Jesus is that Christians understand Nathan's words to David to have been fulfilled in Jesus.

You may remember that when we studied Isaiah's great and glorious king prophecies we tried to separate the original context and meaning of the words from the Christian context and meaning which we have since seen in them. We must do this same thing with the royal psalms. To truly appreciate the psalms we must try to understand their purpose and meaning in their original context.

However, the psalter which we now have does not give us the information we need to place each individual psalm in its original setting. In fact, the primary task of scholars who study the psalms is to find the answers to two questions: "What is the literary form of this psalm?" and "What is the original 'cultic setting' for this psalm?" That is, how was this psalm incorporated into a worship setting? What function did the psalm have in the gathered community?

The function of Psalm 2 seems to have been the renewal and celebration of God's covenant promise to the house of David. The covenant is recalled and renewed each time the people hear God say, "You are my son; today I have begotten you" (Ps 2:7).

Review Questions

1. Did the Israelites have an idea of covenant love before the time of David? Explain. How was this covenant love celebrated?
2. How did the idea of covenant love change at the time of David?
3. How was covenant love celebrated by the time of Solomon?
4. On what occasions might Psalm 2 have been used over the centuries?
5. To whom is the Lord speaking when the Lord is pictured as saying, "You are my son"?
6. Why is it that, to a Christian, the words seem to refer to Jesus?
7. What is the primary task of scholars who study the psalms?

Discussion Questions

1. Do we celebrate covenant love? How?
2. Do you believe that one way God expresses God's love for God's people is to "appoint" their leaders? Why or why not?
3. What is the value of trying to understand the psalms in their original setting rather than simply understanding them in the context of our own lives?

ARTICLE 3

An Individual Lament

Question: "Why did David flee his son Absalom?" (Pss 3,4,5,22)

This question is about the heading of Psalm 3, but it will give us the opportunity to discuss the psalm itself, an example of one of the three major genres found in Psalms, a "lament." First, however, a few words about psalm headings.

The headings which precede many of the psalms are post-exilic additions to the text. Some of the headings are instructions to musicians as to how the psalm should be performed. For instance, Psalm 4 should be accompanied with stringed instruments, Psalm 5 with flutes. Some headings may be instructing the leaders as to the tune by comparing it to a well-known tune. Perhaps "According to The Deer of the Dawn" is such an instruction (see Ps 22).

While Psalm 3 does not have a heading about musical instruments, it does have two other kinds of headings: an attribution to an historical person and the mention of an appropriate historical setting. Neither of these kinds of headings makes any claim to historicity. Since David was known to have played the lyre (see 1 Sam 16:14ff), later tradition attributed the psalms to him, just as later tradition attributed the proverbs to Solomon. In the light of this attribution specific psalms were linked to appropriate settings in David's life as recounted in 1 and 2 Samuel.

David's flight from Absalom was certainly an appropriate choice for a setting for Psalm 3. The reason David fled his son is that Absalom had tried to turn the people against David and take over the throne. David was totally devastated by this act of betrayal. David's troops finally defeated Absalom's troops, but David, at the military leader's request, did not join in the battle. From David's

251

PSALM HEADINGS

- Instructions to musicians
- Attribution to an historical person
- Mention of an appropriate historical setting

---

point of view the Lord had simply chosen to let him prevail over his enemies (see 2 Sam 15–18).

Psalm 3, which has been placed on David's lips, is an example of a lament, more specifically an individual lament. Individual laments occur more than any other genre in the book of Psalms. In Book 1, Psalms 3, 4, 5, 6, 7, 9, 10, 13, 14, 17, 22, 25, 26, 27, 28, 31, 35, 38, 39, 40, and 41 are all individual laments.

The individual lament has a recognizable form. It begins with a call to God.

O Lord, how many are my foes! (Ps 3:1)

Next comes a complaint in which the speaker tells God exactly what has gone wrong.

INDIVIDUAL LAMENTS IN BOOK 1

3	10	26	39
4	13	27	40
5	14	28	41
6	17	31	
7	22	35	
9	25	38	

FORM OF A LAMENT

- A call to God
- A complaint
- An expression of trust
- A petition
- (Priest's words of assurance, usually not in the text)
- Praise and/or a promise to praise God

> Many are rising against me;
>   many are saying to me,
>   "There is no hope for you in God" (Ps 3:1–2).

The complaint is followed by an expression of trust.

> But you, O Lord, are a shield around me (Ps 3:3).

Next is a petition in which the psalmist asks for deliverance for himself and/or destruction of his enemies.

> Rise up, O Lord!
>   Deliver me, O my God! (Ps 3:7)

At this point scholars believe that a priest would speak to the person who is lamenting, assuring the person that God would deliver him. The priest's words rarely appear in the psalter.

In response to this assurance the lamenter responds in an entirely different tone than he has used up to this point. He no longer laments but simply praises God or promises that he will praise God.

> Deliverance belongs to the Lord;
>   may your blessing be on your people (Ps 3:8).

So an individual lament always ends in calm assurance and praise. This is a characteristic of the form.

Even though the individual lament appears to be the complaint of a single person, in the context of the psalter it is a community prayer. When reading the book of Psalms we are not reading "private prayers" as well as "public prayers." Rather we are reading the prayers of the gathered community. Just as this lament would be perfectly suitable for David to have said, so is it suitable for many other settings, including settings in our own lives. The imagery is "non-specific." No matter who the enemies or what the occasion, the words of Psalm 3 would be appropriate, even for a group.

The enemies of the psalmist array themselves not only against him but against God by saying that there is no help for him in God (see Ps 3:2). The psalmist believes that God is constantly helping and protecting him even when he sleeps (see Ps 3:5). However the psalmist's inner confidence is not all he wants. He also wants his enemies to see that they are wrong. He wants God to "break the teeth" of these false speakers. So just as the individual lament is actually public prayer, so is the desired deliverance public deliverance. It is appropriate, then, that the blessing asked for in the last verse be a public blessing, a blessing on all the people (see Ps 3:8).

Before leaving Psalm 3 we might point out one more puzzling detail. In addition to the use of headings and the use of the lament form, characteristics which, by and large, we understand, Psalm 3 includes the word "selah" three times, between verses 2 and 3, 4 and 5, and at the end. Scholars aren't sure what this word means. Perhaps it too is an instruction to the musicians to play some sort of interlude.

Just as some of the headings and musical notations used by the post-exilic compilers are unfamiliar to us, so was the original social setting of each individual lament unknown to the post-exilic compiler. It is for this reason that the compiler selects appropriate settings for individual psalms, settings such as David fleeing his son Absalom.

Review Questions

1. What literary form is Psalm 3?
2. Name three kinds of headings which precede psalms? When were the headings added?

3. Why did David flee his son?
4. Name five parts of the structure of a lament. Why is the fifth part an entirely different tone?
5. Why is an individual lament appropriate for group prayer?
6. What does "selah" mean?

Discussion Questions

1. Why do you think the post-exilic editor of the book of Psalms attributed psalms to particular settings? What do you think might have been his motive?
2. Do you have any reaction to the prayer that the enemy be publicly shown to be wrong? Do you find this offensive? Understandable? Explain.
3. Does music enhance prayer for you? Why or why not?

ARTICLE 4

Scripture: A Process of Revelation

Question: "In Psalm 5 the psalmist claims that God 'hates evil-doers' (see Ps 5:5) and prays that God 'cast out' his enemies (see Ps 5:10). Isn't it wrong to pray for another's destruction? (Pss 5,7,18,21,35)

Students are often shocked by the attitude expressed toward enemies in the book of Psalms. We see such attitudes in many psalms, for instance in individual laments (in addition to Psalm 5 see 7:17–18; 35:1–6), and in royal psalms (see 18:41–49; 21:19–21). What explanation can we offer for an inspired writer praying for another's destruction?

To answer this question we must remind ourselves of one of the contexts within which we need to understand scripture. The Bible represents a two thousand year process of coming to knowledge. Over these two thousand years, from the time of Abraham in 1850 B.C. to the first century after Jesus, people grew in their understanding of God as a loving God.

For many years the Israelites grew in their understanding of God's love for them, but failed to understand God's love for other nations. They believed that their enemies were also God's enemies.

This idea is clearly expressed in the account of God's entering into covenant relationship with Abraham. God is pictured as saying, "I will make of you a great nation, and I will bless you, and make your name great, so that you will be a blessing. I will bless those who bless you, and the one who curses you I will curse" (Gen 12:2–3).

The Israelites acted on this understanding that their enemies were God's enemies. It was their belief that God wanted such ene-

256

A PROCESS OF REVELATION

Coming to Knowledge by Reflecting on Experience

Question: Whom does God love?

Date	Understanding
1850 B.C.	Abraham understood that God is a personal and loving God. He especially loved Abraham. He promised him protection, land, and descendants.
1250 B.C.	The Hebrews understood that God was a personal and loving God. He especially loved the Hebrew people. He freed them from slavery in Egypt.
1200–1000 B.C.	The Israelites understood that God loved them. He helped them conquer Canaan.
537 B.C.	Cyrus, a Persian, conquered the Babylonians and let the Israelites return home.
500–400 B.C.	The author of Jonah understood that God must love other nations. After all, he created them just as he created the Jewish people.
30 A.D.	Jesus taught his followers to love their enemies.
34 A.D.	Peter understood that all people are invited to be God's chosen people and live in a covenant relationship with their God.

mies destroyed (see Deut 7:1–6). When the Israelites conquered a town, they believed that they were doing God's will when they put it under the "ban," that is, when they killed all the inhabitants. We read an account of such destruction in Joshua. "Then they devoted to destruction by the edge of the sword all in the city, both men and women, young and old, oxen, sheep, and donkeys" (Jos 6:21).

The psalms which we are reading in this first book of psalms are an older collection, some undoubtedly having originated at the time of David (1000 B.C.). So these psalms precede the time of the Babylonian exile by five hundred years. At the time the psalms were written, the psalmists did believe that their enemies were God's enemies and that God would want them to be destroyed.

In Psalm 5 the psalmist is expressing his great need for God's love so that he may be among those who enter the temple for worship.

> But I, through the abundance of your steadfast love,
>   will enter your house.
> I will bow down toward your holy temple
>   in awe of you (Ps 5:7).

The psalmist's enemies are those who have "rebelled" against God (see Ps 5:10). They chose the way of evil rather than the way of the Lord.

It is part of the structure of a lament that the individual petitions God, asking for relief from whatever has been the problem. For a person who believed that his enemies were God's enemies, a prayer for relief from the problem would be a request that the enemy be destroyed.

You may remember from reading Isaiah and Job that during and after the Babylonian exile the Israelites grew in their understanding that God loved other nations too. After all, God chose Cyrus, a Persian, to free God's people from the Babylonians. So God must have loved Cyrus (see Is 44:28–45:6).

In the book of Job, written after the exile, we see Job, in an examination of conscience, reveal that he refrained from sinning against his enemies:

If I have rejoiced at the ruin of those who hated me,
   or exulted when evil overtook them
I have not let my mouth sin
   by asking for their lives with a curse (Job 31:29–30).

So, five hundred years after this psalmist prayed for his enemies' destruction, the Israelites had come to realize that because God loves other people, even enemies must be treated as children of God. It is wrong to pray for the destruction of one's enemies.

Why, then, is such a psalm in the Bible? Why is it revelation? Although this psalmist did not have the fullness of revelation which was to come later, he did have spiritual insights which were and are crucial in our understanding of our relationship with God.

This psalmist longed to live in covenant love with Yahweh, to be among God's people praying in the temple. He realized that the ability to do this was not his gift to God but God's gift to him. The psalmist understood that God is in charge of the universe and that God holds God's people accountable for their actions. Those who rebel against God will be held accountable. All of these are important spiritual insights which people of every generation need to realize. True, the psalmist did not understand Jesus' teaching: "Love your enemy," but he did understand the revelation which was available to people of his time.

Review Questions

1. How did the Israelites grow in their understanding of God's love?
2. How did the Israelites treat their enemies? Why did they think this was good?
3. From what time in Israel's history do some of the psalms in Book 1 come?
4. What event helped the Israelites understand that God loved other nations?
5. How did Job think he should treat his enemies?

6. Name four spiritual insights which the psalmist in Psalm 5 did have.

Discussion Questions

1. Have you ever had to forgive an enemy? Do you think the ability to do this is a natural ability or a gift of grace? Explain.
2. Do you think nationalism can be practiced in a Christian country? Why or why not?
3. Do you as a citizen of a certain country or a member of a certain religious tradition sometimes slip into thinking that God loves your group more than others? Were you taught to think this way? Explain. What is dangerous about this way of thinking?

ARTICLE 5

"A Little Lower Than God?"

Question: "What does it mean to say that human beings are 'a little lower than God?' (Ps 8:5) Isn't this a bit grandiose?" (Ps 8)

The person who asked this question is reading the RSV or the NRSV. Other translations picture the psalmist as saying "a little less than the angels" (NAB) or "than the heavenly beings" (New International).

The difference in translations evidently started with the Septuagint, the Greek translation of the Old Testament which preceded Christ by some two hundred years. Scholars suggest that the translators, out of respect for God, translated the passage, "a little less than the angels." If true, these translators also thought the idea that human beings are "a little lower than God" was grandiose.

Psalm 8 is our first acquaintance with one of the major literary types found in the book of Psalms: a hymn. Other psalms which various scholars categorize in this genre are Psalms 19, 29, 33, 66, 100, 103, 104, 111, 113, 114, 117, 145–150.

The hymns have a simple structure. They begin with a call to praise, procede to the reasons why praise is appropriate, a section which begins with the word "for," and often end with a renewed call to praise. In Psalm 8, the call to praise is repeated word for word in the first and last lines (see 8:1; 8:9 if reading NRSV; 8:2, 8:10 if reading the NAB. The NAB assigns v. 1 to the headings and so all succeeding verses are one number higher). The repeated line in the first and last verse is a literary device called an "inclusio."

Whether one translates the line "a little lower than God" or "a little less than the angels," the meaning is much the same. The

---

PSALMS WHICH AT LEAST SOME SCHOLARS CATEGORIZE AS HYMNS

19	100	113
29	103	114
33	104	117
66	111	145–150

---

psalmist is in awe, not only of God, but of the dignity which God has bestowed on human beings.

As was true in wisdom literature, the psalmist's awe is rooted in a meditation on creation.

> When I look at your heavens,
>   the work of your fingers,
>   the moon and the stars that you have established . . . (Ps 8:3).

How is it that so great a God who created such majestic, awesome beauty should care so much about a little human being?

> What are human beings that you are mindful of them,
>   mortals that you care for them? (Ps 8:4).

You may remember that we heard Job ask this same question (see Job 7:17). However, in Job the question was ironic. Job was asking why human beings were so important to God that God would pursue them and test them. Why couldn't God just leave Job alone? The psalmist asks the question in an entirely different mood. His awe of God, of God's majesty and power, has resulted in

---

FORM OF A HYMN

- Call to praise
- Reasons why praise is appropriate
- Renewed call to praise

---

his being in awe of himself as one whom God loves, as one whom God has not only created but has "given dominion" over all else that God has created.

This idea that humans are "godlike" and have dominion over the rest of creation is also present in Genesis. Genesis pictures God as making humankind in God's own image and as giving human beings dominance over every living thing. "Then God said, 'Let us make humankind in our image, according to our likeness; and let them have dominion over the fish of the sea, and over the birds of the air, and over the cattle, and over all the wild animals of the earth, and over every creeping thing that creeps on the earth' " (Gen 1:26).

Are these ideas grandiose or are they an accurate insight into the dignity which God has bestowed upon us?

Judging from the way human beings have acted on earth, how human beings have treated the rest of the created order, many feel that humans have misinterpreted these biblical images. Humans have, it seems, been cruel and selfish "masters," abusing the rest of creation for our own selfish purposes. If one's understanding of these images results in such behavior, then one's understanding is grandiose, but this grandiose posture is a misunderstanding of the images.

In both Genesis and Psalm 8, the idea that humans are "a little lower than God," and that humans have "dominion" over the rest of creation, dignifies human beings. In many cultures humans were understood to be slaves of the gods; in the Israelite tradition humans were understood to be created by one loving God who wanted not a slave but a partner who would extend God's love and care to the rest of creation. God's "dominion," delegated to human beings, is not the dominion of a cruel or selfish God but the dominion of a kind and loving God. For humans to be given dominion over the rest of creation because humans are "a little lower than God" is not a license to "lord it over creation." It is a responsibility to care for and nurture creation.

Is the image grandiose? Not if one understands it correctly. Human beings become more able to love as we learn to love ourselves. As we grow in our understanding of our own dignity, as people made in God's image, we grow in our ability to act lovingly toward all that God has created, other people as well as the whole created order. Since this dignity is a gift from God the creator, understanding our dignity does not lead to false pride but to praise of God who bestowed this dignity upon us.

> O Lord, our Sovereign,
>   how majestic is your name in all the earth! (Ps 8:1)

Review Questions

1. What is the Septuagint?
2. What difference in translation in Psalm 8:5 can be traced to the Septuagint?
3. What literary form is Psalm 8?
4. Name three components usually present in a hymn.
5. What is an "inclusio"?
6. What causes awe in the heart of the narrator of Psalm 5? Why is the psalmist in awe of himself?
7. What two images appear both in Psalm 8 and in Genesis? How might these images be misinterpreted?
8. What is a correct interpretation of the images?
9. How might a correct understanding of the image be helpful to us? To what attitude should it lead?

Discussion Questions

1. What do you think it means to be created in God's image?
2. Do you agree that a positive self-concept is a good thing? Why or why not?
3. If we were to "master" creation as people made in the image of a loving God, how would we change our present behavior?

ARTICLE 6

Psalms: Categorized by Form and Content

Question: "In Psalm 9 are the enemies already defeated (Ps 9:4–6) or is the prayer that they will be (Ps 9:14)? The ideas seem out of order in this psalm." (Pss 9, 10, 11)

Psalm 9 presents a variety of themes, all familiar, such as God defeated the psalmist's enemies (Ps 9:4), God is a just judge (Ps 9:4, 8), God is the God of all nations (Ps 9:5), and God hears the oppressed (Ps 9:9). However, to a person reading the poem in English the ideas seem to lack organization. The reason for this is that the organizing device of the psalm is in its frame and not in the order of its ideas. Psalm 9–10 is an acrostic poem.

You may remember that we read an acrostic poem in Proverbs 31:10–31, the poem on a good wife. An acrostic poem is one based on the Hebrew alphabet in which each successive line begins with the next letter of the alphabet. Acrostic poems are popular in wisdom literature. Other psalms which use an acrostic structure are 34, 37, 111, 112, 119, and 145.

Although Psalm 9 is one-half of an acrostic poem, most scholars do not categorize it as wisdom literature but as a lament or as a psalm of thanksgiving. Since we have not yet introduced the psalm of thanksgiving, the third major literary form found in the psalms, we will do that now.

It is no wonder that scholars disagree on the categorization of some psalms, particularly psalms of thanksgiving, because the category seems to be an outgrowth of a lament.

You will remember that a characteristic of a lament is that it ends

PSALMS WITH AN ACROSTIC STRUCTURE	
34	112
37	119
111	145

in a statement of praise resulting from the word of assurance spoken by the priest. The psalmist is sure that God will save him.

A thanksgiving psalm is one in which the psalmist is proclaiming that this rescue has occurred. Those who categorize Psalm 9 as a psalm of thanksgiving do so because the psalm begins with just such a proclamation.

> I will give thanks to the Lord with my whole heart;
>   I will tell of all your wonderful deeds. . . .
> When my enemies turned back,
>   they stumbled and perished before you (Ps 9:1–3).

Because of such a proclamation the community sees the hand of God in the deliverance and so praises God.

When this element of proclamation receives the greatest emphasis in a psalm, that psalm is considered a psalm of thanksgiving. Other psalms which at least some scholars consider psalms of

PSALMS WHICH AT LEAST SOME SCHOLARS CATEGORIZE AS PSALMS OF THANKSGIVING			
18	41	75	118
30	65	92	124
32	66	103	136
34	67	107	138
40	68	116	

PSALMS WHICH AT LEAST SOME SCHOLARS CATEGORIZE AS PSALMS OF TRUST

11	62	125
16	63	129
23	91	131
27	121	

---

thanksgiving are Psalms 18, 30, 32, 34, 40, 41, 65, 66, 67, 68, 75, 92, 103, 107, 116, 118, 124, 136, and 138.

As you read these psalms you will notice that just as a lament can be a lament of an individual or the lament of a community, so too can psalms of thanksgiving be the proclamation that either individuals or communities have been saved. However, the psalms of individual thanksgiving too are meant for communal prayer. The purpose of the psalm of thanksgiving is to move the community to praise.

Another type of psalm, closely related to the psalm of thanksgiving, is the psalm of trust. Again you will remember that a statement of trust that God would act is a part of the form of a lament. When this statement of trust becomes the predominant feature of the psalm, the psalm is categorized as a psalm of trust. Examples of psalms which at least some scholars consider psalms of trust are Psalms 11, 16, 23, 27, 62, 63, 91, 121, 125, 129, and 131.

Psalm 11 is a psalm of trust, as is evident from its opening lines:

In the Lord I take refuge; how can you say to me,
    Flee like a bird to the mountain? (Ps 11:1)

As in a lament, the psalmist is in trouble. His enemies are arrayed against him. However, the psalmist does not beg God to look his way. He is confident that God already sees him (see Ps 11:4). He does not pray for his enemies' destruction. He simply states that God will destroy the wicked (see Ps 11:6). So the psalmist has no

---

PSALMS CATEGORIZED BY:

Form: Hymns   *Content:* Wisdom
   Laments   Royal Psalms
   Psalms of   Psalms of Trust
   Thanksgiving   Psalms of Zion

---

need to flee town. God is in God's temple (Ps 11:11). The psalmist has nothing to fear.

We have now seen examples of the three main types of psalms: laments, hymns, and psalms of thanksgiving. These three groups are defined primarily by their form. We have also seen some other types of psalms: wisdom psalms, royal psalms, and psalms of trust. We have yet to encounter psalms of Zion. These later kinds of psalms are categorized by their content. They cut across other categories. For instance, a royal psalm could be a lament or a song of thanksgiving. In either case its subject matter is the king.

There is no need for us to try to decide whether a given psalm, such as Psalm 9, is a lament or a psalm of thanksgiving. Obviously the psalm has characteristics of each type or there would be no disagreement. What is important is that we use our knowledge of the characteristics of each form to help us understand the purpose and meaning behind the psalm. The purpose behind Psalm 9 seems to be to move others to praise God, having heard of God's saving acts in the life of the psalmist.

Review Questions

1. Why does Psalm 9 seem disconnected? How is it organized?
2. What is an acrostic poem?
3. What is a psalm of thanksgiving? How is it related to a lament?
4. What two kinds of psalms of thanksgiving are there?

5. What is a psalm of trust?
6. What kinds of psalms are categorized by form? What kinds are categorized by content?

Discussion Questions

1. Do you find it hard to trust others? God? Yourself? What do you think contributes to a person's ability to trust?
2. For what do you feel most thankful? Do you celebrate your thankfulness in any kind of ritual? Explain.

ARTICLE 7

Community Laments for Every Generation

Question: "Psalms 12 and 14 certainly take a dim view of human nature (see Pss 12:1; 14:3). Each says that there are no good people on the earth. Why are these psalms in the Bible?" (Pss 12, 14)

It is true that both Psalms 12 and 14 state that there are no more good people on earth. However, in each case we must put that statement in the context of the literary form within which it appears. When we realize that in each case we are reading a lament, we will see these statements as prefaces to statements of faith and hope.

Psalm 12 is a community lament. As one would expect, it begins with a direct cry to God and a description of just how bad things are.

> Help, O Lord, for there is no longer anyone who is godly;
>> the faithful have disappeared from humankind.
> They utter lies to each other;
>> with flattering lips and a double heart they speak (Ps 12:1–2).

It is interesting to note just what sin the psalmist sees as prevalent among the people. Notice that the sin is treating each other dishonestly. If you remember, Proverbs stressed the same evil that can be accomplished through the misuse of the tongue.

In the prayer of petition the psalmist reveals just why it is that people are using their tongues to lie. Evidently they have lost track of the fact that God holds them accountable for their actions,

> Those who say, "With our tongues we will prevail,
>> our lips are our own—who is our master?" (Ps 12:4)

When we first described a lament, we said that the reason the mood changes so radically is that a word of assurance, usually not repeated in the psalm, is offered by a priest. The final words of trust are in response to this word of assurance.

Psalm 12 is unusual in that the words of assurance do appear in the text:

> "Because the poor are despoiled,
>   because the needy groan,
> I will now rise up," says the Lord;
>   "I will place them in the safety for which they long" (Ps 12:5).

After this sure promise that God will rise up and save God's people, the psalmist is able to trust rather than despair. The promise of the Lord will be fulfilled (see Ps 12:6). God will protect God's people (see Ps 12:7). We see here the movement from despair to petition to trust which is typical of a lament.

Much the same sentiments are expressed in Psalm 14. In this psalm the psalmist states that all are fools. The Lord looks down to see if anyone seeks the Lord, but no one does (see Ps 14:1–3).

Again the problem seems to be that people have forgotten that the transcendent God is also immanent. They have said, "There is no God" (see Ps 14:1) and have forgotten that "God is with" God's people.

Scripture scholars believe that the words "there is no God" are not describing atheism. Evidently no one was an atheist at the time these psalms took form. The argument would have been over whether gods took any interest in humans, whether gods took any active role in events on earth, not whether gods existed.

Opposed to the fool who fails to seek the Lord are those whom God calls "my people" (see Ps 14:14): the "righteous" (see Ps 14:5), the "poor" (see Ps 14:6). These are the people with whom the psalmist identifies himself as he calls out for the deliverance of Israel.

> O that deliverance for Israel would come from Zion!
>   When the Lord restores the fortunes of his people,
>   Jacob will rejoice, Israel will be glad (Ps 14:7).

Scholars debate whether the phrase "restore the fortunes of his people" is a reference to the exile. There seems to be no compelling reason to conclude that it is, since Israel had many occasions during its history when its fortunes needed to be restored.

These psalms, which admit humankind's sinfulness but nevertheless affirm hope in God's power to save, are in the Bible because they express the truth about the human condition. We all do sin. We still lie. We still sometimes act as though we are our own masters, accountable to no one but ourselves. We all know that the "wicked" still do "prowl," and "vileness" still is "exalted" in our midst.

Because we are sinners who believe in God's fidelity to God's promises to save, we can identify with Psalms 12 and 14. The community laments of Israel are just as true when they function as community laments for our own generation.

Review Questions

1. What sin is most lamented in Psalm 12?
2. What have these dishonest people neglected to consider?
3. What is the movement of moods in the lament?
4. What does the phrase "There is no God" mean in the context of this psalm?
5. What does God's "immanence" mean?
6. Why are Psalms 12 and 14 in the Bible?

Discussion Questions

1. Do you find yourself more impressed with the number of good people on earth or with the number of evil people? Why?
2. Do you think of God more often as transcendent or as immanent? Explain.
3. Do you agree that the community gathered in church every Sunday is a sinful community? Why or why not?
4. Do you think it is healthy or unhealthy to admit sinfulness? Explain.

ARTICLE 8

A Rite of Entrance to the Temple

Question: "What is meant by: Who may abide in your tent? Who may dwell on your holy hill?" (Ps 15)

The intent behind the words "Who may abide in your tent?" and "Who may dwell on your holy hill?" (Ps 15:1) is, "Who is worthy to enter the temple to worship God?" Psalm 15 is a rite of entrance to the temple.

Before the temple was built, before David had made Jerusalem the capital of the nation, even before the Israelites had reached the holy land, they had experienced and celebrated God's presence in their midst. While the Israelites were still in the desert and lived in tents, God dwelt in their midst in God's own tent (see Ex 33:7–11). When the Israelites traveled, God traveled with them.

> Then the cloud covered the tent of meeting, and the glory of the Lord filled the tabernacle. . . . Whenever the cloud was taken up from the tabernacle, the Israelites would set out on each stage of their journey (Ex 40:34–36).

The phrase "abide in your tent" recalls this time in the desert.

After David united the twelve tribes and made Jerusalem his capital, David wanted to build God a permanent house. However, it was David's son Solomon who did build the temple on Jerusalem's "holy hill" or on "the mountain of the Lord." You may remember that we saw this image in Isaiah too.

> Come, let us go up to the mountain of the Lord,
> to the house of the God of Jacob (Is 20:3).

ENTRANCE RITE TO THE TEMPLE

- Who is worthy to enter? (Asked by those outside)
- Those who live in covenant love. (Answer, in the form of a covenant code, spoken by priests inside)

We discussed the background for this image in Article 5. The "mountain of the Lord," like "the tent," is a metaphorical way of referring to the place where God dwells.

Once the temple was built it was understood to be God's dwelling place. On great festivals when the people would come to the temple to worship, a rite of entrance would take place.

Scholars think that the questions with which Psalm 15 begins would be asked by those who wished to enter the temple. The answer, starting with verse 2, would be recited by the priests.

Notice that the description of the people who are worthy to enter the temple centers in on some of the very sins we have seen condemned in other psalms, in Proverbs, in Job, and in Isaiah. People must be honest to be worthy to enter the temple. They must "speak the truth from their heart" (see Ps 15:2).

The right use of the tongue, of speech, is again highlighted. People must not speak against their friends, "nor take up a reproach against their neighbors" (see Ps 15:3). Remember how angry God was with Job's friends. They had done just this.

"Despising the wicked" is held up as a virtue. We have already noted that the psalmists do despise the wicked. Over the centuries this attitude has been softened to "despise what the wicked do but not the wicked themselves," since, after all, God loves everyone, even the wicked.

Another sin which is condemned is lending money at interest (see Ps 15:5). Many people in our culture take this to mean "at exorbitant interest," but it means at any interest at all. An excess of material goods was viewed as an opportunity to help those in need, not as an opportunity to exploit people for profit. If a person needed to borrow, a person who was in a position to lend should do so willingly. If the borrower were later able to repay the debt, he should. But no interest could be charged.

A strong statement against taking a bribe is made (Ps 15:5). You may remember that Proverbs acknowledged that bribes sometimes work, but still a person should not accept one. Also, people are to keep their oaths even if things turn out differently than expected and fidelity to the promise turns out to be disadvantageous (Ps 15:4). People of integrity abide by their oaths.

In this rite of entrance to the temple it is clear that heartfelt commitment to the covenant is necessary in order to enter the temple and worship with the community. Worship can never be a ritual action unconnected to daily life. Only those who live lives of covenant love are worthy to abide in God's tent, to dwell on God's holy mountain.

Review Questions

1. What is the intent behind the words, "Who may abide in your tent?"
2. What part of the Israelites' history does the tent recall?
3. To what does the image "the mountain of the Lord" refer?
4. In what cultic situation would Psalm 15 be used?
5. Name six sins which a person who enters the temple should have avoided. Are all of these actions which our culture still considers wrong? Explain.
6. Who is worthy to "abide in God's tent"?

Discussion Questions

1. Does your church have any kind of entrance rite? Explain. Do you have holy water? What is the significance of using it?
2. Do you think a person who has more than he or she needs is obligated to help those in need? Explain.
3. Do you think charging interest on a loan is wrong? Why or why not?
4. Do you think if you make a promise that works to your disadvantage that you should be able to get out of it? Explain.

ARTICLE 9

A Fire-Breathing God of Love

Question: "In Psalm 18:7–15 God is described almost like a fire-breathing dragon. Isn't this an awfully primitive description?"

The array of images used to describe God in Psalm 18 is truly awesome. The images span cultures and centuries. We will discuss the images in Psalm 18:7–15, images which the questioner finds "primitive," but which might better be described as "mythic" or "cosmic." But first, in order to put those images in context, we should see what images precede them.

Psalm 18 is a royal psalm of thanksgiving. The speaker is the king. The psalm is attributed to David not only here but in 2 Samuel 22. While the psalm is perfectly appropriate for that setting, it is also appropriate for many other settings, partly because the images are non-specific. They work in our culture as well as they did in David's.

The psalm begins with the psalmist exultantly shouting out his love because God has saved him from his enemies.

> I love you, O Lord, my strength!
> The Lord is my rock, my fortress, and my deliverer,
>   my God, my rock in whom I take refuge,
>   my shield, and the horn of my salvation, my stronghold (Ps 18:1–2).

In these words we have a whole series of images of God, all presented within the contest of a personal love relationship. The God of the psalmist is known and loved. The psalmist has experienced God's presence in his life. God has been his strength: the very energy within his own body. God has been his rock: solid, completely dependable, immovable. God has been his fortress: the psalmist dwells in God's strength just as God's strength dwells in the psalmist. God has been his deliverer: the saving power of God has reached out and personally delivered the psalmist from danger. The psalmist knows that God is his rock and deliverer, so he turns to God in need; he takes refuge in God. Why? Because God is his shield, his "horn of salvation."

The "horns of salvation" were kept in the temple, at the four corners of the altar. A person in trouble would be guaranteed safety if he fled to the temple and grasped the horn of salvation, just as a person today might be given sanctuary by entering a church. To say that God is "a horn of salvation" means that seeking and clinging to God guarantees safety.

It is within this context of a relationship with a personal loving God that the psalmist goes on to describe God with imagery which reminded our questioner of a dragon.

> Smoke went up from his nostrils,
>   and devouring fire from his mouth:
>   glowing coals flamed forth from him (Ps 18:8).

In the context of the psalm of thanksgiving these verses are part of the account of deliverance. Actually, two accounts are given, one in vv. 6–19, in which mythic imagery is used, and one in vv. 35–45, in which more concrete and realistic imagery is used.

The mythic and cosmic imagery has a long history in Israel. Scholars believe that the imagery originated in the Canaanite culture and was appropriated by Israel. We see the same kind of imagery used in Exodus 15:3–10, where the Israelites are pictured as celebrating God's mighty action in saving them from the Egyptians.

> At the blast of your nostrils the waters piled up;
>   the floods stood up in a heap. . . .
>   You blew with your wind, the sea covered them (Ex 15:8–10).

Such imagery emphasizes God's total dominance over all the earth. Earthquakes, fire and storms are no more than God's breath.

IMAGES OF GOD

God is: rock　　　　　　　　　　*God breathes:*
　　　　fortress　　　　　　　　　　　smoke from nostrils
　　　　deliverer　　　　　　　　　　　fire from mouth
　　　　shield　　　　　　　　　*God acts:*
　　　　horn of salvation　　　　　　strengthens king
　　　　stronghold　　　　　　　　　　trains king

In God all power resides. Nothing is outside God's domain, certainly not an enemy or the outcome of a battle.

In the second account of deliverance more realistic and concrete imagery is used. Instead of God shaking the very bowels of the earth to achieve the king's victory, God strengthens the king so that he can run like a deer, and trains the king so that his arm can bend the bow (see Ps 18:33–34). However, the result is exactly the same. God, in his majesty and power, bends down to earth and orders events so that the king is delivered from his enemies.

Why did God deliver the king? Because God "delighted" in him (see Ps 18:19), because God's love is "steadfast" (see Ps 18:5). The fire-breathing God of the heights and the depths is a God who loves God's people. For the psalmist, the experience of knowing that he is loved is even more overpowering and awesome than the experience of having been saved from the grasp of his enemies. That is why this psalm of thanksgiving begins, "I love you, O Lord, my strength!" (Ps 18:1).

Review Questions

1. What kind of psalm is Psalm 18? Who is the speaker?
2. What does it mean to call God one's "strength," "rock," "fortress," and "deliverer"?
3. What are the "horns of salvation?" What does it mean to say that God is a horn of salvation?
4. What does mythic imagery emphasize about God?

5. How do the images in the two accounts of deliverance differ from each other?
6. For the psalmist what is the more awesome experience?

Discussion Questions

1. Of the images of God in Psalm 18 which is your favorite? Why? Your least favorite? Why?
2. Have you ever been in a fierce storm? If so, did you think of God? Why or why not?
3. What is the difference in meaning between saying God is your "strength" and God is your "fortress"?

ARTICLE 10

From Inadvertent and Willful Sin, Deliver Us, O Lord!

Question: "For something to be a sin, don't you have to know it's a sin and do it anyway? Why is the psalmist worried about 'hidden faults?' " (Ps 19:12; see Pss 19, 32)

Many of us were taught that in order to commit a sin we had to do it purposefully. This is a narrower concept of sin than we find in scripture.

The root meaning of the word "sin" is "to miss the mark." In the context of scripture, "the mark" is God's will. To act contrary to God's will is to sin.

However, not all actions which are contrary to God's will are done purposefully. So the Israelites distinguished two kinds of sin, sin which was willful and sin which was inadvertent. Inadvertent sin could be forgiven through a ritual action. Willful sin, called "high-handed" sin, could not (see Num 15:22–31). Only conversion of heart and God's grace and mercy could bring about forgiveness for such a person.

The psalms give us examples of people asking for forgiveness from both kinds of sin. In Psalm 19 the psalmist asks to be forgiven from inadvertent sin. In Psalm 32 the psalmist is full of gratitude for having been forgiven willful sin.

In Psalm 19 the psalmist arrives at his request that even his inadvertent sins be forgiven through a meditation on God's order as it is revealed in creation and in the law. The psalmist is able to "hear" the heavens "tell" of God's glory and the firmament "proclaim" God's handiwork. Creation "speaks" and imparts "knowl-

---

SIN

To "Miss the Mark"

- Inadvertent Sin: Can be forgiven through ritual action
- Willful Sin: Can be forgiven with a change of heart

---

edge" (see Ps 19:1–2). That knowledge helps a person understand the order which God has designed. In nature that order can be seen in the sun which has a prescribed course which it runs every day with joy.

Humans too have a prescribed course which, if they run, they would run with joy. The psalmist does not express this idea in words but by the placement of a wisdom poem on the law (see Ps 19:7–10) in parallel position to a creation hymn (see Ps 19:1–6). As is often true in wisdom literature, a comparison is implied through the juxtaposition of units of thought rather than stated in explicit words.

The psalmist believes that God's order is established just as surely in the law as it is in the movement of the planets. The sun is joyful in following its assigned path. So too the precepts of the Lord rejoice the human heart. Just as the sun enlightens the day, so does the law enlighten the eye (see Ps 19:8).

The psalmist, with all his heart, longs to follow the law just as faithfully as the sun follows its path. But who can be sure that he or she is not inadvertently missing the mark?

> But who can detect their errors?
>   Clear me from hidden faults. . . .
> Then I shall be blameless,
>   and innocent of great transgression (Ps 19:12–13).

The psalmist concludes his psalm with a beautiful prayer which asks God to permeate his whole being so that his words and thoughts will be just exactly what God wants them to be.

> Let the words of my mouth and the meditation of my heart
> be acceptable to you,
> O Lord, my rock and my redeemer (Ps 19:14).

While the psalmist in Psalm 19 was moved to ask for forgiveness of inadvertent sin through a meditation on God's order, the psalmist in Psalm 32 was moved to ask for the forgiveness of willful sin because he suffered so from sin's effects.

In this psalm of thanksgiving the psalmist begins with a beatitude:

> Happy are those whose transgression is forgiven,
> whose sin is covered (Ps 32:1).

As you know, a beatitude is a form common in wisdom literature. Because Psalm 32 uses a wisdom form and is very didactic in tone, some scholars place it among the wisdom psalms.

The psalmist wants others to learn from his example. When he lived a life of sin he suffered (see Ps 32:3–4), but then he acknowledged his sin and God forgave him (see Ps 32:5). This should be a lesson to others. The faithful should offer prayers to God. God will hear and protect them just as God has heard and protected the psalmist (see Ps 32:6–7).

Scholars debate the meaning of the next verse:

> I will instruct you and teach you the way you should go;
> I will counsel you with my eye upon you (Ps 32:8).

Is the "I" God promising to instruct and watch over the psalmist? Or is the "I" the psalmist promising to instruct the congregation? The more persuasive argument would attribute the voice to God who, once a sinner turns to God, will lead him in the way he or she should go.

Each of these psalms which deal with sin leans heavily on wisdom literature. Each teaches that there is "a way," there is a right path. Each teaches that God has revealed this path to God's people. Whether one wanders from that path through an inadvertent action or a willful action, one has "missed the mark" and needs God's help. Only those who turn to the Lord and follow God's way will find happiness.

Review Questions

1. What is the root meaning of the word "sin"?
2. What is the "mark"?
3. What two kinds of sin did the Israelites distinguish between? How were each of these sins forgiven?
4. In Psalm 19 what does the psalmist learn from nature?
5. In Psalm 19 what is juxtaposed to the creation hymn? What lesson is implicitly taught?
6. For what does the psalmist long?
7. From what does the psalmist in Psalm 32 want to be relieved?
8. For what two reasons do some scholars consider Psalm 32 a wisdom psalm?
9. What lesson does the psalmist want others to learn from his experience?

Discussion Questions

1. Were you ever taught a definition of sin? What was it? Do you agree with it?
2. Has your idea of sin changed as you have grown older? Explain.
3. Do you think one needs to be conscious of wrong-doing to be guilty of sin? Explain.
4. Do you think one needs to be conscious of wrong-doing in order to suffer the consequence of sin? Explain.

ARTICLE 11

Psalm 22 on Jesus' Lips: Why?

Question: "Did the author of Psalm 22 foresee Jesus' passion? He seems to refer to it several times."

To answer this question we will have to draw on some information we learned when studying the book of Isaiah. If you remember, at that point we discussed the fact that the ability to see into the future is not one of the spiritual gifts which God has given God's people. Neither the prophets nor the psalmists were able to foresee the details of inevitable future events.

It is true that several lines of Psalm 22 appear in various accounts of Jesus' death. Mark and Matthew both picture Jesus saying, "My God, my God, why have you deserted me?" (see Mk 15:34; Mt 27:46). Matthew pictures Jesus being taunted with the words, "He trusts in God: let God deliver him now if he wants to" (Mt 27:43). John actually quotes Psalm 22 when he says that the soldiers cast lots for Jesus' clothes. "This was to fulfill what the scripture says, 'They divided my clothes among themselves, and for my clothing they cast lots' " (Jn 19:24).

You may remember when we read the suffering servant songs in Isaiah that we saw other instances of Old Testament passages seeming to refer specifically to details in Jesus' passion. Why is it, then, that we say that the Old Testament authors did not foresee the details which they seem to report?

When we read the four accounts of Jesus' death we are not reading first-hand contemporary newspaper reporting which tells us exactly what we would have seen had we been standing there ourselves. If this were true the accounts would be more similar to each

284

NEW TESTAMENT QUOTATIONS FROM PSALM 22

"My God, my God, why have you deserted me?" Mk 15:34; Mt 27:46

"He trusts in God: let God deliver him if he wants to." Mt 27:43

They divided my clothes among themselves, and for my clothing they cast lots." Jn 19:24

---

other. Rather, we are reading accounts which grew up later, accounts which try to teach their audiences the significance of Jesus' passion, a significance that was not understood at the time the passion occurred. Only after the resurrection and after the post-resurrection appearances did Jesus' followers begin to understand just what had occurred in their midst.

One technique which the gospel editors used to explain the significance of the events of Jesus' passion was to use Old Testament passages which would cast light on the events. In other words, the Old Testament passage, such as Psalm 22, is used to explain the meaning of Jesus' crucifixion. Jesus' crucifixion does not explain the psalmist's intent in writing the words as our questioner presumed.

Why did the gospel editors find Psalm 22 useful in teaching the significance of Jesus' passion? In order to answer this question let us first look at what the psalm has to say in its own right. We will then see how the gospel editors used the psalm to teach about Jesus.

Psalm 22 is an individual lament. While it does not perfectly conform to the structure of a lament, the elements of the structure are still present. In vv. 6–8 and 12–18 the speaker laments his situation. Like Job, he is not only suffering physically but, because he is suffering, his neighbors have judged him guilty of sin. When his neighbors shake their heads and say:

> Commit your cause to the Lord;
> let him deliver—
> let him rescue the one in whom he delights (Ps 22:8),

their words are dripping with irony. They do not believe God delights in him at all. Otherwise he would not be suffering.

In vv. 3–5 and 9–10 the psalmist states his trust that God will answer his plea. After all, the psalmist's ancestors had also been in dire straits and had called out to God, and God had saved them. Vv. 11 and 19–21 contain the usual petition. The psalmist begs that God be not far away, but rescue him.

The words of assurance spoken by the priest do not appear. However, with verse 21b the psalm completely changes tone. Unlike the usual lament, the psalmist does not express faith and confidence that he *will be saved* but that he *has been saved.*

> From the horns of the wild oxen you have rescued me.
> I will tell of your name to my brothers and sisters. . . .
> For he did not despise or abhor the affliction of the afflicted;
> he did not hide his face from me,
> but heard when I cried to him (Ps 22:21–24).

The concluding words of trust and praise in a lament are usually a line or two. In Psalm 22 the praise goes on for verse after verse (see Ps 22:21–31). It moves from the individual psalmist's praise, to the congregation's praise, to a universal chorus of praise.

> Posterity will serve him;
> future generations will be told about the Lord,
> And proclaim his deliverance to a people yet unborn,
> saying that he has done it (Ps 22:30–31).

Now that we have looked carefully at the psalm, we are ready to answer the question, "By using the psalm in their accounts of Jesus' passion, what were the gospel editors saying about the significance of Jesus' passion in the life of their readers?"

To picture Jesus as praying the psalm as he died on the cross is to bring to bear on the event of Jesus' passion the entire psalm, not just the first line. To picture Jesus as the lamenter, who prays "My

God, my God, why have you forsaken me?" is to identify Jesus with all of humankind who, when in terrible distress, feels deserted and afraid even though we are not deserted and need not be afraid. God was with Jesus even as God was with Jesus' ancestors in their distress and will be with Jesus' followers in their distress.

The exultant, universal praise which the psalmist pours out after having been saved takes on new meaning when read in the context of Jesus' life. In hindsight, in the light of the resurrection, the gospel editors realized:

> To him [Jesus] indeed shall all who sleep in the earth bow down;
>> before him shall bow all who go down to the dust,
>> and I shall live for him.
> Posterity will serve him;
>> future generations will be told about the Lord,
> And proclaim his deliverance to a people yet unborn,
>> saying that he has done it (Ps 22:29–31).

The gospel writers, by the very fact of writing the gospel, hope to help their audiences realize the significance of Jesus' passion. Because Jesus fulfilled his Father's will, revealed his Father's love, and accepted death, even death on a cross, the words of Psalm 22 have been fulfilled in him. Salvation has been accomplished. Deliverance is proclaimed to a people yet unborn. *Jesus has done it!*

By placing the words of the psalm on Jesus' lips the gospel editors helped their audiences and us see the significance of Jesus' life in the light of the words of the psalm. So even though the psalmist did not foresee the events of Jesus' life, the words of the psalmist could be used to explain the significance of those events to each succeeding generation.

Review Questions

1. Did Old Testament authors see details of inevitable future events?
2. When the gospel editors give accounts of Jesus' passion, what is their purpose?
3. Why did the gospel editors use Psalm 22?

4. What kind of psalm is Psalm 22?
5. What is different about the final words of confidence?
6. How do the words of Psalm 22 become "fulfilled" in the light of Jesus' passion, death and resurrection?

Discussion Questions

1. What does it mean to say that the psalm is used to explain the significance of events, not the events used to explain the meaning of the psalm?
2. What advantage does hindsight give when explaining an event? How does a hindsight explanation differ from one contemporary with events?
3. Did you think God did give some psalmists the ability to see the details of future events? Do you wish God had? Why or why not?

ARTICLE 12

A Song of Procession with the Ark of the Covenant

Question: "In Psalm 24 it sounds as if God is actually entering the temple. What is going on here?" (Ps 24:7–10; see Pss 15, 24)

From the point of view of the participants, God was actually entering the temple, most probably as represented in the ark of the covenant. Although we do not know the specific occasion on which this ritual was enacted, we can reconstruct the spirit and meaning of the occasion.

You may remember that when we were discussing Psalm 15 we called it a rite of entrance to the temple. Psalm 24 contains a similar entrance rite. The question:

> Who shall ascend the hill of the Lord?
> And who shall stand in his holy place? (Ps 24:3–4)

once again means, "Who is worthy to enter the temple for worship?" As we saw in Psalm 15, the priests respond by naming specific behaviors which are core to covenant love (Ps 24:4–6). Those who live in covenant love are worthy to enter the temple.

Instead of ending here, as did Psalm 15, Psalm 24 continues with a processional hymn (Ps 24:7–10). Again the song is antiphonal. Those outside the temple would say:

Lift up your heads, O gates!
and be lifted up, O ancient doors!
that the king of glory may come in (Ps 24:7-9).

Those inside the temple would respond:

Who is the king of glory?
The Lord, strong and mighty,
the Lord, mighty in battle! (Ps 24:8-10)

What actions would have been taking place as the psalm was sung? What would have been the occasion?

Scripture scholars cannot say with certainty. It seems most likely that the ark of the covenant was being taken into the temple.

The ark, containing the ten commandments, was built during the time when the Israelites were in the desert (see Ex 25:10-22). For the Israelites God was enthroned upon the ark. Where the ark was, there was God.

We read of several occasions in the history of the Israelites during which the ark was brought in with great ceremony. When the ark was brought into the battle camp during the war with the Philistines, it was greeted with such rejoicing that the "earth resounded" (see 1 Sam 4:5-10). When David brought the ark into Jerusalem, he did it with such glee and abandon that he embarrassed his wife (see 2 Sam 6:16). The narrator tells us: "David and all the house of Israel were dancing before the Lord with all their might, with songs and lyres and harps and tambourines and castanets and cymbals" (2 Sam 6:5).

By the time of the second temple there were three main festivals celebrated at the temple. The festival of Passover, originally a celebration of the spring barley harvest that was reinterpreted to recall Passover, the festival of "Weeks" or "Pentecost," originally a celebration of the summer wheat harvest which eventually recalled the reception of the law at Sinai, and the festival of "Booths" or "Tabernacles," originally a celebration of the fall fruit harvest which became the occasion to celebrate the years when the Israelites were nomads and lived in "booths" or tents.

Each of these three major feasts was a pilgrimage feast. Pilgrims

---

MAJOR FEASTS CELEBRATED IN THE SECOND TEMPLE

- Passover: spring
- Pentecost or Festival of Weeks: fifty days after Passover
- Festival of Booths or Tabernacles: fall

---

would come to Jerusalem for a one or eight day celebration at the temple. Psalms 120–134 are each entitled "a song of ascent." Scholars believe that the "songs of ascent" were songs to be used by pilgrims on their way to Jerusalem.

On what occasion would Psalm 24 have been used? Perhaps in one of these three great pilgrimage festivals, such as the fall "new year" festival of Booths. While scholars can surmise, they have no sure proof. However, it seems extremely likely that the words "Lift up your heads, O gates . . . that the King of glory may come in" (see Ps 24:7) were sung annually by generations of pilgrims who, like David, processed and sang before the ark of the covenant.

Review Questions

1. How is God entering the temple?
2. What does Psalm 24 have in common with Psalm 15?
3. What does Psalm 24 add to the entrance rite?
4. Name two occasions in the Israelites' history when there was a great celebration in honor of the arrival of the ark.
5. Name the three main festivals celebrated at the temple by the time of the second temple.
6. What is a pilgrimage feast? What are psalms of ascent?

Discussion Questions

1. The Israelites concretized God's presence in the ark of the covenant. How do we concretize God's presence?

2. Have you ever been part of a procession? What was being celebrated? What is the purpose of a procession?
3. Why is it important to recall the great events in one's history?
   On what occasions do we do this as a church? As a nation? Do
   you do it as a family? When?

ARTICLE 13

Psalms: Honest Prayers from the Heart

Question: "Doesn't Psalm 39 present a terribly depressed view of life? Is this psalm compatible with Psalm 8 in which the psalmist claimed that we are a little lower than God? (Pss 8, 23, 39)

Psalm 39 does present a depressed view of life. The psalm is an individual lament, but instead of ending on a positive note, as is typical of a lament, this psalm ends with the psalmist unable to solve the mystery with which he is confronted. He prays:

> Turn your gaze away from me, that I may smile again,
> before I depart and am no more (Ps 39:13).

In terms of its content, Psalm 39 has a great deal in common with wisdom literature. Since we have read Job we can see the similarities. Job, too, early in his suffering, prayed:

> Will you not look away from me for a while,
> let me alone until I swallow my spittle (Job 7:19)?

Although scholars are not sure of the exact situation in which the psalmist finds himself, it seems likely that he, like Job, was suffering from a life-threatening illness, suffering which "the wicked" interpreted as being punishment for his sins.

The psalmist begins by claiming that he had tried to keep silent; he had tried not to give a retort to the wicked.

One gets the impression that the psalmist thought that if he remained silent he would be rewarded with improved health because

293

he says that he was silent "to no avail" (see Ps 39:2). When the psalmist speaks, he addresses not his enemies but God.

> Lord, let me know my end,
>   and what is the measure of my days;
> Let me know how fleeting my life is (Ps 39:4).

The psalmist's meditation on the transitory nature of human life on earth is true. Because he has no knowledge of life after death, he has lost his sense of purpose. What, after all, does it all mean? The psalmist's hope is in God (see Ps 39:7), but, at the same time, God is the cause of his distress.

> It is you who have done it (Ps 39:9b).

So while the psalmist tries to hold on to his hope, he still feels hopeless.

Is this view compatible with the idea that humans are a little lower than God? Is birth compatible with death? Is joy compatible with grief? Is the prayer, "Leave me, Lord," compatible with the prayer, "Be with me, Lord?"

Remember that the book of Psalms was collated to be used in liturgical settings in the second temple. If you think about the liturgical celebrations which we celebrate during the course of a year, you will realize that we turn to God in prayer in completely opposite circumstances. We do not pray only when we are joyful, but when we are angry as well. We do not pray only when we are full of hope, but when we are full of despair as well. The psalms are honest prayers. In them human beings pour out whatever is in their hearts.

The questioner saw this psalm in contrast with Psalm 8 in which the psalmist claims that we are a little lower than God, for in Psalm 39 the psalmist says, "Surely everyone is a mere breath" (see Ps 39:11). An even greater contrast exists between Psalm 39 and Psalm 23, "The Lord is my shepherd," for in Psalm 39 the psalmist longs for the very peace and security which the psalmist in Psalm 23 already has.

Notice that each psalmist feels that he is in the presence of his enemies. The psalmist in Psalm 39 does not feel God's presence and solace with him as does the Psalmist in Psalm 23.

> You prepare a table before me
>   in the presence of my enemies;
> You anoint my head with oil;
>   my cup overflows (Ps 23:5).

The psalmist in Psalm 39 has kept silent in hopes that he will be restored, but his silence is to no avail. The psalmist in Psalm 23 feels that God constantly "restores" his soul (see Ps 23:2).

The psalmist in Psalm 39 expects a short, unhappy life, while the psalmist in Psalm 23 expects a long, blessed life.

> Surely goodness and mercy shall follow me
>   all the days of my life,
> And I shall dwell in the house of the Lord
>   my whole life long (Ps 23:6).

Are these two psalms compatible, with their opposite points of view? Each derives from a different life experience, but at various times of life each of these psalms could have been on the same person's lips. Prayer is an honest conversation with God. Whatever is in the heart is what we have to offer God. The author of Psalm 39, at the time he composed this prayer, had only his despair to offer.

Review Questions

1. What kind of psalm is Psalm 39? How is the ending of Psalm 39 unusual for this form?
2. How is the psalmist similar to Job?
3. Why is the psalmist in such distress? What does he not know which we do know?
4. What is the difference in experience between the psalmist in Psalm 39 and the psalmist in Psalm 23?
5. Are Psalms 8, 13 and 39 compatible? Explain.

Discussion Questions

1. Do you think it is all right to pray when you are mad at God? Why or why not?
2. What are we "celebrating" on Ash Wednesday? On Good Friday? On Easter Sunday? Are these "compatible"?
3. Do you think you are able to pray as honestly as the psalmist in Psalm 39? Why or why not? Do you think God wants you to? Why or why not?

ARTICLE 14

Integrity: God's Gift

Question: "In Psalm 41 isn't the speaker awfully proud to say that God saved him because of his own integrity?" (Ps 41:12; see Pss 26, 41)

If the psalmist means by "integrity" something he has accomplished, then his claim to "integrity" does seem proud. However, in the context of this psalm and also of Psalm 26, in which the psalmist claims to "walk in my integrity" (see Ps 26:1, 11), "integrity" seems to be a quality which God has accomplished in the person, not a quality which the person has accomplished in himself.

Psalm 26 has a chiastic arrangement (ABCBA) in which the psalmist begins and ends not only by referring to his right relationship with God, his integrity, but also by asking to be "redeemed:"

> Vindicate me, O Lord,
> for I have walked in my integrity (Ps 26:1).

> But as for me I walk in my integrity;
> redeem me, and be gracious to me (Ps 26:11).

The psalmist has walked in integrity because God's "steadfast love" is always with him, and he has walked in faithfulness to that love.

In a chiastic arrangement the core of the psalm is in the center. So the core of Psalm 26 is vv. 6–8.

> I wash my hands in innocence,
> and go around your altar, O Lord,
> singing aloud a song of thanksgiving,
> and telling all your wondrous deeds.

297

HEBREW POETRY USES

- *Chiastic Form:* ABCBA The central idea is in the middle of the poem

- *Beatitude:* "Happy is the one who. . ." or "Blessed is the one who. . ."

- *Doxology:* Short prayer of praise to God

> O Lord, I love the house in which you dwell,
>   and the place where your glory abides (Ps 26:6–8).

Scholars surmise that this psalm was sung by priests during a ritual washing of the hands just before they offered sacrifice, much as Roman Catholic priests ritually wash their hands before the eucharistic prayer. As the priests wash their hands they are thanking and praising God for all God's wondrous deeds. Among those wondrous deeds is the integrity of the psalmist who has received integrity as a fruit of God's steadfast love.

With this context in mind we can see that the psalmist in Psalm 41 has also received rather than achieved integrity. The psalm begins with a traditional wisdom form, a beatitude.

> Happy is he who has regard for the lowly and the poor;
>   In the day of misfortune the Lord will deliver him (Ps 41:1).

However, as the psalm proceeds the voice changes from third person (i.e. "he") to first person (i.e. "I"). In hindsight we realize that the speaker was speaking of himself as that "happy man."

Far from claiming a past life of virtue, the speaker recalls the time when he was a sinner.

> Once I said, "O Lord, have pity on me,
>   heal me, though I have sinned against you" (Ps 41:5).

In a recalled lament the speaker elaborates on the sufferings he endured not only because of his illness but because of the treatment which he received at the hands of his enemies.

Unlike the psalmist in Psalm 39 which we discussed in our last article, this psalmist did experience healing (see Ps 41:11). He interpreted the healing as a sign of God's love and as vindication over those who had mistreated him.

> That you love me I know by this,
>> that my enemy does not triumph over me (Ps 41:12).

The vindication is not a claim that he didn't need forgiveness. He did, and asked for it. The vindication is that, in his friends' eyes, his return to health proved God's steadfast love. Because of God's love the psalmist lives in right relationship to God. Because of God's love the psalmist has integrity in his own eyes and in the eyes of his enemies.

The last verse of Psalm 41 is not really the end of Psalm 41 but the end of the first book of Psalms. Each of the five books which make up the psalter (the collection of "praises") ends with such a doxology or "hymn of praise."

> Blessed be the Lord, the God of Israel,
>> from everlasting to everlasting. Amen and Amen (Ps 41:13).

Such praise is always appropriate, but it is particularly appropriate when one realizes, as the psalmists do, that all that exists comes from the hand of a loving God. The psalmist in Psalm 41 realized that among God's many gifts was the psalmist's own integrity.

Review Questions

1. What is a "chiastic" arrangement?
2. In Psalm 26 what has made it possible for the psalmist to walk in integrity?
3. On what occasion might Psalm 26 have been used?
4. What is a beatitude?
5. Did the psalmist in Psalm 41 earn his integrity?
6. What motivated the psalmist to repent?

7. Why did the psalmist in Psalm 41 feel vindicated?
8. What does the word "psalter" mean?

Discussion Questions

1. What does the word "integrity" mean to you?
2. Think of a person who, in your eyes, has integrity. Do you think of this person as having achieved or received the integrity? Why?
3. Think of a quality in yourself which is important to you in your own eyes. Do you feel you earned or received this quality? Explain.
4. For what would you like to praise God the most? Why?

Endnote

We have now read Isaiah, Job, Proverbs and the first book of Psalms. What have we learned from this study that will help us in our everyday life?

The most obvious lesson is that we have learned how to understand, and so accurately quote, the Bible. All of the books which we have just read are quoted liberally in our culture. Which of us has not heard reference to "Immanuel," to "the patience of Job," to "spare the rod and spoil the child," and to "My God, my God, why have you deserted me?"

However, we now know that each of these quotations is very often misunderstood when it is referred to in our culture. Isaiah did not know that God would become a human being. Job was not patient, yet God was very pleased with him. The Bible should not be used to support corporal punishment. The lament on Jesus' lips did not reveal that Jesus suffered despair on the cross.

Through reading each of these books we have learned that we simply cannot understand quotations from the Bible unless we put them in context. We must know the literary form of the book and the historical setting of the author to know what the author is saying to his audience as well as what God is saying to us.

God is saying something to us, both as a group and as individuals. The Bible is a living word which can form our minds and hearts according to God's will. We are to love this living word with all our minds and all our hearts. Part of loving the word with our minds is to study it. Without study our hearts can be led astray.

In addition to learning how to understand, and so accurately quote scripture, we can learn another very important lesson from reading prophecy and wisdom. Our study can help us see how reason must struggle to integrate revelation and experience. This is a task which those of us who live in a post-Vatican II church have in common with the post-Babylonian exile church. Both generations lived at a time of immense change.

All of the books we have read reveal this struggle. Recall that Isaiah, Job, Proverbs, and Psalms all preserve the context of covenant love, the context within which the Israelites saw their relationship with God. All admonish their readers to live lives appropriate for those in covenant love. From First Isaiah through the psalms of the second temple the people are reminded that worship without a life lived according to the law is useless.

In addition all of the books emphasize the Davidic covenant theology which started with Nathan's promise to David. From Isaiah's urging Ahaz to trust God's promise, through the royal psalms used in the second temple, the idea that God will be with the house of David endures. This is remarkable, since Persian governors, not Davidic kings, were in power after the Babylonian exile.

All four books, in addition to maintaining tradition, reveal the kind of re-evaluation that had to be done after the Babylonian exile. In Third Isaiah's questions about who should be admitted for temple worship, and in Job's agonizing questions about whether or not God really is present and faithful, we see the role reason had to play in integrating ongoing experience with inherited tradition. In Proverbs reason integrates the wisdom of other nations into Israel's concept of "fear of the Lord." In the book of Psalms inherited tradition continues to be honored as the "praises" from centuries of festivals are integrated into worship in the second temple.

In both of these lessons, how to interpret scripture correctly and how to use reason to integrate inherited tradition with present experience, we can see how important our minds are as we grow spiritually. True, wisdom literature shows us the limits of reason and the necessity of revelation. But it also shows us the essential role that reason plays in integrating revelation into daily life. The gift that prophecy and wisdom literature offer us is that they give us a model we need in our century. They teach us how to be faithful to covenant love and faithful to our inherited tradition as we face the challenges confronting us in a rapidly changing society.

Glossary

Acrostic Poem: An alphabetical poem in which each successive line begins with the next letter of the alphabet.

Adultery: Sexual intercourse between a married person and a person who is not the spouse.

Ahaz: King of Judah (the southern kingdom) from 735 to 715 B.C. during the time when Isaiah was a prophet. Ahaz was considered a bad king because he relied on the Assyrians for political protection rather than on God.

Amen-em-ope: The name which appears in an Egyptian Instruction that was appropriated and used in Proverbs.

Analogy: A correspondence between two things which overall may be dissimilar.

Anthology: A collection of literary works such as oracles, psalms, proverbs, etc.

Antithetic Parallelism: Parallelism in which the second line expresses the opposite thought of the first line.

Apocalyptic Literature: A kind of literature written to a persecuted audience to give them hope that their "end time," the end of their persecution, is near. It is written in code so that only the persecuted will understand it.

Appropriate: To take and use for one's own purposes.

Aram: Syria. Aram was the ancestor of the Arameans. The Arameans are also called the Syrians. Syria was between Egypt and Mesopotamia.

Ark of the Covenant: The gold-plated box in which were kept the ten commandments.

Ashdod: A Philistine city which revolted against Assyria in 714 B.C.

Assyria: The Assyrians rose to power and dominated the near east from the eleventh to the seventh centuries. They threatened to destroy Jerusalem during the reign of Hezekiah. They were finally defeated by the Babylonians.

Babylon: The capital of the Babylonian empire. The Babylonians destroyed Jerusalem in 587 B.C. They were defeated by the Persians in 539 B.C.

Babylonian Exile: 587–537 B.C. The time when the southern kingdom was conquered and many of its citizens were taken to Babylon.

Ban: Those under the ban were killed. Enforcing the ban was seen as a way of acknowledging that victory belonged to God.

Beatitude: A beatitude begins, "Blessed is the one who . . ." or "Happy is the one who . . ." "Beatitude" is a common form in wisdom literature.

Bildad: One of Job's "friends" who believed Job was guilty or he wouldn't be suffering.

Birth Narrative: The stories about a great person's birth which appear in the Bible. Examples are the stories about Jesus' birth which appear in Matthew's and Luke's gospels.

Canaan: The land to which Abraham traveled. It is west of the Jordan River. Once settled by the Israelites, Canaan became the holy land.

Canonical Text: The canon is the body of writing which the believing community identifies as "inspired," as "authoritative," as "revelation." A "text" is the wording, what is actually written in the book. A canonical text is a text that is part of the accepted canon.

Chiastic Arrangement: ABCBA. In a chiastic arrangement the main focus is in the middle. The ideas presented before that middle are presented after, but in the opposite order. Thus you begin and end with the same idea.

Concrete Imagery: A concrete image is one which relies on the material world rather than mythic or cosmic abstractions to make a point. "Rock" as an image for God is a concrete image.

Cosmic Imagery: An image is a mental conceptualization of something not present to the senses. A cosmic image is an image that embraces the cosmos rather than something local and specific. Cosmic imagery might include planets, the course of the stars, the foundations of the earth, etc.

Covenant: A solemn ritual agreement which could not be broken. The word "covenant" is used to describe the relationship between God and God's people.

Covenant Theology: "Covenant" refers to the bond of love between God and God's people. Theology refers to one's understanding of God. Covenant theology refers to the fact that the Israelites believed that God chose to express God's covenant love through the house of David. Because they believed this, some thought that Judah and the house of David could never be destroyed.

Cult: A community or system of religious worship and ritual. The word has come to have a negative connotation which it has not always had. Mass is religious worship in a cultic setting.

Cyrus: A Persian who conquered the Babylonians in 539 B.C. and let the Israelites return home.

David: King of Israel from 1010 to 970 B.C. He united the twelve tribes. He became the image of God's "anointed," the "messiah." Nathan's prophecy about God's fidelity to the Davidic line was made to David.

Deuteronomist: The name attributed to the editing tradition which produced the Deuteronomistic history.

Deuteronomistic History: Joshua, Judges, 1 and 2 Samuel, 1 and 2, Kings. Also called the Former Prophets.

Didactic: Intended to instruct.

Dramatic Irony: Dramatic irony exists when an author or narrator (the voice telling the story) and an audience share information which the characters in a story do not share. The book of Job uses dramatic irony because the audience knows that Job is innocent but the characters in the story, such as Eliphaz, do not.

"E": The Elohist editor. The editing tradition which originated in the northern kingdom.

Egypt: The country around the valley of the Nile River, bordering the south side of the Mediterranean.

Elihu: A character who appears in Job 32–37. He is verbose and arrogant and doesn't help to solve the problem which the book confronts.

Eliphaz: One of Job's "friends" who believed that Job was guilty or he would not be suffering.

Elohim: "Lord." The word used to refer to God in the Elohist tradition up until the time of Moses.

Emmanuel: See Immanuel.

Ephraim: Joseph's son who received preference over his older brother, Manassah. The whole northern kingdom is sometimes referred to by the name Ephraim.

Ethiopia: In northeast Africa. Also called "Cush" by the Israelites.

Exile: 587–537 B.C. when many of the Israelites were exiled in Babylon.

Ezekiel: A prophet before and during the Babylonian exile.

Festival of Booths or Tabernacles: A fall festival originally celebrating the fruit harvest. It came to recall the time of wandering in the desert.

Festival of Weeks: Held fifty days after Passover. Originally an agricultural feast. Later came to be associated with the reception of the law. Also called Pentecost.

Figure of Speech: An expression, such as a comparison, exaggeration, image, etc., in which the intended meaning of the words is not identical to the literal meaning of the words. Figures of speech are used to add effect.

Gentile: A non-Jew.

Grandiose: More "grandeur" than is appropriate, so it seems pompous and affected rather than true and moving.

Hebrew: This word is used to name the Israelites in their relationship with "foreigners."

Hebrew Language: The language in which the Old Testament was written.

Hezekiah: King of Judah from 715 to 686 B.C. Succeeded Ahaz, his father. During his reign the Assyrians were a constant threat. Isaiah begged him to trust God.

Hyperbole: Exaggeration.

Idolatry: The worship of idols rather than of the one true God.

Image: A mental representation of something not present to the senses. A concrete way of thinking about an abstract concept.

Immanent: To exist within. God's immanence refers to God's closeness as opposed to God's transcendence, i.e. God's independence of the material world.

Immanuel: The word means, "God with us." Isaiah used this word to name the hoped-for infant in Isaiah 7:10–17. Matthew refers to Isaiah's words in his account of the annunciation to Joseph (Mt 1:23).

Incarnate: To "enflesh." To put in a human form.

Inclusio: A structuring device in which the same point is made in both the beginning and the end of a literary unit.

Infancy Narrative: See birth narrative.

Instruction: A literary form appropriated from Egypt in which a teacher passes on good advice to his students or "son."

Integration: To make part of the whole, not just a "tack-on" or an after-thought.

Irony: A tone used so that the literal meaning of words is different than the intentional meaning, sometimes even opposite.

Isaiah: The prophet who lived at the time of Ahaz and Hezekiah (735–715 B.C.). Referred to as First Isaiah or Isaiah of Jerusalem.

Isaiah: The name of a prophetic book of the Bible which contains the work of three prophets from three historical periods.

Isaiah, First: Chapters 1–39 of the book of Isaiah. Also used to refer to the prophet whose work appears in these chapters.

Isaiah, Second: Chapters 40–55 of the book of Isaiah. The setting for Second Isaiah is the Babylonian exile (587–537 B.C.).

Isaiah, Third: Chapters 56–66 of the book of Isaiah. The setting for Third Isaiah is the post-exilic period.

Israel: The tribes united under Saul. After the kingdom split, the northern kingdom.

"J" Editor: Another name for the Yahwist editing tradition.

Jerusalem: The city David chose as his capital. It became the center of worship, the "city of God."

Job: The name of the book which addresses the question "Do innocent people suffer?" as well as the name of the book's main character. An historical Job, known for his virtue, may have lived at the time of the patriarchs.

Jubilee Year: A celebration every forty-nine years in which property was redistributed and forgiveness and freedom were granted.

Judah: A southern tribe. Later the name of the southern kingdom.

Juxtaposition: To "juxtapose" is to place things side by side for the purpose of comparing or contrasting them.

Lament: A type of psalm in which the psalmist is expressing grief. Laments move from grief to faith and praise.

Lebanon: Two mountain ranges, extending for one hundred miles through Syria and Palestine, are called the Lebanons. The "cedar of Lebanon" is from these mountains.

Legend: A symbolic and imaginative story with an historical core.

Maher-shalal-hash-baz: One of Isaiah's children. The name means "quick spoils, speedy plunder."

Messiah: Hebrew for "anointed one." "Messiah" and "Christ" are synonyms. Both are used to identify Jesus as God's saving instrument.

Messianic Prophecy: A prophecy of hope that reminds people of God's fidelity to God's promise to the house of David. An "anointed one" would come, so keep the faith.

Metaphor: A comparison that does not use the word "like" or "as."

Metonymy: A figure of speech in which the real meaning is expressed through a word closely associated with that meaning— e.g. "The White House said . . ."

Moab: Moab was Israel's neighbor in the Jordan highlands east of the Dead Sea and a traditional enemy.

Monotheism: A belief in one God.

Mythic Imagery: An "image" is a mental conceptualization of something not present to the senses. A mythic image is the kind of image that appears in a myth, such as primordial beings, fire breathing dragons, evil creatures, etc.

Narrator: The "voice" telling the story. The narrator cannot always be equated with the author. The author may create a character who tells the story and is thus the narrative voice.

Nathan: The prophet during David's kingship who prophesied that David's line would be secure forever.

Nebachadnezzar: The Babylonian king who destroyed Jerusalem in 587 B.C.

Nomads: People who are on the move rather than settled in one location.

Numerical Proverb: A proverb that begins with a linguistic formula such as "Three things are . . . Four . . ." The similarity among the four things is then pointed out.

Oracle: The form of a prophetic utterance. It begins with a formula such as, "Yahweh says this . . ."

Parable: A parable is a story which, at base, rests on a metaphor. The comparison is between the audience and the story itself. The function of the parable is to correct the audience and to call the people to conversion.

Parallelism: A structural device used in Hebrew poetry in which units of thought are juxtaposed in synonymous or antithetical relationship to each other.

Parody: A literary work which criticizes or pokes fun by mimicking. It imitates but is purposefully no good at all.

Passover: The celebration which reminds Jews of the night on which they escaped from Egypt because the angel of death passed over their homes during the last plague.

Patriarch: The male head of a family. A patriarchal society is one in which the men have all the power and women are treated as subordinate.

Pentateuch: Genesis, Exodus, Leviticus, Numbers, Deuteronomy. Also called the "law," or the "Torah."

Pentecost: See Festival of Weeks.

Persia: Persia became dominant under Cyrus. Cyrus conquered the Babylonians and let the Israelites return home.

Personification: Describing inanimate objects or abstract ideas with human characteristics. Wisdom described as a woman who speaks is an example of personification.

Philistine: The Philistines lived along the southern coast of Palestine. They were in constant battle with the Israelites during the period of the judges and during David's time.

Polytheism: A belief in many gods.

Prophet: One who speaks for God. The prophet's spiritual gift is the ability to see the ramifications of covenant love.

Proverb: A short pithy saying that expresses practical advice known from experience.

Psalter: The song book containing the psalms. The word means "praises."

Redeem: To set free. To redeem a person or animal was to set it free by offering something else in its place.

Remnant: The word refers to the small group among the chosen people who would return to Yahweh, be converted, and so carry on the covenant relationship.

Revelation: That which makes known God's will or truth. When we claim that the Bible is revelation, we claim that it reveals the truth about God, our relationship with God, and what we should be doing to build up rather than tear down the kingdom.

Rite: The prescribed form for conducting a religious ceremony.

Royal Psalm: A psalm in which the king is either the subject or the speaker.

Satan: The adversary. The character in the book of Job who challenged God, saying that Job did not honor God "for nothing." "Satan" was not identified with the devil at this stage in Israel's thinking.

Second Temple: The temple rebuilt by the Jews after the Babylonian exile.

Secular: Worldly rather than spiritual.

Selah: A direction given between verses in the book of Psalms. Scholars don't know exactly what it means.

Sennacherib: King of Assyria from 704 to 681 B.C. Son of Sargon II. He threatened Jerusalem during the reign of King Hezekiah.

Septuagint: The Greek translation of the Old Testament begun about 250 B.C.

Shear-jashub: One of Isaiah's children. The name means "A remnant shall return."

Simile: A comparison that uses the word "like" or "as."

Solomon: Son of David and Bathsheba. King of Israel from 961 to 922 B.C. Built the temple.

Southern Kingdom: After the kingdom split, the two tribes, Judah and Benjamin, who remained faithful to the house of David made up the southern kingdom. Also called Judah.

Symbol: Something that stands for or represents something else.

Synecdoche: A figure of speech in which a part is used to refer to a whole or the whole is used to refer to a part—e.g. "The lips of the righteous feed many."

Synonymous Parallelism: A device used in Hebrew poetry in which the second line repeats the thought of the first except in different words.

Synthetic Parallelism: Parallelism in which the second line elaborates or completes the thought of the first line.

Syro-Ephramite Alliance: "Syro" refers to Syria, also called "Aram." "Ephraim" refers to the northern kingdom. The Syro-Ephramite alliance was the alliance of these two nations against Assyria. They wanted Ahaz to join them.

Testament, New: "Testament" means "covenant." The New Testament is the collection of Christian Greek scriptures.

Testament, Old: "Testament" means "covenant." The Old Testament is the collection of Jewish Hebrew scriptures.

Tone: The pitch of a word which determines its meaning or the general effect or atmosphere created.

Torah: See Pentateuch.

Transcendent: Above and independent of the material world.

Usury: Charging interest on a loan.

Uz: Job's homeland. Scholars disagree on its location. The important point is that Job was not an Israelite.

Vindicate: To clear of charges made against someone.

Wisdom Literature: Proverbs, Job, Ecclesiastes, Ecclesiasticus, Wisdom, Song of Songs, Psalms. Wisdom literature deals with practical behavior and bases its conclusions on reason and experience.

Wisdom Psalms: Psalms which resemble wisdom literature in tone (didactic) or interest (i.e. the two ways; the order of creation, etc.)

Yahweh: The name of God revealed by God to Moses at the burning bush.

Zadok: A priest during David and Solomon's time who became chief priest at the temple. His descendants were the priests in the second temple.

Zedekiah: King of Judah in 587 B.C. when Jerusalem was conquered by the Babylonians.

Zion: "Zion" refers to the hill on which Solomon built the temple or to the city of Jerusalem.

Zophar: One of Job's "friends" who believed that Job was guilty or he wouldn't be suffering.

Index of Biblical References